Rejuvenate

A 21-DAY NATURAL DETOX PLAN

FOR OPTIMAL HEALTH

Helene Silver

THE CROSSING PRESS

FREEDOM, CALIFORNIA

Copyright ©1998 by Helene Silver
Cover design by Tara M. Eoff
Cover photograph by ©1998 Frederic Jorez/The Image Bank
Line art illustrations by Kathleen Savage
Interior woodcut print by Tom Killion

The information contained in this book is based on the experience and research of the author. It is not intended as a substitute for consulting with your physician or other health care provider. Any attempt to diagnose and treat an illness should be done under the direction of a health care professional. The publisher does not advocate the use of any particular health care protocol, but believes that the information in this book should be available to the public. The publisher and author are not responsible for any adverse effects or consequences resulting from the use of any of the suggestions, preparations, or procedures discussed in this book. Should the reader have any questions concerning the appropriateness of any procedure or preparation mentioned, the author and publisher strongly suggest consulting a professional health care advisor.

For information on bulk purchases or group discounts for this and other Crossing Press titles, please contact our Special Sales Director at 800/777-1048, ext. 203.

Visit our Web site on the Internet: www.crossingpress.com

Typeset in Janson Text and Weiss

Library of Congress Cataloging-in-Publication Data

Silver, Helene (Helene M.)
    Rejuvenate : a 21 day natural detox plan for optimal health / by
Helene Silver.
        p. cm.
    Includes index.
    ISBN 0-89594-938-5 (pbk.)
    1. Rejuvenation. 2. Health. 3. Toxicology. 4. Nutrition.
RA776.75.S53 1998
613--dc21   98-27320
                                                                   CIP

                0   9   8   7   6   5   4   3

Dedication

Dedicated to the loving memory of my father, Sam Silver, whose persistent health problems stimulated my interest in natural health principles and cures.

And to John, whose encouragement, love, support, and belief in me over the years has increased my belief in myself.

Acknowledgments

I gratefully acknowledge my teachers, Walt and Magana Baptiste, pioneers in the natural health movement, for their loving guidance. I developed many phases of the nutritional, breathing, and yoga portions of the 21-Day Program, from their teachings. The holistic health philosophers and teachers Edgar Cayce, Dr. Norman Walker, Dr. Bernard Jenson, Dr. Paavo Airola, Dr. Randolph Stone, and Ann Wigmore were all sources of inspiration and information for me through the years.

Special thanks to Kathleen Anderson Ross, who did a beautiful job of testing, refining, and quantifying my recipes.

I express my appreciation to Dr. Elson Haas for his support and medical advice throughout the many years of our association and friendship.

Love and thanks to my close friends and family, especially Joanne Brown, Weslynn Hants, Bill Henley, Virginia Kihn, Dona Monet, Cheryl Silver, and Shirley Silver, for encouraging and nurturing me when I needed it most.

Many thanks to Esther Mitgang, Rita Aero, and Kathleen Goss for their innumerable contributions to an earlier first edition.

Finally, much admiration and gratitude to all of my loyal clients and readers, whose trust, discipline, and commitment have taught me so much.

Contents

Foreword
by Elson Haas, M.D.

To describe and understand symptoms and disease in the simplest way I combine Western thinking, Chinese medicine, and naturopathy. Problems in the body and mind often arise from either deficiencies or congestion. In a state of deficiency, we are not acquiring enough nutrients to meet our bodily needs; in a state of congestion, we are suffering from excessive intake and reduced eliminative functions from the overconsumption of foods and non-foods, such as caffeine, alcohol, nicotine, refined sugar, and chemicals.

Those who are deficient may experience symptoms such as fatigue, coldness, hair loss, or dry skin. They need to be nourished with wholesome foods to aid the healing process. Congestive problems, however, are more common in Western, industrialized civilizations. Many of our acute and chronic medical diseases and dilemmas result from the clogging of our tissues and tubes and from the suffocating of our cells and, consequently, of our vitality.

Colds, flus, cancer, cardiovascular diseases, arthritis, and allergies are all examples of congestive disorders. These medical problems may be prevented or treated, at least in part and often quite dramatically, by a program of cleansing and detoxification. The incorporation of dietary changes such as those presented in the Pure Body Plan—consumption of more fresh fruits, vegetables, and water and the reduction of animal fats, heavy proteins, and abusive substances—is the beginning of the rejuvenation process for the human body. This was discovered long ago and is still true today, although conventional medical science may make light of it in deference to the "quick solution."

I consider the cleansing and detoxification process to be the missing link in Western nutrition and a key to the health and vitality of our civilization. It will be a crucial therapy in twenty-first century medicine. In my twenty-five years of medical practice, I have extensively used various cleansing and rejuvenation practices for myself and literally thousands of patients. I truly believe that these practices are some of the most powerful healing therapies I have seen. They initiate a true healing of ailments rather than simply a suppression of symptoms.

I have written extensively about detoxification in my book *Staying Healthy With Nutrition*, as well as in my most recent book, *The Detox Diet*, wherein I discuss both the medical and health factors of this important process. However, you have in your hands a beautiful and powerful book, *Rejuvenate: A 21-Day Natural Detox Plan for Optimal Health*, that can help guide you along your path of healing toward the attainment and maintenance of optimum health.

I have known Helene Silver for more than 20 years. She is a knowledgeable and devoted practitioner and educator for the achievement of both inner and outer beauty. In truth, both Helene and I are encouraging you, through our private practices and writing, to take back the responsibility for your health. So much of it is really up to you. It matters how you live—what you do, what you eat, how you think, how you feel. Take hold and do what you can to be vital and healthy. It is really worth it!

Be Well,
Elson M. Haas, M.D.

Dr. Elson M. Haas is a practicing physician of Integrated Medicine and founder and medical director of the Preventive Medical Centers of Marin and Sonoma in San Rafael, California. He is the author of Staying Healthy with the Seasons, Staying Healthy with Nutrition, A Diet For All Seasons, *and* The Detox Diet.

Introduction

My program can change your life. I know, because I have supervised hundreds of clients on this deep-cleansing program. I have watched the pounds and the signs of aging melt away, to be replaced by a clarity and optimism that enable people to realize their full potential.

For the past eighteen years, I have been director of the Inner Beauty Institute in Sausalito, California. My clients are well-informed, active adults ranging in age from twenty to eighty—people seeking the most effective, up-to-date methods to maintain their vitality. Whether they find me on their own or are referred by physicians, chiropractors, massage therapists, or skin-care specialists, they all want to experience the benefits of peak health that come from inner cleansing. I place my clients on programs that address their specific concerns—excess weight, constipation, abdominal gas and bloating, skin problems, low energy, premature aging. As they cleanse their bodies of toxins, they enjoy a dramatic rejuvenation of body and mind.

I have been studying the various philosophies and techniques presented in the 21-Day Program for almost twenty-five years. I have personally experienced and refined many of these healing procedures and feel better now at fifty than I did at thirty. I used to have painful cramping and breast discomfort with my menstrual periods. Thanks to my cleansing and diet program, I no longer have such problems. My skin used to break out all the time; now I receive frequent compliments on my complexion. Ending my old pattern of constipation increased my mental clarity and released a flow of energy that allows me to get through my busy days with enthusiasm and pleasure.

In the past, comprehensive rejuvenation and cleansing programs were available only in expensive spas, where people could retreat to a peaceful, restricted environment, away from the pressures and temptations of their daily lives. Now, using techniques adapted from my Inner Beauty Institute program, you can create a luxurious spa for yourself in the comfort and privacy of your own home. I will show you how to turn many of your normal daily activities into enjoyable healing rituals. At the end of three short weeks, you will look and feel younger, more attractive, mentally clearer, and energized. And you will realize that you can continue to feel this way throughout your life, because you have learned new ways to renew your beauty from the inside out.

My 21-Day Program fine-tunes all the systems of elimination, or "body filters"— your skin, your lungs, your lymphatic system, your liver and kidneys, and your colon. Some cleansing methods, such as bathing and skin brushing, may already be familiar to you. Some, such as breathing exercises, fasting, and colonic irrigations, may be completely new. Through these techniques, you will learn how to release the toxic substances that are clogging up your body and robbing you of youthful beauty and vitality.

Your most important tool in this cleansing process is clear, pure water. Your body is about 70 percent water. You depend on water to maintain your body temperature, to carry away wastes and toxins, and to renew your body's cells and tissues and fluids. In your at-home spa, you will learn to gently suffuse every part of your body with the miraculous, rejuvenative power of water, through bathing, special drinks, and flushes.

To aid in cleansing and detoxifying your body, you will explore the principles of food combining to provide maximum nutrition to every cell in your body, making you more youthful on the outside and healthier inside. You will discover a safe and comfortable approach to fasting. You will learn to stimulate the cleansing action of your lymph system through massage and exercise. You will clear your mind of stressful thoughts by learning how to relax, let go, and return naturally to a positive attitude. And perhaps most important, at the end of the 21-Day Program you will have learned how to guarantee that the new cells you build will be perfect and healthy because they are free of DNA-damaging toxins.

It takes about three weeks to instill new health and beauty habits that you will carry forward into the rest of your life. You will have more knowledge about how your body works and be able to make more informed choices. You will find that many of these invigorating techniques, activities, and special recipes will become favorites that you will integrate into your daily life. Thus, the program will last much longer than 21 days, and you will use *Rejuvenate: A 21-Day Natural Detox Plan for Optimal Health* as a resource guide for many years to come.

A convenient weekly shopping list will help you assemble the foods and supplies you will need for the coming week.

You can follow this richly rewarding program while you continue to go to work and attend to your personal life. Each day's special activities require no more than about one hour. It's an investment of time and pleasurable effort with a big health and beauty payoff. The program works for me. It works for my clients. And it will work for you!

Orientation to the Program

I will tell you everything you need to know to prepare for your 21-Day Program—what you'll need to buy, what to have on hand, how to schedule your time. Once you have made your preparations, I will lead you, step-by-step, day-by-day, through the same kind of program you would experience at the Inner Beauty Institute. So relax, pamper yourself, and wake up the beauty that slumbers within you!

If you are like most of my clients, you want to look and feel the very best you can. You may have decided it is time to lose weight or to clean the toxins out of your body, or to do something about your low energy or poor complexion or constipation.

The rejuvenation program is designed to promote a positive overall change in your lifestyle. While you will undoubtedly lose weight on this program, you will also learn health habits that will stay with you over your lifetime, improving the quality of your life. Your body will last you many youthful-looking years longer; you will be able to give more of yourself to others; and you will experience a greater sense of well-being.

Overview of the 21-Day Program

Food, Water, and Air:
The Principles of the Program

You may be wondering how you can incorporate all the activities of a comprehensive rejuvenation program into your busy daily life. The 21-Day Program transforms the activities that you do every day—bathing, breathing, walking, eating, thinking, sleeping—into positive, enjoyable, rejuvenating rituals. We all have spent a great deal of time and money going to diet doctors, having facials, and attending exercise classes and gyms. As you learn the principles of this program, you will be able to provide much of this health and beauty care for yourself at home.

As an expert with twenty-five years in the field of health education, I have discovered many high-quality products that promote the goals of cleansing and rejuvenation. These products are discussed throughout the book and can often be found in your local health food store. For your convenience, I have also made them available by mail order. For a resource list, contact me (Helene Silver, POB 3116, Sausalito, CA 94966, (415) 332-6566).

The Rejuvenate Food Philosophy

We begin with food, eliminating the toxins that you are putting into your body needlessly and unintentionally. I encourage you to buy only organically grown fruits and vegetables. Commercially grown produce is treated with a frightening variety of chemicals—pesticides, herbicides, fungicides, bleaches, and gases, among others. In fact, more than four hundred pesticides are currently licensed for use on America's foods, and every year more than 2.5 billion pounds of pesticides are dumped on croplands, forests, lawns, and fields. Because the body is not designed to metabolize these man-made compounds, many of them are stored as toxic waste. If you are not able to obtain organic fruits and vegetables, I will show you how to cleanse your produce so you will not introduce more toxins into your body.

Because much animal protein today is also contaminated with drugs and chemicals, I will ask you to limit your animal-flesh consumption to organic chicken and deep-water ocean fish such as swordfish, tuna, sea bass, and halibut. By eating whole, fresh, uncontaminated foods as often as possible, you will be furnishing your cells and tissues with all the nutrients they require for youthful beauty and vitality. Today it's easier than ever to find organic foods. Due to increased demand, many grocery chains now carry organically grown fruits and vegetables, free-range chickens and eggs, additive-free meats, and filtered water. In addition, many farmer's markets are popping up in metropolitan areas, offering organic options.

I will show you how to combine foods properly so you will get the greatest possible benefit from them, create the smallest amount of toxic residue, and reduce the strain on your digestive system.

On the Rejuvenation Diet, which you will begin tomorrow evening, you will be eating delicious, nourishing meals that will leave you feeling rejuvenated and happy. Most people shed five to twenty pounds during the program. My program also allows for individual variation. Some people simply do not do well on a light breakfast of fruit alone. Please pay attention to your body's messages and plan for the suggested mid-morning protein drink if your energy level has a tendency to drop before lunchtime or if you tend to have an appetite in the morning. Similarly, if you really feel better having your protein meal in the evening, you are free to adjust your menus accordingly, as long as you continue to adhere to the rules of food combining you will be learning in this program. Those of you who choose not to eat animal products will also find it easy and convenient to follow the principles of the Rejuvenation Diet.

The Water Prescription

Just as important as your food is the water you drink. Every cell in your body is constantly flushed and bathed by an exchange of water, which brings in nutrients to build new cells and carries away waste. Pure, clean water is a very important element of your daily intake. The quality of tap water in the United States varies widely from place to place. More than seven hundred toxic compounds have been identified in water drawn from U.S. water systems. Even if your municipal water supply is free of bacteria, it may contain high levels of chlorine and rust, which, combined with other substances, can form unhealthy compounds.

The best health protection today is to use purified water. Many people drink bottled water—which may be distilled, filtered spring water or well water—because they distrust the water from their taps. Unfortunately, water bottling is an essentially unregulated industry. One bottled-water company was found to be selling municipal tap water that had been labeled spring water. Another company was getting its water from a well adjacent to a toxic dump site. If you are not confident about the purity of the bottled water available to you, I recommend that you install a water purifier on your tap. It is very easy to do. The water purifier that I prefer uses an activated charcoal-block filter, which can remove organic chemicals, bacteria, chlorine, toxic metals, dirt, and other suspended matter, while leaving the beneficial natural minerals dissolved in the water. In some areas, where the water is very contaminated, it may be necessary to use a reverse osmosis filter, which removes contaminants by means of a semipermeable membrane, in combination with a charcoal-block filter. Whichever you choose, I recommend that you change the filter in your water purifier twice as often as recommended by the manufacturer.

In any case, use nothing but purified water during your 21-Day Program for making all your teas, beverages, soups, and recipes, as well as for your daily drinking water. If you must resort to bottled water, do not use carbonated water, because it just adds gas and bloating to your system. You should also be suspicious of European bottled waters since the Chernobyl incident, because they may contain radioactive particles.

Besides the water you drink, you will be exploring the external uses of water for healing and rejuvenation. Your daily showers and baths will be one of the most enjoyable aspects of this program. Bathing is an essential practice in all the world's great health spas. To enrich your bathing rituals and make them even more pleasurable, I will show you how to use aromatic essential oils to relax your body and your mind and to produce specific healing and beautifying effects. They also create wonderful scents in your bath.

Essential Breathing

I will help you to become aware of your breathing and to use it to cleanse your body and free your mind of stress. Stress reduction is one of the most important parts of any rejuvenation program. I will show you many techniques for becoming more aware of where you are holding stress in your body and releasing that stress. I will encourage you to get plenty of rest, using bathing and stress-releasing evening activities to ease yourself into sleep. The quality of your sleep reflects the quality of your waking state. By learning to have a more relaxed, vital, and joyful daytime life, you will also enjoy a more pleasant, restful, and beneficial sleep. Finally, as you clean out your body, I will also encourage you to clear your mind of negative thoughts and to use your thinking in a positive, constructive way.

Populations renowned for their longevity and vitality have much to teach us about how to eat right, relieve stress, and maintain an active lifestyle and a positive mental attitude. My 21-Day Program includes proven health, beauty, and rejuvenation secrets from around the world—foods such as sea vegetables, garlic, onions, and fermented foods, and healing practices such as bathing and massage. In addition, my program brings you the very latest discoveries in nutrition and life-extension research, introducing you to supplements and skin-care products that promise to be the most exciting new beauty and health-care products of the coming decade.

The Three Weeks of the Program

The rejuvenation program consists of three weeks of scheduled activities. Each day begins a new chapter, introducing you to important components of the program and lifelong optimal wellness.

A final chapter will show you how to create essential one-day, three-day, or week-long revivers for rejuvenation tune-ups throughout the rest of the year.

Before I provide you with an overview of the program, I want to encourage you not to strive to be perfect or expect to follow the program exactly as it is presented.

Please, be gentle with yourself and make this an enjoyable experience. Part of the benefit of this program is that it is fun and helps you to feel good about yourself. If you wish, you may repeat the program several times during the next year or two, and each time you can expect more of yourself.

Whether you follow the program to the letter or not, I am certain you will find it a valuable resource for many years to come. You will have more knowledge about how your body works, and you will be able to make more informed, responsible choices as you care for yourself. Over the years, I have done variations of this program many different times. It always works! You will discover your own individual path through the 21-Day Program—scheduling, meal plans, and activities. That is absolutely fine, and I know that you will be pleased with the results.

The First Week

The 21-Day Program has three phases. During the first, or elimination, phase, you will begin to clean out your body by eliminating sources of toxins in your diet, concentrating on whole, organic foods and clean, pure water. You will take a look at your habits and eliminate sources of toxicity. At the same time, you will gradually develop positive new habits, as you learn how to make the best possible use of exercise, breathing, bathing, and massage to promote cleansing, rejuvenation, beauty, and a feeling of vitality.

The Second Week

During the deep-cleansing phase, you will be clearing your body of wastes more intensely, because you will be eliminating animal protein from your diet and consuming an array of fruits and vegetables and finally, only juices or broth for two days. By this time, you will have eliminated many of the foods to which people are often unknowingly sensitive. You may experience some minor symptoms, such as a light headache or a pimple or two, as your body begins to throw off the toxins that are being released from the cells. You will also learn techniques for colon cleansing, and your body will become progressively cleaner, clearer, and lighter. You will discover that the cleansing process is not only physical but also psychological. Often, as people clean out their bodies, they find that they are also releasing long-held emotions that have been held in the abdominal area, and they may experience profound personal insights. In working with my clients, I have been amazed to see how the cleansing process brings the mind and body into greater harmony.

The Third Week

As you return to a normal diet during the third, or integration, phase, I will teach you techniques to conquer constipation and eliminate cellulite forever. Did you know that laxatives are the best selling over-the-counter remedy in this country? Many people reading this book have suffered from constipation or poor elimination habits and may be seeking help for this problem. Constipation results in the buildup of toxic-waste material in your colon—wastes that are periodically absorbed into your body, aging it. I am going to help you get rid of this toxic waste, and show you how to prevent it from building up in the future. This toxic waste is also a major factor in the formation of cellulite—those unattractive, lumpy deposits of fat, water, and waste that ruin many otherwise good figures. By showing you how to avoid constipation forever, I will also help you to keep cellulite from forming in your body. In addition, my cleansing program, along with special cellulite-reducing activities, will help you to reduce any cellulite you may now have.

Getting the Most Out of the Program

Self-Assessment

I always begin my first appointment with clients by helping them to examine their health and set realistic goals. I help them to evaluate every aspect of their lives—diet, exercise, stress tolerance, relationships, the environment they live in. I have adapted my questionnaire so that you can go through this process on your own. In filling out this questionnaire, try to be totally honest with yourself. Sometimes it takes my clients weeks or months before they feel comfortable telling me certain things, but you can start out with a completely honest inventory of your own health practices and concerns. You may become aware of some aspects of your life that you never thought of as contributing to how you look and feel.

After you have filled out and scored the questionnaire, make time to take a walk for at least thirty minutes. On an unconscious level, what you have learned about yourself in the questionnaire will be sinking in, so that you will be ready to come back and set goals for what you hope to accomplish in your 21-Day Program.

Questionnaire

In order to make changes in how you look and feel, it will be helpful to evaluate your present health practices and level of awareness. This questionnaire will help you to identify areas you may want to work on during the 21-Day Program.

Instructions: For each question, answer Y for yes or often, S for sometimes or somewhat, and N for no or rarely. After you have completed the questionnaire, refer to the Scoring Key to determine your score on each section. I will then tell you how to use your scores for goal setting.

1. Diet

	Y	S	N
a. Do you make a point of eating natural, whole foods?	❑	❑	❑
b. Do you eat animal protein more than once a day?	❑	❑	❑
c. Do you eat packaged or processed foods?	❑	❑	❑
d. Do you make an effort to avoid insecticides and other chemicals in foods?	❑	❑	❑
e. Do you ever notice any physical or mental symptoms (e.g., headache, stomach pain, rash, drowsiness, irritability) after eating a certain food?	❑	❑	❑
f. Do you eat fresh fruits or vegetables every day?	❑	❑	❑
g. Do you drink six to eight glasses of water every day?	❑	❑	❑
h. Do you drink tap water?	❑	❑	❑

2. Eating Habits

	Y	S	N
a. Do you eat in a calm, relaxed setting, without distractions?	❑	❑	❑
b. If you are angry or upset, do you try to calm down before eating?	❑	❑	❑
c. Do you chew your food well?	❑	❑	❑
d. Do you tend to overeat?	❑	❑	❑
e. Do you eat when you are not hungry?	❑	❑	❑
f. Do you regularly eat out in restaurants?	❑	❑	❑

3. Weight Control

	Y	S	N
a. Are you comfortable with your present weight?	❑	❑	❑

b. Are you overweight? ❑ ❑ ❑

c. Are you underweight? ❑ ❑ ❑

d. Do you have a history of crash dieting? ❑ ❑ ❑

e. Do you tend to eat compulsively to avoid dealing
with emotional issues? ❑ ❑ ❑

4. Digestion

	Y	S	N

a. Do you often feel bloated and full after eating? ❑ ❑ ❑

b. Do you notice after eating particular foods that
you tend to be bloated or uncomfortable? ❑ ❑ ❑

c. Do you experience heartburn or gas pains after eating? ❑ ❑ ❑

5. Elimination

	Y	S	N

a. Do you move your bowels every day? ❑ ❑ ❑

b. Do you move your bowels in direct proportion
to what you eat (i.e., two meals a day equals two
bowel movements)? ❑ ❑ ❑

c. Are your stools hard? ❑ ❑ ❑

d. Are you generally constipated? ❑ ❑ ❑

e. Do you get constipated before your menstrual period? ❑ ❑ ❑

6. Energy Level

	Y	S	N

a. Would you describe your energy level as generally low? ❑ ❑ ❑

b. Are you aware of the fluctuations in your energy level
during the day? ❑ ❑ ❑

c. Are these changes in energy level so dramatic that they
keep you from doing things you would like to do? ❑ ❑ ❑

d. Does your energy level seem to increase or decrease
in relation to meals? ❑ ❑ ❑

e. As you grow older, do you notice your energy level
decreasing? ❑ ❑ ❑

7. Exercise

	Y	S	N

a. Would you describe yourself as physically fit? ❑ ❑ ❑

b. Do you do some form of aerobic activity, such as brisk walking, for one-half hour at least three times a week? ❑ ❑ ❑

c. Do you do yoga or other stretching exercises? ❑ ❑ ❑

d. Do you walk or ride a bicycle regularly, rather than taking a bus or car? ❑ ❑ ❑

8. Breathing   *Y*   *S*   *N*

a. Do you have frequent respiratory infections or bronchitis? ❑ ❑ ❑

b. Does your abdomen expand when you breathe? ❑ ❑ ❑

c. Do you tend to breathe through your mouth? ❑ ❑ ❑

d. Do you do any regular breathing exercises? ❑ ❑ ❑

e. Do you notice that you hold your breath or hyperventilate when you are nervous or angry? ❑ ❑ ❑

9. Rest and Sleep   *Y*   *S*   *N*

a. Do you sleep six to eight hours a night? ❑ ❑ ❑

b. Do you sleep more than nine hours at night? ❑ ❑ ❑

c. Do you have trouble falling asleep? ❑ ❑ ❑

d. Do you have trouble getting up in the morning? ❑ ❑ ❑

e. Do you wake up during the night? ❑ ❑ ❑

10. Stress Level   *Y*   *S*   *N*

a. Would you rate the general stress level in your life as high? ❑ ❑ ❑

b. Do you hold a lot of stress in your body? ❑ ❑ ❑

c. Do you know which parts of your body tend to become tense or painful when you are under stress? ❑ ❑ ❑

d. Does your job produce stress for you? ❑ ❑ ❑

e. Do your family or your personal relationships produce stress for you? ❑ ❑ ❑

f. Are you able to express your anger? ❑ ❑ ❑

11. General Appearance and Personal Hygiene   *Y*   *S*   *N*

a. Do you feel that you are too rapidly showing signs of aging? ❑ ❑ ❑

b. Do you floss your teeth every day? ❑ ❑ ❑

c. Are your teeth in need of repair? ❑ ❑ ❑

d. Do you have bad breath? ❑ ❑ ❑

e. Do you have an unpleasant body odor? ❑ ❑ ❑

f. Do you look bloated or puffy? ❑ ❑ ❑

g. Do you have a protruding tummy, in spite of all
your efforts at diet and exercise? ❑ ❑ ❑

12. Skin, Hair, and Nails   Y   S   N

a. Is your skin either extremely dry or very oily? ❑ ❑ ❑

b. Do you often have blemishes on your face, back,
or other parts of the body? ❑ ❑ ❑

c. Is your hair dry and dull? ❑ ❑ ❑

d. Are your nails weak, ridged, or bitten? ❑ ❑ ❑

e. Do you have cellulite? ❑ ❑ ❑

f. Do you use antiperspirants or deodorants containing
aluminum or other chemical compounds? ❑ ❑ ❑

13. Menstrual Cycle   Y   S   N

a. Does your menstrual period occur in a regular cycle? ❑ ❑ ❑

b. Is the flow about the same every cycle? ❑ ❑ ❑

c.. Do you have severe menstrual cramps? ❑ ❑ ❑

d. Do you have a lot of bloating before your period? ❑ ❑ ❑

e. Do you have an increased tendency to get angry,
anxious, or depressed just before your period? ❑ ❑ ❑

f. Are you having any uncomfortable symptoms as a
result of nearing or undergoing menopause? ❑ ❑ ❑

14. Sexuality   Y   S   N

a. Are you satisfied with your sexual drive? ❑ ❑ ❑

b. Does decreased or excessive libido cause problems
in your relationship? ❑ ❑ ❑

c. Do you crave more touch or nurturing than you
are presently receiving? ❑ ❑ ❑

d. Do you practice "safe sex"? ❑ ❑ ❑

15. Emotional and Mental Health

	Y	S	N
a. Do you notice mood swings throughout the day, the week, or the month?	❑	❑	❑
b. Do you get angry easily?	❑	❑	❑
c. Do you cry easily?	❑	❑	❑
d. Do you laugh a lot?	❑	❑	❑
e. Do you use any stimulants, depressants, or other drugs (legal or illegal) to affect your mood or alertness?	❑	❑	❑

16. Substance Use

	Y	S	N
a. Do you drink more than one caffeine beverage each day?	❑	❑	❑
b. Are you concerned about your tobacco use?	❑	❑	❑
c. Do you drink alcohol more than you think you should?	❑	❑	❑
d. Do you need support in dealing with your use of any of these substances?	❑	❑	❑

17. Environment

	Y	S	N
a. Are you pleased with the overall appearance and atmosphere of your home environment?	❑	❑	❑
b. Do you have natural light, fresh air, and green plants or access to nature in your living space?	❑	❑	❑
c. Is there a quiet place in your home where you can have complete privacy for an hour or more?	❑	❑	❑

SCORING KEY

Use the following key to score your responses on the Orientation Questionnaire. Circle your answers, and total the scores for each section. Record them in the box provided. If your score for a given section is equal to or higher than the Goal Trigger Score, this may indicate an area of special concern for you.

1. Diet

	Y	S	N
a.	0	1	2
b.	2	1	0
c.	2	1	0
d.	0	1	2
e.	2	1	0
f.	0	1	2
g.	0	1	2
h.	2	1	0

Total ____
Goal Trigger Score: 7

2. Eating Habits

	Y	S	N
a.	0	1	2
b.	0	1	2
c.	0	1	2
d.	2	1	0
e.	2	1	0
f.	2	1	0

Total ____
Goal Trigger Score: 5

3. Weight Control.

	Y	S	N
a.	0	1	2
b.	2	1	0
c.	2	1	0
d.	2	1	0
e.	2	1	0

Total ____
Goal Trigger Score: 4

4. Digestion

	Y	S	N
a.	2	1	0
b.	2	1	0
c.	2	1	0

Total ____
Goal Trigger Score: 4

5. Elimination

	Y	S	N
a.	0	2	4
b.	0	1	2
c.	2	1	0
d.	2	1	0
e.	2	1	0

Total ____
Goal Trigger Score: 5

6. Energy Level

	Y	S	N
a.	2	1	0
b.	0	1	2
c.	2	1	0
d.	2	1	0
e.	2	1	0

Total ____
Goal Trigger Score: 6

7. Exercise

	Y	S	N
a.	0	2	4
b.	0	1	2
c.	0	1	2
d.	0	1	2

Total ____
Goal Trigger Score: 4

8. Breathing

	Y	S	N
a.	2	1	0
b.	0	1	2
c.	2	1	0
d.	0	1	2
e.	2	1	0

Total ____
Goal Trigger Score: 4

9. Rest and Sleep

	Y	S	N
a.	0	1	2
b.	2	1	0
c.	4	2	0
d.	2	1	0
e.	2	1	0

Total ____
Goal Trigger Score: 6

10. Stress Level

	Y	S	N
a.	4	2	0
b.	2	1	0
c.	0	1	2
d.	2	1	0
e.	2	1	0
f.	0	1	2

Total ____
Goal Trigger Score: 6

11. General Appearance and Personal Hygiene

	Y	S	N
a.	4	2	0
b.	0	1	2
c.	2	1	0
d.	2	1	0
e.	2	1	0
f.	2	1	0
g.	2	1	0

Total ____
Goal Trigger Score: 8

12. Skin, Hair, and Nails

	Y	S	N
a.	2	1	0
b.	2	1	0
c.	2	1	0
d.	2	1	0
e.	2	1	0
f.	2	1	0

Total ____
Goal Trigger Score: 6

13. Menstrual Cycle

	Y	S	N
a.	0	1	2
b.	0	1	2
c.	2	1	0
d.	2	1	0
e.	2	1	0
f.	4	2	0

Total ____
Goal Trigger Score: 6

14. Sexuality

	Y	S	N
a.	0	1	2
b.	2	1	0
c.	2	1	0
d.	0	2	4

Total ____
Goal Trigger Score: 4

15. Emotional and Mental Health

	Y	S	N
a.	2	1	0
b.	2	1	0
c.	2	1	0
d.	0	1	2
e.	2	1	0

Total ____
Goal Trigger Score: 5

16. Substance Use

	Y	S	N
a.	2	1	0
b.	2	1	0
c.	2	1	0
d.	4	2	0

Total ____
Goal Trigger Score: 6

17. Environment

	Y	S	N
a.	0	2	4
b.	0	1	2
c.	0	1	2

Total ____
Goal Trigger Score: 4

Circle the boxes where your totals are equal to or higher than the Goal Trigger Score. Keep these areas in mind as you read the Goal Setting section.

Goal Setting

When you filled out your questionnaire and scored yourself, you no doubt became aware of things that you would like to focus on during the course of the 21-Day Program. Goal setting is one of the most crucial parts of your whole program, because you chart the course that you will follow for the next three weeks.

It is important to establish realistic goals. Do not strive to be perfect, or expect to achieve your goals or make meaningful changes overnight. Part of the benefit of this program is that it is fun and helps you to feel good about yourself. You may repeat the program several times during the next year, and each time you can set more advanced goals. The key is to be gentle with yourself, and to make this an enjoyable experience.

Try to define your goals in the form of positive statements. For example, instead of saying, "I don't want to have a bloated stomach after meals," you can say, "I want to feel clean and clear and light after meals." Instead of saying, "I don't want to feel angry and tense at work," make your goal, "I want to be calm and good-humored at work." Stating your goals in an affirmative way reinforces your positive self-image.

Do not try to define goals in every area on the questionnaire. I want you to concentrate on setting goals only in those areas of your life that are especially important to you, where your own choices can make a difference. Keep in mind that changing your attitude is just as important as changing your behavior. Feel free to set goals that do not involve spectacular outward changes. As you change yourself internally, the external things will improve noticeably.

Go back and review your scores on the Orientation Questionnaire. For each section of the questionnaire, I have provided a Goal Trigger Score. If your score is equal to or higher than this Goal Trigger Score, circle or highlight your score. This is an area where you will probably want to set some goals. Finally, go back over the questionnaire and see if there are any areas that are of special concern to you, even if your score for that section is not high. Mark those sections also.

Now, look below at the areas of concern that have been triggered in the scoring of your questionnaire, or that you have marked as significant for you. Here you will find some suggestions that will help you to state your goals. Record your goals under the corresponding headings in the 21-Day Goals Contract on page 32.

1. *Diet Practices*—Most of your concerns in this area will be taken care of simply by eating natural, whole foods and eliminating processed foods on the Rejuvenation Diet I will introduce on Sunday: Day 2. If a sweet tooth is an area of special concern, an example of a realistic and positive goal might be, "I will replace my craving for sugar with an enjoyment of fresh fruits."

2. *Eating Habits*—As I will explain on Monday: Day 3, your emotional and mental state have a direct bearing on your ability to digest your food. You will learn many ways to calm and center yourself during this program, for example, through relaxing baths, through yoga postures, and through the breathing exercises you will learn on Thursday: Day 6. A possible goal might be, "I will eat only when I am calm," or "I will eat slowly, chew my food well, and pay attention to its flavor, texture, and smell."

3. *Weight Control*—If you want to lose (or gain) weight, set a realistic goal for yourself. Although your weight will tend to normalize on the 21-Day Program, the main objective is not rapid weight loss, but lifelong dietary change. The Rejuvenation Diet, accompanied by the tips I will offer during Week 3 for lifelong bowel health, will help to keep your weight where you want it to be.

4. *Digestion*—In this program, you will learn how your digestive system works and why you may have been having problems with digestive upset in the past. Special cleansing beverages and digestion-toning postures will help to flush and heal your digestive system during Week 2. If digestive problems are one of your reasons for undertaking this program, you may want to set a positive overall goal, such as, "I will learn how to select foods in such a way that I will feel light and comfortable after my meals."

5. *Elimination*—If you are troubled by constipation, the Rejuvenation Diet will automatically help you to resolve this problem. The cleansing process will become more intense during Week 2, as you flush all your systems of elimination. Finally, you will learn about colon cleansing and rules for eliminating constipation forever. A realistic goal might be, "I will use natural methods for keeping my bowel function regular."

6. *Energy Level*—As you eliminate the toxins from your system through proper diet, you will begin to experience an increase in your energy level. Your exercise program and yoga postures are also designed to improve your energy level, as are the invigorating baths used throughout the program. If low or fluctuating energy levels

have been limiting your activity or keeping you dependent on caffeine, state a goal such as, "I will become aware of the daily fluctuations in my energy level and learn natural ways to increase my energy when I need an extra boost."

7. *Exercise*—On Tuesday: Day 4, I will introduce a simple, pleasant program of brisk walking that can keep you in shape for the rest of your life. If you have been irregular in your commitment to exercise in the past, a general goal might be, "I will walk whenever possible, for pleasure, exercise, and transportation."

8. *Breathing*—The essential breathing exercises on Thursday: Day 6 and the breath-awareness activities that accompany your daily exercise will improve your breathing capacity. A general goal might be, "I will pay attention to my breathing and learn how to use breathing exercises for health and relaxation."

9. *Rest and Sleep*—It is important to get plenty of sleep during the program to support the physical and emotional changes that you will be experiencing. Commit yourself to a certain number of hours of sleep every night. If you suffer from insomnia or early awakening, the 21-Day Program will provide many aids to help solve these problems, such as the relaxing baths described on Monday: Day 3 and the various forms of massage described on Friday: Day 7. A general goal might be, "I will practice natural methods for inducing sleep."

10. *Stress Level*—Everyone experiences stress. The first step in learning to control stress is to learn to recognize it in your body and your mind. Awareness exercises, such as the tense-and-relax Yoga Stress Releaser you will learn on Saturday: Day 1, can help you take a regular inventory of your stress points. You will then be able to use breathing, exercise, bathing, and mental reprogramming—all explained in this program—to control the stress you have identified. A realistic goal might be, "I will learn to recognize the signs of stress in my body, and I will practice techniques to release my daily stress."

11. *General Appearance and Personal Hygiene*—Even with all the pleasurable bathing activities recommended throughout the 21-Day Program, it is still up to you to maintain high standards of cleanliness and personal care. You may find that the intensive cleansing during Week 2 will help resolve some troublesome problems, such as unpleasant body odor, bad breath, or a protruding tummy. Other issues will require your specific attention and resolve. An example of a realistic goal might be, "I will establish the habit of flossing my teeth every day."

12. *Skin, Hair, and Nails*—As you follow the Rejuvenation Diet and the skin-care program described on Monday: Day 3, your complexion should become clear and glowing with youthful radiance. Special unsaturated-oil supplements introduced on Monday: Day 3 will help make your hair shiny and your nails healthy and strong. Still, there are some areas where you may need to make personal decisions and commitments. A realistic goal might be, "I will replace my cosmetics and skin-care products with all natural products," or "I will devote extra effort to the special activities to rid my body of cellulite."

13. *Menstrual Cycle*—A special section "Monthly Women's Retreat" at the end of this book will provide helpful suggestions for overcoming menstrual discomfort naturally. The regular exercise program you will establish on Tuesday: Day 4, as well as reducing your overall toxicity, should also help to keep your cycle normal and regular. A realistic goal might be, "I will become more in tune with my monthly cycle and use it as an opportunity for cleansing."

14. *Sexuality*—Some, but by no means all, sexual problems are related to toxicity and stress. The conscious breathing techniques you will learn on Thursday: Day 6 may prove especially useful in helping you to relax and open yourself sexually, and on Friday: Day 7 you will learn how to use massage to satisfy the normal human need for nurturing, nonsexual touch. You may also be surprised to discover during Week 2 that colon cleansing can produce a dramatic improvement in many people's sex lives. A realistic goal in this area might be, "I will learn new ways to give and receive pleasure and express caring."

15. *Emotional and Mental Health*—Emotional and mental problems are often the result of toxicity, lack of exercise, or excessive stress. During Week 2, you will undergo an intensive cleansing, accompanied by the use of affirmations to reprogram your negative thinking into positive attitudes. The 21-Day Program provides many natural techniques for feeling good about your whole self. A realistic general goal might be, "I will be more easygoing and cultivate a sense of humor about the little things that bother me," or "I will spend my time with positive, upbeat, like-minded people."

16. *Substance Use*—This is an area where you will really need to take a look at what kind of commitment you want to make. I do not insist that you quit drinking coffee, smoking, or drinking alcohol completely. If you want to eliminate or cut down on any of your toxic habits, set realistic goals for yourself, so you do not waste energy and create stress by blaming yourself for slipping. At the beginning of Week 1, I will offer

some suggestions that may help you reduce your caffeine and alcohol consumption, and on Thursday: Day 6, I will give you some ideas about how to cut down on smoking.

17. *Environment*—I encourage you to think of ways to make your home more peaceful and pleasing. What changes would you like to make in your personal environment? It may not be realistic to set a goal of moving to the country, but you can think of ways to help keep the air in your house clean or to protect yourself from excessive noise. A positive goal might be, "I will create a quiet, private place where I can enjoy being by myself."

Now, fill in your goals on the 21-Day Goals Contract. Remember, make commitments only in those areas where you have real concerns. You will be reviewing those goals again at the end of the program, on Friday, Day 21.

21-Day Goals Contract

During the 21-Day Program and after its completion, I commit myself to making the following changes:

1. Diet: _____
2. Eating Habits: _____
3. Weight Control: _____
4. Digestion: _____
5. Elimination: _____
6. Energy Level: _____
7. Exercise: _____
8. Breathing: _____
9. Rest and Sleep: _____
10. Stress Level: _____
11. General Appearance and Personal Hygiene: _____
    _____
12. Skin, Hair, and Nails: _____
13. Menstrual Cycle: _____
14. Sexuality: _____
15. Emotional and Mental Health: _____
    _____
16. Substance Use: _____
17. Environment: _____

Your Personal Support System

Support from your friends or family is vital when you commit yourself to a program of intensive whole-body cleansing. I encourage you to go on the program with a partner. You can create a buddy-support system, arranging for someone you can call on to share your experiences. You may want to surprise a close friend with a copy of this book and then plan to do the program together. If you have a family, share your plans to do this program with your parents, your spouse, and your children. With luck, they will understand and support your commitment to improve your health and vitality—to be the very best you can be, for them and for yourself.

Human nature being what it is, some people will simply not support your efforts to improve yourself. They may discourage you or tease you and make you feel self-conscious. Reduce the negativity in your life during this time. Share your plans only with positive, loving, upbeat people who will make you feel good about the new direction your life is taking.

Many of my clients like to keep a journal during the twenty-one days of mind/body cleansing. After your evening bath, when you get into bed, is a good time to take a moment and write down any thoughts or impressions that may have come to mind. What were the high points and the low points of the day? What new discoveries did you make? How are you feeling about your body? Have you found any new ways to deal with stress? You may make these observations in any form you choose—journal notes, drawings, or poetic affirmations. By recording your personal experiences on a daily basis, you support yourself and reinforce your twenty-one-day commitment.

Fitting the 21-Day Program Into Your Life

Many people spend a great deal of time and money on extended stays at health spas. Part of the reason they do this is because the spa environment eliminates the distractions of everyday life. One of the advantages of the rejuvenation program is that you can enjoy the personal benefits of a spa while you carry on with your normal life. You can continue to eat in restaurants, you can continue to socialize with friends, you can still take care of your family and loved ones, and you can continue to go to work.

To help you get the most out of the program, I ask you to commit yourself to a schedule for the regular activities—mealtimes, exercise, reading the lecture portion of each chapter, evening activities, bathing, and writing in your journal. Arrange plenty of private time for yourself on weekends for the extended sessions in your cleansing program. I know there will be special dates you just won't want to miss or meetings you must attend. However, concentration and personal commitment are essential, so look at your schedule and pledge the necessary time to yourself.

Take a deep, self-indulgent breath—relax and enjoy yourself. My 21-Day Program is designed to be fun—three weeks of self-awareness and new approaches to things you do every day. I do not encourage extremism. Do not feel you must give up forever the things you enjoy. I encourage my clients to enjoy life, to be happy. I have developed a moderate cleansing program with which everyone can feel comfortable. I assure you that there is room in this program for variation, and I will help you to discover where you need to make adjustments in the recommended program to fit your personal energy level and emotional needs. One of my great personal lessons has been not to be hard on myself. If you go off the program, please take it with good humor. Just give a little shrug, forgive yourself, and get back on. Be gentle with yourself, and do the best you can. You'll still get great results. Next time, you'll do more.

Personalizing Your Rejuvenation Schedule

The schedule provided for each day of the 21-Day Program must be personalized to your own requirements. You need to decide at what time you will eat your meals, do your exercise, read the lecture, perform your evening activities, and write in your journal. Of course, you may need to make some adjustments, but it is important that you make a commitment to set aside time each day to do all the scheduled activities.

Lecture

Each day during the program, you will read the background information about the activities described in the chapter. Do not read the lecture material at meals, since I want you to relax and eat slowly without distractions. A good idea is to pour yourself a cup of Inner Beauty Herbal Tea and sip it while you read the day's lecture. Consider reading the lecture before or after breakfast, during your afternoon break, or before bedtime.

Meals

It is important to space your meals at specific intervals, so you can derive the greatest nutritional benefit from your food and allow your system to cleanse itself. The 21-Day Program is built around three meals a day, with mid-morning and mid-afternoon snacks if you feel your energy flagging. As you look over the recommended meals, please feel free to make individual adjustments based on the preparation time you have available and your personal tastes. For example, some prefer to prepare the Potassium Broth and use it throughout the program rather than making any of the other soups and bisques. Others choose one salad dressing or protein drink and use that throughout the program. All of this works! I am providing you with a program and encouraging you to personalize it as you wish. Enjoy!

Exercise

Every day of your 21-Day Program you will do at least thirty minutes of brisk walking or other vigorous exercise. If you are exercising regularly at present, you already have an exercise schedule. If not, think about what time of day you would most enjoy taking a thirty-minute walk. You may decide to gradually increase your exercise time during the course of the program, but for now simply commit yourself to a half hour of exercise daily. Each day you will also be given a warm-up or stretch to precede your exercise schedule.

Evening Activities

Each evening, your 21-Day Program will provide special activities that are fun, relaxing, and rejuvenating. Your evening schedule may vary, but you will need to commit about an hour a night to your evening activity and your bath. Because these activities have a relaxing and stress-relieving effect, I recommend that you do them right before bedtime. I understand that there will be nights when this will not be possible, but it is very important for you to go through the learning experience that each of these evening activities provides. Think ahead now, and decide on an alternate time (such as right after work or early in the morning) that you will be able to commit, when necessary, to each day's special activities.

Journal Entries

Sometimes you will be asked to write in your journal in the course of reading a lecture or during an evening activity. Besides these self-affirmation exercises, I want you to make regular daily notes about the feelings that occur to you during the day. A convenient time to make such journal entries is right at bedtime, but some people may prefer to make their entries on rising in the morning, during a morning commute, or at some other time during the day when they are free of distractions. To help establish a regular habit of writing in your journal, commit yourself now to a time that you think will be best for you.

21-Day Time Commitments

I commit myself to carrying out the activities of the 21-Day Program at the following times each day:

Lecture: _____

Meals: _____

    Breakfast: _____

    Lunch: _____

    Dinner:_____

Exercise: _____

Evening Activity: _____

    Alternate Time: _____

Journal Entry: _____

Commonly Asked Questions

How do I fit this into my schedule?

If you already plan time for daily exercise, you will only need an additional thirty minutes daily to include the other activities.

I have provided recommendations for how to follow the program if you are eating out in restaurants. It is always possible to order a healthy meal, and it's simply up to you to make the necessary requests. Don't be shy! Ask for what you want. You'll be surprised how accommodating most restaurants will be. If they are not willing to prepare what you have requested, find a restaurant that will. I'm sure there's one just down the street.

If you travel a lot for business, I suggest that you wait to follow the entire program until you know that you will be at home for at least three weeks. However, the diet for week one is a great way to begin the cleansing process and can be sustained indefinitely until you have the time to go further on the program. You will find increased vitality and will probably lose weight simply by eliminating many of the heavier and more congestive foods from your diet. You may even find that many undesirable symptoms of toxicity disappear or are greatly reduced simply by cleaning up your diet. Follow weeks two and three as soon as your schedule allows.

I have recommended that you begin the program on a Saturday so that you have the weekend to organize yourself for the coming week. Preparation will reduce the daily time required to follow the program. If you have days off other than Saturday and Sunday, please feel free to set the program up so that it best suits your schedule.

It is possible to do only *some* of the program and still get great results. Do the parts that *you* feel ready to do. Each time you follow the 21-day program, you will probably be more comfortable adding new activities. After awhile you will find that you have more energy than ever! You'll feel great in the morning, and it will be easier to get up and spend the extra time doing your cleansing activities.

Do I have to do it perfectly to get results?

Definitely not. I have done many variations of this program over the last twenty-five years and get great results each time. I have supervised, literally, thousands of clients on individualized variations of the program and have continuously seen improvements in their overall health and vitality and corrections of many of the problems discussed throughout the book. I have shared many of these personal stories with you throughout, and you can expect these same results for yourself.

If you fall off the diet, you don't need to start the 21-day program over. Simply get back on and continue. It's truly okay. Please don't spend time being hard on yourself. No one, including myself, is perfect. A slip will not degrade the experience or the results, but a negative attitude will.

If certain recommended foods or recipes don't appeal to you, simply exchange them for the ones that do. You will still get great results.

If you're uncomfortable with the recommended colon cleansing activities, you can still achieve positive results by following the other parts of the program. However, the results are greatly enhanced by colon cleansing. If you are frightened of colon cleansing, please find a qualified health professional with whom to discuss the issues. For some, this phase of the program may be too extreme. For others, simply communicating with a qualified professional may ease your fears and allow you to feel comfortable.

What if I can only schedule my massage or colonic on days other than you recommend in the course of the twenty-one days?

Please keep in mind that it is impossible to write a book that will fit everyone's schedule, and there *is* room for individual variation in every aspect of the program. For example, you may get better results on the program by having more than the recommended number of colonics. It is impossible for me to know that, but I have attempted to give you the basic guidelines so that you can make your own self-evaluation. By tuning in to what your body is telling you, you will learn to know yourself even better than you already do.

It truly doesn't matter whether your massage or colonic falls on days other than I suggest. The most important thing is to do them, to feel good about doing them, and to congratulate yourself for your accomplishments.

Some cleansing programs are much more extreme than the one you recommend. Will I still get results on this more moderate plan?

There are certainly more intense cleansing programs available, but I believe in a moderate approach that will more easily integrate into your daily life and provide you with long-term benefits. I encourage you to adapt your favorite cleansing techniques from this program into your every day life rather than get into the "binge and purge" cycle so common today.

How will I feel during the 21 days?

Whenever you change your habits or lifestyle, there is bound to be a transitional period. There will probably be times that you will feel more energized than usual and other times that you feel more tired or sluggish. Please read my discussion of cleansing reactions on pages 211-213. This will help you to understand that annoying symptoms such as headaches, skin eruptions, coated tongue, low energy, grouchiness, and cold or flu-like reactions may be caused as toxins are being released from your organs, cells, and tissues, and dumped into your system to be eliminated through the various body filters. These reactions are telling you that your body is eliminating wastes that have probably been stored in your system for some time. Any minor discomfort that you experience now means fewer problems in the future.

Be sure to drink lots of liquids and get enough rest to assist your body in dealing with this process. Use the various cleansing techniques I recommend throughout the book to help you get through these reactions as quickly as possible.

You will feel great by the end of the twenty-one days, and each time you do the program you will find fewer and fewer of these symptoms.

Do I have to be really strict with food combining? I have read so many different philosophies about it that I am confused.

My philosophy of food combining is more moderate than many other health professionals. In fact, over the years I have found that most of my clients have responded well to simplified food combining, and that only those who have extremely sensitive digestive systems need to be quite strict.

If you want to eliminate gas and bloating, it really is imperative that you don't mix fruit with other foods. Papaya may be an exception since it is full of enzymes which may help with the digestion of heavier foods. Other than papaya, I recommend that you eat fruit *only* in the morning rather than in-between meals or for dessert. If you follow this guideline, you will be guaranteed that the fruit is not mixing with an earlier meal that still may be digesting in your stomach. Otherwise, the fruit will ferment in combination with these other foods and cause gas and bloating. It will also inhibit the absorption of nutrients.

It is also important not to mix your animal proteins (fish and chicken) with your processed starches (bread and pasta). I have found that this modified food combining principle is successful for most people. Whole grains and potatoes are basically unprocessed foods and seem to be tolerated in combination with animal proteins by most people. If you follow this modified combining recommendation and continue to notice gas and bloating, then I recommend that you become more stringent with the combining principles and eliminate even the grains and potatoes with animal proteins.

If you are a vegetarian and are confused about whether you can combine tofu, beans, and other legumes with rice or other grains, please read on. You will probably be able to combine tofu and beans with whole grains. However, if you notice gas and bloating or any other discomfort after eating, experiment with *Beano*, an enzyme which helps digest beans. If this doesn't work, then you are probably one of those people who will benefit from a very strict adherence to food combining principles. In that case, it will probably be better to eat tofu and beans with vegetables only, or rice and other whole grains with vegetables only, rather than mixing them all together. Only experimentation will tell you what is best for your body.

Program Recipes

The recipes in this chapter are specially designed for use during the 21-Day Program. They contain no chemicals, preservatives, refined starches and sugars—no toxins of any kind. When you make these recipes, be sure to use organic produce (or produce you have treated with the Cleansing Soak on page 116) and cold-pressed vegetable oils, to ensure that your meals are clean and clear.

Some of the ingredients may be unfamiliar to you. Part of the purpose of this program is to introduce you to the flavors and nutritional benefits of foods you may not have used before. I am sure that many will become lifelong favorites.

The yield for each recipe is given in terms of small servings, the equivalent of side dishes. If you are going to use the dish as a main course, the yield is half as many servings. These recipes are free of fattening and hard-to-digest ingredients, so do not hesitate to eat as large a helping as you wish.

Cleansing Beverages

Hot Lemon-Water Flush

You will drink the Hot Lemon-Water Flush first thing each morning, to help complete the cleansing process that has been going on during the night. This drink flushes all the systems of elimination, especially the kidneys, the liver, and the colon. It helps to cleanse waste from the digestive tract and keep your breath sweet.

8-ounce glass of warm purified water
Juice of ½ lemon

*Pinch of cayenne pepper or 1 drop of cayenne
   tincture*

Heat eight ounces of purified water until it is quite warm, pour the water in a glass, and add the lemon juice and cayenne. You may increase the amount of cayenne gradually (up to one-eighth teaspoon of the powder or eight drops of tincture) as you continue to make your Hot Lemon-Water Flush each morning.

Lemon juice helps to break up and dislodge the sticky mucus deposits that tend to clog up the system. Its powerful enzymes and high vitamin-C content are natural cleansers, helping to flush your system of toxic wastes. The bioflavonoid in the white inner rind and fibrous strands are also very cleansing, so use a squeezer to derive the benefits of these fibrous parts of the lemon as well. Cayenne pepper aids digestion by stimulating the production of digestive juices and helps to eliminate mucus. Some people find that drinking hot water, even by itself, helps to encourage a bowel movement in the morning.

Inner Beauty Herbal Tea Blend

This blend was developed by Walt Baptiste of San Francisco. I have studied yoga and meditation with him for the last twenty-five years and have learned many wonderful techniques from him, including this mineralizing tea.

You will enjoy the pleasantly soothing, minty taste of this tea as a daily beverage. Not only is it a delightful substitute for caffeine drinks, but it also promotes cleansing and nourishes the cells and tissues. Begin by making up a large batch of the dried herbs for the Herbal Tea Blend, so that you can use this premixed blend each morning to prepare your tea.

1 cup dried peppermint	*½ cup dried alfalfa*
½ cup dried oat straw	*½ cup dried sage*

Combine all the herbs, mix together well, and store in an airtight container.

Each morning, boil four cups of purified water, remove it from the heat, and pour it into a teapot. Add four teaspoons of Herbal Tea Blend and steep for twenty minutes with the teapot covered. Strain the tea into a thermos or other container and drink it between meals throughout the day. You may reheat the tea if you wish, or drink it cold.

Peppermint is an excellent aid to digestion and relieves flatulence and bowel spasms. Oat straw is rich in the mineral silica, an essential component of teeth, hair, skin, and nails. Oat-straw tea is also a traditional remedy for chest ailments. Alfalfa is one of nature's richest sources of a variety of vitamins and minerals, including potassium and iron. Sage is an antispasmodic and helps to eliminate mucus in the respiratory passages and stomach.

Hydrating Drink

You can enhance the hydrating properties of your purified drinking water by adding a small amount of natural sugar. This Hydrating Drink was developed by two Australian doctors who were working in Africa with malnourished children. The doctors found that infants who were dehydrated from diarrhea were not helped when given water alone, but if some sugar was mixed in the water, it helped to rehydrate their tissues. Using sugar water for oral-hydration therapy is based on the same theory as giving intravenous glucose, or sugar water, to people in the hospital who cannot eat solid food.

You may prepare the Hydrating Drink using either pure maple syrup or apple juice, in the proportions given below. Be sure to use juice from organically grown apples, or pure maple syrup (not a maple-flavored, refined-sugar syrup). Both are excellent sweeteners. Try them, and see which suits your own taste.

6 ounces of purified water	or	*8 ounces of purified water*
2 ounces of organic apple juice		*1 teaspoon of pure maple syrup*

Pour the pure maple syrup or apple juice into an empty glass and fill it to the top with purified water.

Drink a glass of Hydrating Drink between meals throughout the day, whenever you are thirsty. Bring some sweetener of your choice to work. Fill a glass with water from the cooler, add the sweetener, and sip it at your desk. This Hydrating Drink helps your body absorb water at a cellular level. This keeps the tissues plump and moisturized and promotes the cleansing activity of lymphatic fluid as water is moved in and out of the cells. Regular use of this Hydrating Drink keeps your system constantly flushed with fresh water, pushing the stagnant fluids out from between the cells and overcoming a tendency to bloating by removing salt. It also keeps your colon hydrated and discourages constipation.

Potassium Broth

Potassium Broth is one of the mainstays of your 21-Day Program. It is delicious all by itself, either thin or thick, hot or cold. You will also be using it as a stock for nourishing vegetable soups. Have some of today's batch of Potassium Broth with a vegetable or starchy food for dinner tonight, and store the rest for later this week. Potassium Broth is rich in minerals and is the quintessential cleanser for the intestines and the blood.

You will use my recipe to make both a thick bisque for a satisfying meal and strained to make a thin broth. The thin broth will be used as a base for other soups and as a mineral-rich drink during the cleansing phase of the program.

14 carrots, with tops	*4 cloves of garlic*
14 celery stalks, with tops	*3 summer squash*
Beet tops from 2 bunches	*3 zucchini*
4 potatoes	*2 handfuls of parsley*
2 onions	

Chop all of the vegetables, place them in an eight-quart soup pot, and cover them with purified water. Bring the water to a boil. Turn the heat down and simmer, uncovered, for thirty minutes. Turn off the heat, cover the broth, and allow it to sit for another thirty minutes. Remove and discard the greens from the pot. Their nutrients are now in the stock. Remove the rest of the vegetables, put them into your food processor or blender, and purée them into a bisque. (Depending on the size of your appliance, you may need to do this in batches.) Add about one-fourth cup of the broth to each batch that you purée until it is the consistency you like. Empty the bisque into a storage container and refrigerate it until you are ready to use it—you will have eight servings. Put the rest of the clear broth into a separate container to use as a base for your other soups or as a quick pick-me-up whenever you wish.

Helpful Hints:

- Both the thick bisque and the thin broth can be stored in the refrigerator for up to five days. You may wish to make a double batch of the recipe and freeze it in four-cup containers to be used throughout the program. (If you do this, you will need to use a larger pot.)

- Take either the bisque or broth along with you in your thermos to use as a mid-afternoon snack, or have a cup of the nourishing mixture before going to bed.

- Use the thick bisque as an alternative to the other vegetable soup recipes suggested throughout the 21-Day Program if your schedule during the week does not allow for further preparation time.

Variations:

- Add a packet of Knox unflavored gelatin to a cup of the broth or bisque to add protein richness. The gelatin will also assist the absorption of vitamins and minerals into your system.

- Add one tablespoon of granulated lecithin to each cup of bisque or broth for additional cleansing power.

- Add additional cloves of garlic to your soup pot as desired.

- If desired, add one bunch of spinach as well.

- For a different flavor and extra nutrition, dissolve one-half to one teaspoon of miso in one-fourth cup of hot broth and add it to your bowl of bisque or cup of broth.

Ionic Cocktail

The Ionic Cocktail is a blend of minerals that are absorbed very readily through the walls of the intestine and colon. Drink this mixture just before you exercise each day.

Into an eight-ounce glass of purified water, stir:

1 Emergen-C packet or 1 teaspoon of
vitamin-C powder

1 tablespoon liquid minerals
1 ounce aloe vera juice

Along with this drink, take:

10 drops of wheat-germ oil on the tongue
1 40-milligram tablet of ginkgo-leaf extract
or 1 dropperful of ginkgo-leaf tincture

Emergen-C, which contains vitamin C and some minerals, can be purchased in any health food store. You can also use powdered vitamin C (ascorbic acid). Vitamin C helps form collagen, so vital to repairing and rejuvenating the skin. Along with vitamin E and the trace mineral selenium, vitamin C is well known for its anti-aging action and for preventing the accumulation of destructive free radicals in the cells.

Aloe vera juice, when taken internally, promotes cleansing of the digestive tract. It has also been reported helpful in the treatment of arthritis and allergies. Externally, aloe juice is a remedy for burns, sunburn, skin irritation, and minor cuts and scratches. You may increase the amount of aloe vera in this recipe by one ounce per week, up to three ounces. Ginkgo-leaf extract is derived from an ancient species of tree native to China. Ginkgo leaf has long been valued in Chinese herbal medicine and is just now being recognized in the West for its powerful antiaging activity. Besides combating harmful free radicals, it helps to increase the flow of nutrients and oxygen to the circulatory system, eyes, ears, and brain.

Wheat-germ oil contains the active ingredient octacosanol. When taken just before your exercise, octacosanol exerts a powerful cleansing action, bringing oxygen into the muscle tissues and flushing the blood vessels.

On Thursday: Day 6, I am going to amplify your Ionic Cocktail with the powerful nutrients germanium and co-enzyme Q-10, which will help to deliver oxygen to all the cells in your body. During Week 2, I will add liquid chlorophyll to aid in the cleansing process.

Rejuvelac

Rejuvelac is a fermented grain drink. It has been valued by women for centuries for its ability to impart a beautiful complexion. Furthermore, Rejuvelac is high in the friendly bacteria that are so important for a healthy colon. The tonic can be made from either barley or millet. The taste varies depending on which grain is used. Barley is my personal favorite; it imparts a nut-like flavor to the Rejuvelac and is delightfully fragrant as it ferments. Millet has a tangy, lemony flavor. Experiment to find a taste that you enjoy.

1 cup of barley or millet
1 quart of purified water

Soak the raw grain in water for twenty-four hours without refrigerating. After twenty-four hours, pour off the water and refrigerate it to drink throughout the day as a refreshing and rejuvenating between-meal beverage. If any beverage is left over at the end of the day, add it to your bath water, and prepare a new batch of Rejuvelac for tomorrow.

Reuse the grain base at least three times and up to five times, if you wish. The flavor will get stronger with each use.

Oxygenation Cocktail

This powerful, space-age, nutrient-rich cocktail helps prepare your body for any kind of exercise by ensuring that all the muscles, tissues, and other cells are supplied with oxygen.

Fill a glass with eight ounces of purified water and add:

1 Emergen-C packet or 1 teaspoon vitamin-
C powder
Pinch of germanium (about $^1/_{16}$ teaspoon)

1 ounce aloe vera juice
1 tablespoon liquid minerals

Along with this drink take:

10 drops of wheat-germ oil on the tongue
1 co-enzyme Q-10 capsule
1 50-milligram tablet of pycnogenol

1 40-milligram tablet of ginkgo extract
or 1 dropperful of the liquid tincture in 1
ounce of water

Called the "nutrients of the nineties," co-enzyme Q-10 and germanium are being widely used in Japan. Germanium and co-enzyme Q-10 are available in a number of forms—sublingual, powder, and capsules. All are equally effective.

Germanium has been nicknamed the "oxygen nutrient," because its oxygen-rich molecular structure facilitates the oxygenation of tissues. It also protects against harmful free radical molecules and stimulates the immune system. By increasing oxygenation, it promotes cell and tissue rejuvenation and improved metabolism. Due to FDA regulations, it is sometimes difficult to find germanium. Watch for any changes in its availability.

Co-enzyme Q-10 protects against heart disease and high blood pressure, stimulates the immune system, slows the aging process, and guards against the gum disease that so often accompanies aging. As we grow older, our bodies become less capable of producing co-enzyme Q-10. Taking it as a supplement assists our cells and tissues in rejuvenating themselves. Co-enzyme Q-10 also helps athletes to meet their bodies' increased energy demands, and it can aid in weight loss, because it increases the body's ability to burn stored fat.

Pycnogenols are naturally-occurring chemicals found in pine bark, grape seeds, and a variety of fruits and vegetables. They are nearly twenty times more powerful than vitamin C and fifty times more powerful than vitamin E. Studies have shown that pycnogenols improve capillary action, restore elasticity and strength to connective tissues, and, unlike many other antioxidants, are able to cross the blood brain barrier and provide free radical protection to central nervous tissue. Anecdotal evidence indicates that pycnogenols may help alleviate a wide variety of conditions, including seizures, poor vision, allergies, asthma, Alzheimer's, Parkinson's, varicose veins, depression, stroke, and more.

You can benefit from these powerful health-promoting nutrients by adding them to your daily supplement program. The Oxygenation Cocktail, combined with exercise and correct breathing, will promote a dynamic oxygenating and cleansing action within your cells in a matter of minutes.

Inner Beauty Tea with Chaparral

On Saturday and Sunday of Week Two, you will begin the deep cleansing phase of the 21-Day Program by drinking this enhanced version of the Inner Beauty Herbal Tea Blend. The addition of chaparral to the basic recipe produces a powerful cleansing effect on all the organs of elimination. If you do not wish to prepare this tea, there are many Detox Teas available in health food stores.

2 tablespoons Inner Beauty Herbal Tea Blend   6 cups purified water
   (pages 42-43)
2 teaspoons dried chaparral herb[*]

Boil the water, remove from heat, and add the Inner Beauty Tea Blend and the chaparral herb. Cover and steep for one hour, then strain it into a thermos or other container to drink, a cup at a time, throughout the day.

You may drink the tea cool, or you may warm it again if you wish. Sweeten the tea with a little honey if you'd like.

Chaparral protects against infection and promotes elimination of toxins through the kidneys, lymph, and blood. It is a powerful herb used specifically for cleansing; it is not appropriate to drink as an everyday beverage.

[*]Due to FDA regulations, dried chaparral is sometimes not available. However, you will find a chaparral tincture, of which you may use 1 dropperful per cup of Inner Beauty Tea.

Herbal Purification Tea

On Monday: Day 10 through Friday: Day 14 you will drink two cups of Herbal Purification Tea in the morning, and another cup just before going to bed. This pleasant-tasting herbal flush helps to eliminate congestion and toxicity in the digestive and lymph systems.

¼ cup of fennel seeds   *½ cup of flax seeds*
¼ cup of fenugreek seeds   *½ cup of peppermint leaves*
¼ cup of licorice root

Prepare a supply of Herbal Purification Tea blend by combining all ingredients and storing the mixture in an airtight container. To make a supply of the tea for the day, add four teaspoons of this blend to four cups of cold purified water, bring to a boil, and simmer, covered, for seven to ten minutes. Strain out the herbs and save the strained tea to drink at the specified times. You do not need to refrigerate the tea, and you may reheat it if you wish.

This tasty, fragrant herbal blend has powerful detoxifying effects, helping to expel mucus, remove gas from the intestines, promote digestion, cleanse the digestive system and the urinary tract, and soothe the mucous membranes. It is so effective at flushing the lymph system that people have reported a shrinking of swollen lymph nodes shortly after drinking this tea.

If you do not wish to make this tea, you will still get great results by using the Intestinal Cleanser on page 52.

Liver Flush #1

This detoxifying drink, which you will take on Monday, Wednesday, and Friday mornings of Week Two, helps to eliminate poisons stored in the liver. The liver filters pollutants out of the blood, but as long as more poisons are being put into the system, it does not have a chance to eliminate them all through the intestines. During a cleansing program, while you are giving your liver a rest, you can help flush the stored toxins out and restore its natural vitality.

juice of 1 to 2 lemons, freshly squeezed
juice of 1 orange, freshly squeezed
1 teaspoon of grated fresh ginger
pinch of cayenne pepper or 1 drop of cayenne
   tincture

1 to 3 cloves garlic, crushed
1 tablespoon safflower oil, cold-pressed
1 tablespoon olive oil, cold-pressed

Combine all the ingredients and drink the Liver Flush early in the morning. Do not eat anything for two hours, to allow this potent flush to act undisturbed by food in your body. During this two-hour period, drink Herbal Purification Tea to support the cleansing process.

Begin with a pinch of cayenne pepper or a drop of cayenne tincture, and increase gradually as you get used to the hot taste, up to no more than one-eighth teaspoon of the powder or eight drops of the tincture. Do not use more of the cayenne than is pleasant and comfortable for you. You may also begin with a smaller amount of ginger and gradually increase it to one teaspoon or more, and with one clove of garlic, increasing to three.

Liver Flush #1 amplifies the benefits of the Hot Lemon-Water Flush you began drinking in the first week. The addition of orange juice enriches the drink with an extra boost of vitamin C, a powerful protective cleanser. The white inner peel and fibrous strands of the orange contain cleansing bioflavonoids, so be sure to include some in the juice. Do not worry if you get some seeds in the juice; they contain beneficial enzymes, vitamins, and minerals and stimulate the liver and gallbladder. Orange juice helps combat viruses, lowers blood cholesterol, and reduces the risk of some kinds of cancer. Garlic promotes the detoxifying activity of the liver, and olive oil stimulates the secretion of bile, flushing out the liver though the hepatic duct.

Liver Flush #2

On Tuesday and Thursday mornings of Week Two, you will drink another liver-flushing beverage, based on organic apples. Apple juice contains malic acid, which helps to cleanse the intestines and heal inflammation of the mucous membranes. If you do not have a juicer, look for fresh organic apple juice in the refrigerator section of your health food store. Do not use commercial juice or nonorganic apples, since they may add to the toxic load on your liver.

1 cup of organic apple juice, freshly made
juice of two lemons, freshly squeezed
1 teaspoon of grated fresh ginger
pinch of cayenne pepper or 1 drop of cayenne
  tincture

1 to 3 cloves garlic, crushed
1 tablespoon of safflower oil, cold-pressed
1 tablespoon of olive oil, cold-pressed

Combine all the ingredients and drink early in the morning. Do not eat anything for two hours, to allow the Liver Flush to stimulate the detoxification of the liver. During this two-hour period, drink Herbal Purification Tea to support the cleansing process.

You may increase the amount of cayenne pepper, ginger, and garlic, as described for Liver Flush #1.

Diuretic Tea

The combination of special herbs in the Diuretic Tea promotes cleansing through the kidneys and bladder. It helps to relieve the water retention that often lies at the root of premenstrual stress and will overcome uncomfortable and unsightly bloating. Juniper berries and uva-ursi leaves are well known for their diuretic effects. Parsley root is a remedy for water retention, as well as for ailments of the liver and gallbladder. Licorice root imparts a sweet taste to the tea and soothes the mucous membranes of the urinary passages. On Monday through Friday of the deep cleansing week of this program, you will drink one cup of Diuretic Tea one hour before dinner.

3 tablespoons of juniper berries, crushed   *3 tablespoons of licorice root*
3 tablespoons of uva-ursi leaves   *3 tablespoons of parsley root*

Prepare a supply of this Diuretic Tea blend by combining all ingredients and storing in an airtight container. To make a cup of tea, add one teaspoon of this blend to one cup of boiling water, cover, and let it steep for fifteen to thirty minutes. Strain out the herbs and drink the strained tea.

As an alternative, look in your local health food store for a Diuretic Tea.

Intestinal Cleanser

Seeds and their hulls are an excellent source of the fiber that helps to cleanse the bowels. On contact with water, the mucilaginous seed coatings swell, softening the stool and helping it to move quickly and easily through the colon. Every day during Week 2, you will be taking an intestinal cleanser before bedtime, so it can gently sweep out your digestive tract while you sleep.

Make your own intestinal cleanser to use in the 21-Day Program. The seeds and husks, ground to a powder, are available in bulk in health food stores.

½ teaspoon psyllium husks, powdered   *4 to 6 ounces of purified water*
1 teaspoon flax seed, powdered

Add the psyllium husks and flax seed to the water and stir thoroughly. The consistency of the mixture will change as it begins to gel. Use enough water so you can swallow the mixture easily. Drink it all at one time; you will notice that the flax seeds impart a slightly nut-like flavor.

If you prefer, you may purchase an intestinal cleanser at a health food store. There are many good brands of ready-mixed intestinal cleansers on the market. These products generally contain a combination of seeds, including psyllium and flax, and sometimes beneficial bacteria as well. If you use a commercially prepared product, be sure to follow the instructions on the package.

Apple-Cider Vinegar Drink

Apple-cider vinegar is a popular folk remedy for aiding the digestion process. It is believed to be a supplement for the hydrochloric acid in the stomach, helping the digestion of proteins and the absorption of minerals and vitamins B and C.

1 teaspoon apple-cider vinegar   *2 ounces purified water*
½ teaspoon honey with royal jelly

Combine all ingredients and drink before eating a protein meal. You can make up a mixture of the vinegar and honey and take it with you to work. Add purified water to the basic mixture and drink a glass before you go to lunch.

Cleansing Juice Blends

Use only fresh-squeezed juices from raw organic vegetables or the vegetables that you have treated with the Cleansing Soak for Fruits and Vegetables (page 116).

Constipation Cure: Six ounces carrot juice and two ounces spinach juice.

Blood Builder: Six ounces carrot juice, one ounce beet juice, and one ounce parsley or watercress juice.

Complexion Tonic: Three ounces carrot juice, three ounces cucumber juice, and two ounces beet juice.

Breath Freshener: Two ounces of any combination of parsley, spinach, watercress, comfrey, and alfalfa juices, with three ounces carrot juice and three ounces celery juice.

Calming Cocktail: Five ounces carrot juice and three ounces celery juice.

Digestive Toner: Four ounces carrot juice and four ounces cabbage juice.

Breakfasts

Fresh Apple Breakfast

The old adage about "an apple a day" has a basis in fact. Researchers have found that people who added two or three apples a day to their diet showed a 10 percent decrease in their blood cholesterol levels. Apples contain a fruit fiber known as pectin, which helps to sweep out and detoxify the alimentary canal. Pectin is the active ingredient in the pharmaceutical Kaopectate, a classic over-the-counter remedy for diarrhea.

Apples provide sweetness while keeping blood sugar on an even keel and aid in controlling appetite by producing a satisfying feeling of fullness. They are also good for cleansing the teeth and stimulating the gums.

If you possibly can, buy organic apples that are free of pesticides and other chemicals. Apples grown with chemicals have toxins even in the core. Many supermarkets are now beginning to carry apples and other produce that have not been sprayed. Choose your favorite sweet red apples (I prefer Red Delicious), and eat them raw, up to three small apples or two large ones for your breakfast. Be sure to eat the skin, which is very high in pectin fiber. Some people even like to eat the seeds, because of their rich supply of nutrients.

Sliced Pineapple Breakfast

Choose a fresh pineapple that is very, very ripe, so it doesn't irritate the mouth. Slice and eat as much as you want. Fresh pineapple contains the enzyme bromelain, which interacts with stomach acid to digest excess protein and burn body fat.

Many digestive upset problems can be alleviated by providing the body with enzymes to help break down undigested proteins and other food residues. I recommend the use of a digestive-enzyme supplement whenever you miscombine foods or eat too much protein. The bromelain in pineapple works much the same as the enzymes in the human digestive system. For this reason, pineapple is a great cleansing meal for any day after you have indulged in too much rich food. Fresh pineapple juice is also a helpful home remedy for relieving sore, raspy throats.

Papaya Complexion Breakfast

Papaya is a delicious tropical fruit with an incomparable flavor and unsurpassed nutritional value. Richer in nutrients than just about any other fruit, papaya has an abundance of vitamins A, C, D, E, and K, as well as the minerals calcium, phosphorus, and iron. Papaya contains hardly any starch; it is made up of simple, natural sugars that are readily absorbed into the bloodstream. Not only has nature already broken down its sugars, but the papaya enzyme papain also helps in the digestion of other foods. This is such a powerful enzyme that the American Indians wrapped meat in the leaves of the papaya plant in order to tenderize it.

Papaya is very good food for digestive disorders, because it can be tolerated by the stomach when other foods cannot. It cuts excessive mucoid material that accumulates in the digestive tract, aids in breaking down proteins and other hard-to-digest foods, helps to cleanse the intestinal tract of decayed matter, and promotes regular elimination. It even protects against bad breath and offensive body odors and cleans the mouth and teeth.

Select a large ripe papaya, cut it in half, and scoop out the seeds. Then you may either scoop out the flesh with a spoon or peel it and eat it in slices. Eat as much as you want, up to one whole papaya.

Berry Breakfast

The high fiber content of berries sweeps the intestinal walls of toxic wastes. Their rich mineral content has earned them a reputation as potent blood purifiers. When you add their sweet-tart flavor to their health benefits, you have an irresistible concoction.

½ pint strawberries, sliced or halved   *½ cup blueberries or raspberries*
¼ cup fresh orange juice

Soak the sliced strawberries in orange juice for fifteen to thirty minutes. Puree the blueberries or raspberries in a blender or food processor and pour the topping over the strawberries.

Strawberries are valued for their blood-cleansing properties, owing to their high vitamin C and mineral content. They have been used for disorders of the intestinal tract, liver, heart, and kidneys, and for gout and rheumatic problems. They have also been used as a dentifrice. High in the fruit fiber pectin, strawberries help to lower blood cholesterol. Recent research indicates that people who eat strawberries have a reduced incidence of cancer. Strawberries have also been found to help kill disease-causing viruses.

Blueberries kill both viruses and bacteria, owing to compounds called anthocyanosides, which may also protect against heart disease and stroke by preventing cholesterol from penetrating blood-vessel walls, especially in the brain. Blueberries are a popular folk remedy for diarrhea.

Raspberries are a mild intestinal cleanser. Raspberry-leaf tea is a great traditional "female remedy," used to relieve nausea in pregnancy, ease childbirth, and reduce menstrual cramps.

Fresh Cantaloupe Breakfast

Cantaloupe has been valued by peoples all over the world as a healing fruit. In China, it is used to treat hepatitis; in the Philippines, to treat cancer and induce menstruation; in India, as a diuretic; and in Guatemala, the seeds are used to expel worms. Such traditional uses of cantaloupe are now being authenticated by scientific research. Like other orange-colored fruits, cantaloupe is high in beta-carotene and other carotenoids, which are believed to aid in the prevention of cancer, according to epidemiological studies comparing diets and cancer rates.

Recent medical findings show that cantaloupe also helps to inhibit blood clotting, thereby protecting against heart disease and stroke. The chemical believed responsible for this anticlotting effect is adenosine, the same compound that accounts, at least in part, for the similar anticoagulant action of garlic and onions.

Like all melons, cantaloupe is very high in water content. Because it moves out of the stomach very quickly, it should not be eaten in combination with other fruits. Eat one-half to one whole fresh cantaloupe for breakfast. The high water-soluble fiber content is extremely effective for cleansing the digestive tract.

Cleansing Watermelon Breakfast

Watermelon is filled with sweet water, and when eaten alone for breakfast, it helps to flush the entire digestive system. It is the breakfast of choice at some of the cleansing-oriented spas. Eat as much watermelon as you wish. This fun fruit breakfast completes your body's natural nocturnal cleansing process.

Healing Grape Breakfast

Grapes have long enjoyed a popular reputation as a healing fruit. In the late 1920s, grapes were in vogue when a South African woman, Johanna Brandt, wrote a book claiming that she had cured her abdominal cancer with a grape diet and grape packs. The high levels of caffeic acid in grapes may explain their reported anticancer action, although no studies have been done using humans. Grapes, grape juice, raisins, and grape-based wines have been shown to kill disease-causing viruses in test-tube experiments. Best of all, grapes taste wonderful. Eat as many as you wish for a breakfast rich in natural sugars and cleansing enzymes. Be sure to choose organically raised grapes, or cleanse them thoroughly with the Cleansing Soak for Fruits and Vegetables to remove contaminating sprays.

Mineralizing Soups

The following vegetable soup recipes use Potassium Broth as a base. Take any of these delicious bisques along with you in a thermos for a quick, satisfying lunch or snack on a busy day, or combine them with a salad for a complete evening meal. These recipes provide four small or two large servings. You can freeze separate portions for later in the program.

Squash Bisque (SERVES 4)

1 medium butternut squash or acorn squash
1 onion
1 tablespoon olive oil
2 tablespoons sweet white miso

4 cups Potassium Broth
2 tablespoons granulated lecithin
¼ teaspoon ginger or curry (to taste)

- Cube the squash and place it in a pot with the Potassium Broth. Bring it to a quick boil and turn it down immediately. Simmer for 15 to 20 minutes.

- While the squash is simmering, slice the onion and sauté it in the olive oil until it is golden. Add the onion to the squash. Add ginger or curry, your choice. Continue simmering for another 10 minutes or until the squash is soft. Let it sit for another 15 minutes.

- Remove one-fourth cup of broth and dissolve the miso in it. Set aside for a moment.

- Transfer the soup into a food processor or blender and purée. Add the lecithin and miso broth just as you are finishing.

- Garnish with a handful of chopped parsley, toasted almond slivers, toasted sesame seeds, chopped scallions, or nori flakes.

Helpful Hint:

Winter squashes, like butternut squash, are fairly starchy and should not be combined with protein. They may be combined with salad or cooked vegetables for a complete Rejuvenation meal.

Variation #1

Carrot Bisque (SERVES 4)

8 carrots	¼ teaspoon grated ginger
2 potatoes	4 cups Potassium Broth
1 onion	2 tablespoons granulated lecithin

Follow cooking and preparation instructions for Squash Bisque, substituting carrots and potatoes for the squash.

Variation #2

Cauliflower Bisque (SERVES 4)

1 head cauliflower	¼ teaspoon curry
2 potatoes	4 cups Potassium Broth
1 yellow onion	2 tablespoons granulated lecithin
1 clove garlic, minced	

Follow cooking and preparation instructions for Squash Bisque, substituting cauliflower and potatoes for the squash.

Yam Delight (SERVES 4)

2 yams	1 tablespoon fresh grated ginger
1 large onion	2 cups Potassium Broth or purified water
1 tablespoon olive oil	1 handful parsley, chopped
2 cloves garlic, minced	sea salt to taste

- Bake the yams at 350 degrees until they are soft.

- While the yams are baking, chop the onion and sauté it in the olive oil with the garlic and ginger until the onion is translucent.

- Peel and cube the baked yams.

- Place the yams and the sautéed onion mixture in a blender or food processor. Purée the mixture while slowly adding the Potassium Broth.

- Garnish with chopped parsley and add sea salt to taste.

Helpful Hint:

Yams are a starchy food and should not be combined with protein. Combine this bisque with a salad or steamed vegetables.

Variation:

Yam Delight is a delicious topping for steamed vegetables; reduce the amount of Potassium Broth to create a thick mixture.

Beet Borscht (SERVES 4)

1 bunch fresh beets	*2 cups Potassium Broth*
2 carrots	*1 cup nonfat yogurt*
1 onion	*juice of ½ lemon*
1 teaspoon caraway seeds	*pinch of sea salt*
1 tablespoon olive oil	

- Trim the greens from the beets and save them for your next batch of Potassium Broth. Scrub the beets well. Place the beets in 2 inches of water in a covered pot. Bake them at 350 degrees for about an hour, until soft. Check occasionally to be sure the water has not evaporated, and add a bit more water if necessary.

- While the beets are cooling, slice the carrots and onions. Sauté carrots and onions in olive oil with the caraway seeds at a very low temperature until the carrots are soft and the onions are golden.

- Drain and cool the beets. Slip off the skins with your fingers and slice the beets.

- Place all of the ingredients except lemon juice and salt into a blender or food processor. Purée while slowly adding the Potassium Broth and yogurt. Add the lemon juice and sea salt to taste. Return the borscht to a pan, heat it slowly, and serve.

Helpful Hint:

Because this soup contains yogurt, it is a protein dish and should not be combined with starches.

Variations:

Serve Beet Borscht chilled if desired.

During the cleansing phase of the program, you may delete the yogurt and add an additional cup of Potassium Broth.

Raw Soups

These delicious uncooked vegetable soups will be featured during Week 2. These soups are a potent source for all the vitamins and minerals available in the raw vegetables themselves. Their fiber content helps to sweep the intestines of waste, assisting the intense cleansing that takes place during the second week of the program.

Raw Vegetable Delight (SERVES 4)

2 ½ cups tomatoes, chopped
2 cloves garlic, minced
4 cups onion, chopped
2 cucumbers, peeled and sliced
2 yellow squash, chopped
2 zucchini, chopped
2 cups celery, diced

4 cups red bell pepper, diced
1 ear of corn
4 teaspoons sea salt
1 tablespoon umeboshi vinegar
1 tablespoon dried dill or 2 tablespoons fresh dill

- Cut the corn off the cob and combine it with all the other ingredients in a blender or food processor. Purée the mixture and pour it into a serving bowl.

- Garnish the soup with thin slices of cucumber and a sprinkle of fresh dill.

Raw Vegetable "Cream" Soup (SERVES 4)

1 ½ cups carrots, chopped
2 cloves garlic, minced
1 cup alfalfa sprouts
1 tablespoon olive oil
1 tablespoon Herbamare (a seasoning found
   in health food stores)

2 cups Potassium Broth
1 avocado, diced
pinch of nori flakes (found in health food
   stores or Asian markets), as garnish

- Blend the first six ingredients in a blender or food processor. Add the avocado and blend again for a few seconds.

- Pour the mixture into a serving bowl and garnish it with nori flakes.

Helpful Hint:

These raw soups are excellent for tasty hot-weather meals after you have completed the 21-Day Program.

Variations:

Substitute broccoli, cauliflower, or spinach for the carrots for a different taste treat.

Combine carrots, broccoli, cauliflower, and spinach for a mixed vegetable soup that is packed with nutrients.

Miracle Salads

These salads are excellent sources of vitamins and minerals. Adding a salad dressing containing GLA-rich oils helps to ensure healthy skin, hair, and nails and to control cholesterol levels in your blood.

To provide a daily helping of miracle foods and antiaging vegetables, you will eat the Super Salad regularly during the 21-Day Program. Later on, make it a part of your lifetime eating habits. Combine these salads with either a protein or a starchy food for a complete meal.

Super Salad (SERVES 4)

2 cups mixed sprouts (sprouted sunflower seeds, mung beans, alfalfa seeds, garbanzo beans, lentils, radishes, and wheat berries)

8 cups organic mixed greens (Do not include iceberg lettuce. It is difficult to digest and tends to be constipating.)

½ red and/or green cabbage, shredded

2 carrots, grated

1 zucchini, grated

½ pound broccoli, broken into florets

1 sliced cucumber

garlic, minced, up to 2 cloves

granulated lecithin, 2 tablespoons

½ cup sunflower and pumpkin seeds, hulled and unsalted (optional, as a protein source)

- Steam the broccoli and the cauliflower.

- Toss the first seven ingredients together in a large salad bowl. When ready to serve, top with the sliced cucumber, minced garlic, lecithin, and seeds.

- Toss the salad with the Fat-Loss Dressing of your choice (pages 63 to 65) and serve immediately.

Helpful Hints:

This recipe provides four generous servings. You may make up enough for two or three days and store it in an airtight container in the refrigerator.

Many health food stores and quality supermarkets now carry prewashed, mixed salad greens. They also have many of the sprouts. This makes it much easier to prepare your salad.

Do not add the garlic, cucumber, lecithin, sunflower or pumpkin seeds, or salad dressing until you are ready to serve the salad.

Vary the garlic to suit your taste. Try to build up to 2 minced cloves per serving. If you prefer, you may get your garlic from the salad dressing. Remember, you can chew fresh parsley after eating garlic to mask the odor.

If you are having the Super Salad as a complete meal or combining it with a steamed vegetable dish, add the sunflower seeds and/or pumpkin seeds to provide excellent protein.

High-Iron Salad (SERVES 4)

1 bunch beets   Lemon-Mustard Dressing (page 64)
1 bunch watercress

- Trim the greens from the beets and save them for your next batch of Potassium Broth. Scrub the beets well. Place the beets in 2 inches of water in a covered pot. Bake them at 350 degrees for about an hour, until soft. Check occasionally to be sure the water has not evaporated, and add a bit more water if necessary. Drain and cool the beets. Slip off the skins with your fingers and slice the beets.

- Wash the watercress well, remove large stems and wilted leaves, and arrange it on a plate.

- Place the beets over the bed of watercress.

- Top with Lemon-Mustard Dressing.

Fat-Loss Dressings

These salad and vegetable dressings help to flush fat from your system because of the beneficial omega-6, or GLA, oils in safflower and sesame oil. Be sure to use cold-pressed vegetable oils to ensure that you are deriving the full benefits of the GLA oils. Make up a batch of your favorite Fat-Loss Dressing and store it in your refrigerator. Take some with you in a small container when you go to a restaurant, and you will always be able to enjoy a healthy, properly combined salad. (If you forget, you can request olive oil and lemon or vinegar on the side.)

Helpful Hints:

To make a creamier dressing or a tangy dip, add one-fourth to one-half cup of yogurt or 2 to 4 ounces of tofu to any of these recipes.

Remember that the dressing is then a protein food; do not combine it with other proteins or with starches.

Garlic-Tarragon Dressing (SERVES 4)

⅓ cup safflower oil
3 garlic cloves, minced
½ teaspoon tarragon

2 tablespoons balsamic vinegar
pinch of sea salt

Place all ingredients in a blender and blend thoroughly. Store the extra dressing in a glass jar in the refrigerator.

Raspberry-Vinaigrette Dressing (SERVES 4)

3 tablespoons olive oil
2 tablespoons safflower oil
1 tablespoon raspberry vinegar
1 teaspoon umeboshi vinegar
juice of 1 lemon

Herbamare to taste
1 clove garlic, minced
⅛ cup fresh parsley, chopped
pinch of peppermint
dash of pepper

Place all ingredients in a blender and blend thoroughly. Store the extra dressing in a glass jar in the refrigerator.

Lemon-Mustard Dressing (SERVES 4)

juice of ½ lemon
2 tablespoons tahini
1 tablespoon olive oil
1 tablespoon safflower oil

½ tablespoon brown-rice miso
1 teaspoon Dijon mustard
⅛ cup Potassium Broth
1 teaspoon honey

Place all ingredients in a blender and blend thoroughly. Store the extra dressing in a glass jar in the refrigerator.

Variation:
Lemon-Mustard Dressing is delicious heated and poured over steamed vegetables.

Lemon-Parsley Dressing (SERVES 4)

¼ cup sesame oil

¼ cup safflower oil

2 tablespoons brown-rice vinegar

½ cup chopped parsley

juice of ½ lemon

1 teaspoon sweet white miso

handful of toasted sunflower seeds

Place all ingredients in a blender and blend thoroughly. Store the extra dressing in a glass jar in the refrigerator.

Rejuvenating Toppings

These Rejuvenating toppings are divided into two groups. The first five are based on vegetables and may be combined with starches and proteins as well as with vegetables. The last four are made with protein. These should be used as toppings for vegetables, but should not be combined with other proteins or with starches.

Helpful Hint:

All the Rejuvenating Toppings may be kept in the refrigerator for up to three days.

Green Goddess Topping (SERVES 4)

1 cup broccoli, divided into florets and steamed

⅛ cup olive oil

⅛ cup fresh basil

1 clove garlic, minced

1 teaspoon sweet white miso

Herbamare to taste

• Steam the broccoli.

• Combine all ingredients in a blender and blend until creamy.

Golden Goddess Topping (SERVES 4)

1 small butternut squash
1 carrot

1 clove garlic
½ tablespoon brown-rice miso

- Cut the squash into large pieces.

- Place the cut-up squash in a pot with the carrot and garlic and cover with purified water. Boil until the squash is tender (about 20 minutes). Drain and reserve the water.

- Scoop the flesh of the squash out of the skin.

- Place the vegetables in a blender and purée. Add a little of the cooking water if necessary to create a smooth consistency.

Spa Salsa (SERVES 4)

3 tablespoons cilantro
¼ cup green bell pepper, chopped
¼ cup red bell pepper, chopped
1 tomato, chopped

½ red onion, chopped
2 scallions, chopped
juice of 1 lemon
1 garlic clove, minced

Combine all the ingredients in a bowl and toss.

Variations:
Add 1 diced jalapeño pepper to make a spicy salsa topping.

This recipe makes a delicious topping for fish as well as for steamed and raw vegetables.

Carrot-Leek Purée (SERVES 4)

3 cups sliced carrots
1 cup sliced leeks
dill to taste

fresh lemon juice to taste
sea salt to taste

- Steam the carrots until just tender (10 to 15 minutes, depending on the maturity of the carrots).

- Add the leeks to the carrots and steam until the leeks have wilted.

- Transfer the vegetables to a blender or food processor and purée until smooth.

- Season the purée with a pinch of dill, sea salt, and a few drops of fresh lemon juice to taste.

Variations:

Substitute steamed white turnips for the carrots to make a sweet, high-potassium and high-calcium topping.

Use carrots and turnips together for another variation.

Warm Garlic Dressing (SERVES 4)

2 tablespoons olive oil
2 tablespoons sliced garlic

3 tablespoons red-wine vinegar or lemon juice

- Warm all ingredients in a small saucepan for 5 minutes.
- Pour the dressing immediately over freshly steamed vegetables, or pour it over raw spinach or lettuce to create a "wilted" salad.

Helpful Hint:

This quick and easy dressing is a great way to add a healthy dose of garlic topping to your cooked vegetables.

Tahini-Tofu Topping (SERVES 4)

4 ounces tofu
2 tablespoons tahini
1 tablespoon brown-rice vinegar
⅛ cup Potassium Broth or purified water

2 scallions, chopped
1 tablespoon sesame oil
1 tablespoon umeboshi vinegar
pinch of sea salt

Combine all ingredients in a blender and blend until smooth.

Helpful Hint:

The tahini in this recipe imparts a nut-like sesame taste and provides beneficial GLA oils.

Carrot-Yogurt Topping (SERVES 4)

1 cup yogurt
1 tablespoon honey
1 tablespoon grated onion

1 tablespoon apple-cider vinegar
1 carrot, grated

Combine all ingredients in a blender and blend until smooth.

Tofu-Ginger Topping (SERVES 4)

8 ounces tofu
2 tablespoons sesame oil
2 ½ tablespoons brown-rice vinegar
1 tablespoon toasted sesame oil
1 ½ tablespoons sweet white miso

1 tablespoon sesame seeds
1 tablespoon chopped fresh parsley
pinch of sea salt
½ teaspoon fresh grated ginger, garnish

Combine all the ingredients except the ginger in a blender and blend until smooth. Spoon the topping over raw or cooked vegetables and garnish with the fresh grated ginger.

Tofu-Miso Topping (SERVES 4)

G cup Potassium Broth
8 ounces tofu

1 to 1 ½ tablespoons brown-rice miso
1 tablespoon sesame oil

Combine all ingredients in a blender and blend until smooth.

Sea Vegetable Specialties

These sea vegetable recipes are rich in iodine, a nutrient essential to proper functioning of the thyroid gland and the regulation of the metabolism. Seaweed also contains a wealth of other trace minerals found in the ocean. You will use these recipes during Week Three of the program. The hijiki and wakame called for in these recipes are dried seaweeds. They can be purchased in a health food store, a Japanese food store, or in the Oriental foods section of a well-stocked supermarket. These recipes provide four small or two large servings. The yield for each recipe is given in terms of small servings, the equivalent of side dishes. If you are going to use the dish as a main course, the yield is half as many servings.

Hijiki Stir-Fry (SERVES 4)

½ cup hijiki
1 tablespoon sesame oil
2 cloves garlic, minced
1 tablespoon grated ginger
½ onion, chopped
½ cup celery, chopped
1 cup carrots, chopped
1 cup broccoli, broken into florets, and/or chopped cabbage

juice of ½ lemon
1 tablespoon tamari
¼ cup purified water
1 teaspoon maple syrup
1 tablespoon mirin (sweet cooking sake available in Asian markets)
1 tablespoon white sesame seeds, to garnish

- Rinse and soak the hijiki for 15 minutes.

- Heat the sesame oil in a frying pan or wok. Add the garlic, ginger, and onion. Sauté until the onions are translucent (about 2 minutes). Add the hijiki, celery, carrots, broccoli, and/or cabbage, and continue to sauté.

- Mix the lemon juice, tamari, water, maple syrup, and mirin and add them to the vegetables. Simmer, covered, for 5 minutes.

- Spoon the stir-fry into a serving dish. Garnish with raw sesame seeds and serve immediately.

Variation:

Allow the Hijiki Stir-Fry to cool and spoon it over a bed of organic greens and shredded cabbage for a tasty, iodine-rich salad.

Miso Sea Soup (SERVES 4)

4 cups Potassium Broth	*8 ounces tofu*
2 or 3 dried shitake mushrooms	*3 tablespoons brown-rice miso*
½ cup wakame	*2 scallions, chopped*

- Soak the mushrooms in 1 cup of purified water for 10 minutes. Cut off and discard the stems and slice the mushrooms into thin strips.

- Soak the wakame in enough water to cover for 10 minutes.

- . Bring the Potassium Broth to a boil in a 3-quart soup pot. Reduce the heat to a simmer and add the mushrooms and wakame. Cook, covered, for 7 minutes.

- While the soup is cooking, cut the tofu into cubes. Add it to the soup and cook, covered, for another 5 minutes.

- Thin the miso with a few tablespoons of the cooking broth and add it to the soup, stirring until smooth. Remove the soup from the heat immediately.

- Serve and garnish with the chopped scallions.

Protein Drinks

The base for these protein drinks is seeds and nuts, which are a source of excellent protein. Seeds and nuts also contain protease inhibitors, protective factors that have anti-aging benefits and may help prevent cancer. These drinks are a delicious alternative to dairy products for a protein-rich beverage. Soaking the nuts and seeds overnight before blending them enhances their digestibility and triggers the release of the nutrients.

Helpful Hints:

These protein drinks can be refrigerated for a full 24 hours, but it is best to make them daily and use them as soon as possible to derive their nutritional value.

Fill a thermos and bring it to work for a mid-morning or mid-afternoon snack.

If your schedule demands, you can buy ready-made almond milk in your local health food store or substitute ready-made low fat soy milk for the nut and seed milks.

These drinks are protein-rich, so be sure to wait at least two hours after your fruit breakfast before using a protein drink as a mid-morning snack.

Almond Milk (YIELDS 3 CUPS)

½ cup almonds	*1 tablespoon honey*
purified water to soak almonds	*pinch of sea salt*
3 cups purified water	*1 teaspoon flax seed oil*

- Soak the almonds overnight in enough purified water to cover.

- In the morning, pour off and discard the soak water. Slip the skins off the almonds with a gentle squeeze.

- Place the almonds, 3 cups of purified water, honey, sea salt, and flax oil in a blender and blend. If desired, you may strain the drink through a cheesecloth. (I like the crunchiness of the unstrained drink. If you do not strain it, be sure to chew your drink well!)

Sesame Seed Milk (YIELDS 3 CUPS)

½ cup sesame seeds	*1 tablespoon rice syrup or honey*
3 cups purified water	

- Grind the seeds in a coffee grinder or blender.

- Blend all of the ingredients in a blender.

- Strain the hulls through a strainer or cheesecloth.

Sunflower Seed Milk (YIELDS 3 CUPS)

⅓ cup sunflower seeds, hulled and unsalted
purified water to soak sunflower seeds

3 cups purified water
1 tablespoon rice syrup, if desired

- Soak the seeds overnight in enough purified water to cover.

- Pour off and discard the soak water. Place the soaked seeds and 3 cups of water in a blender and blend.

- This mixture is sweeter than the Almond Milk and Sesame Seed Milk, but you may add 1 tablespoon of rice syrup or honey if you wish.

The following four protein drinks use the first three recipes as a base. Each of these recipes makes one serving. If you find that you like to have two protein drinks a day, double the recipes.

Hot Mock Chocolate (SERVES 1)

1 tablespoon carob powder
1 tablespoon honey

1 cup nut or seed milk

- Add the carob powder and honey to one cup of any of the nut or seed milks.

- Warm the mixture and drink it immediately, or store it in a thermos for later use.

Maple Nut Shake (SERVES 1)

1 tablespoon almond butter
1 teaspoon pure maple syrup

1 cup Almond Milk

Place all the ingredients in a blender and blend thoroughly.

Tahini Shake (SERVES 1)

1 tablespoon tahini   1 cup Sesame Seed Milk
1 teaspoon honey

Place all the ingredients in a blender and blend thoroughly.

Carrot Shake (SERVES 1)

4 ounces fresh carrot juice
4 ounces Sesame Seed Milk

Place the carrot juice and the Sesame Seed Milk in a blender and blend.

Variation:

For a different flavor, try the Almond or Sunflower Seed Milk in place of the Sesame Seed Milk.

Elimination Phase

INTRODUCTION:
The Rejuvenation Diet

Back in my twenties, I was teaching in a public school, where I was encouraged to teach my students traditional dietary ideas about eating from the "four food groups" at every meal. Knowing how sluggish I felt when I followed the rules I was supposed to be teaching my students, and how wonderfully light and energetic I felt when I followed the principles of food combining, I began to wonder if we were damaging our children by bringing them up with this misinformation about foods.

I have adapted the classic principles of food combining to create the Rejuvenation Diet that you will follow during most of the 21-Day Program. Each day's menu starts with a single raw fruit breakfast, a protein-and-vegetable lunch, and a light dinner of vegetables and starch. You will be amazed at how energized you will feel as your body adjusts to this truly "balanced" diet. It may seem strange at first not to feel so full after meals. This lack of fullness is not because you won't be well nourished, but because you won't be so bloated. It may take a while for you to get used to this new sensation, as you begin to digest your foods in an easier way. As a side benefit, you will quickly notice a flatter tummy.

This week's Rejuvenation Diet is an absolutely essential preparation for the intensive cleansing your body will be undergoing in the second and third weeks of my program. This is why I want you to eat foods that are free of chemicals and contaminants, in combinations that are easy to digest. Such a diet will not add any more toxicity to your system, and it will minimize any cleansing reactions you may have later on. It is also the best diet for clearing your body of cellulite once and for all. In fact, the Rejuvenation Diet is so healthy and satisfying that it will change your eating habits permanently.

How Food Combining Works

Although we eat for many different reasons, the ultimate physiological purpose of eating is to get nutrients into the blood, so we can build new cells to replace the ones that are constantly dying. Dead cells and other body wastes are removed from the body through the systems of elimination. When food is not properly digested, nutrients are not released, and extra energy is needed to remove the undigested waste from the system. This is why you may have noticed low energy and digestive discomfort when you eat heavy meals that are not properly combined.

The principles of food combining are based on an understanding of how the digestive process works. Different foods are digested in different ways, and they require different digestive juices to release the nutrients that can be used by your cells. Therefore, foods are eaten in combinations that promote efficient digestion and make the process extremely efficient. Conscious food combining has helped many people with long-standing digestion and elimination problems.

A good example is a client of mine named Marc, a Frenchman with a very successful import business. For fifteen years, he had gone from doctor to doctor to get help for his heartburn. Of course, he was used to eating the typical rich French foods. The doctors generally prescribed antacids, without giving him much advice on his diet.

When Marc came in to see me, his chief complaints were gas, bloating, and a feeling of burning and pressure after eating. I began with some intestinal cleansing for immediate relief. But mainly I worked with him on food combining principles. By learning how to combine foods properly, Marc completely eliminated his heartburn and no longer needed antacids. It sounds amazingly simple, and it is. From time to time, however, Marc will eat a rich meal that combines a full spectrum of foods, but now he knows the reason when he has a feeling of burning afterward. He also knows that he can prepare his body for such occasions by taking digestive enzymes to support the digestive process. Marc is now in control of his body.

Heartburn and indigestion are only one kind of penalty you may pay for combining foods improperly. Constipation, flatulence, bloating, bad breath, cellulite, and overweight can all be signs that you are eating the wrong combinations of foods.

This week's Rejuvenation Diet follows five simple rules that work best for people whose main goals are relief from indigestion and gas, rejuvenation, weight loss, and renewed energy. You may wish to refer to the Food Combining Chart on page 81 to see what foods fall into each of the food categories I refer to.

The Five Food Combining Principles

1. Eat fruit alone.

Every morning this week you will have a breakfast consisting of fresh fruit. This is a wonderful way to start the day, because fruit is a marvelous detoxifier. It has the highest water content of all foods and travels through the body very quickly. Besides the nutrients that it provides, the fiber in fruit acts like a brush to keep the intestinal walls clean and clear. The soluble fibers in fruit also help lower cholesterol in the blood.

Fruit is a very simple food. It contains sugars that are ready for the body to use and provides its own enzymes, so it does not need much time to be digested in the stomach. Your goal is to pass fruit out of the stomach as quickly as possible, so its nutrients will be absorbed rapidly through the walls of the small intestine and the colon. This is why you should not combine fruit with other foods or have it too soon after eating protein or starch. If you do, the sugar in the fruit will ferment in the stomach, causing bloating and gas pain.

Generally, fruits may be combined with each other, but melons should be eaten alone, because they are made up almost entirely of water and need very little time to digest. Combining melon with another kind of fruit will cause it to be held up in the stomach, and it will begin to ferment.

After eating fruit, allow at least two hours before eating any other kind of food. Morning is the best time to eat fruit, because then you can be certain other foods have already left the stomach. Please do not eat fruit for dessert after a meal. It will be held up in your stomach by the other foods, causing it to ferment.

You may wonder why I recommend a light fruit breakfast, when traditionally dietitians advise us to eat a hearty breakfast consisting of foods from all four food groups. Your body really does not need much food in the morning, because it is still utilizing the nutrients from the food you ate the night before. Fruit helps to raise your blood sugar and cleanse the wastes from your system.

If you find this light breakfast is not enough for you, please honor that message from yourself, as there are several metabolic types of people. We all differ slightly in our nutrient needs. This is why I recommend the protein drink two hours after the fruit breakfast for some of you.

If you have found that fruit simply does not agree with you due to its high sugar content, feel free to completely eliminate the fruit breakfast and substitute a protein drink. You may have an additional drink in mid-morning if you wish.

2. Do not combine protein with starch.

Protein foods and starchy foods require different digestive juices in order to be properly broken down and used by the body. The digestion of starches begins in the mouth with the enzyme ptyalin, which is contained in your saliva. Proteins are mainly broken down in the stomach by hydrochloric acid and the protein-splitting enzyme pepsin. Please avoid the traditional American dinner of meat and potatoes, or meat and other starches, as well as sandwiches containing cheese, meats, eggs, or other proteins. When you think about how regularly we consume these combinations, it is no wonder that indigestion remedies are among the best-selling over-the-counter medicines in this country.

When protein and starch are eaten together, ptyalin is not effectively produced in the saliva, and so the starch is not predigested in the mouth. It enters the stomach and begins to ferment, producing gas. To make matters worse, protein needs to be digested in an acid environment and starch in an alkaline environment. So, when starches and proteins are combined, the acid and alkaline digestive juices neutralize each other! All this decaying food is held up in the stomach, causing gas and discomfort. More important, the nutrients you need to rejuvenate and replenish your cells are destroyed in the decaying and fermenting process. This dietary cycle can eventually lead to premature aging and illness.

When I speak of protein foods, I am referring mainly to animal proteins. Some plant foods, such as beans, contain natural combinations of starches and proteins. If these foods are eaten alone, the body is able to digest them properly by releasing the proper digestive juices in the proper sequence. Even so, some people do feel uncomfortable after eating beans.

3. Protein with vegetables is okay.

Your mid-day meals in this first week of the program will consist of a protein food—fish or chicken or tofu—and non-starch vegetables. Vegetables are high in water content and are relatively easy to digest. They can be broken down in either an acid or alkaline environment, so they can be combined with proteins as well as with starches. The enzymes in the vegetables actually enhance the digestion of protein. The fiber contained in vegetables helps to move the fiberless protein foods rapidly through the intestines.

4. Starches with vegetables are okay, too.

Since vegetables do not require their own specific digestive juices, they can be digested in the alkaline environment required by starches. Your evening meal each day this week will be based on vegetables and starchy foods. You will feel and see the benefits right away when you begin to eat your lighter meal in the evening rather than at lunchtime. Your body will respond by speedily digesting your dinner while you sleep. By morning, your body will be clean and clear again, ready for its final flushing with a fruit breakfast.

5. Do not drink with meals.

If you drink water, tea, or any other beverage along with your meal, you dilute the digestive juices that are needed to break down your food, preventing it from being properly digested. The best time to drink fluids is between meals—at least one-half hour before or two hours after. Remember, you will be drinking at least eight full glasses of water each day, including herbal tea and other rehydrating drinks I will recommend. If you are eating fruits and vegetables, which are high in water content, or beans and grains that are prepared with water, then the food itself will provide plenty of fluid, and you should not feel thirsty after your meal. If you do find that you are thirsty after eating, you may be consuming too much salt.

Food Combining for Your Busy Lifestyle

Do you ever experience a mid-afternoon slump, when you just seem to run out of energy? These low points may be caused by a drop in your blood sugar level. Part of the reason you will be eating protein at lunchtime is to help boost your blood sugar level and keep you on an even keel throughout the afternoon.

FOOD COMBINING CHART

Eat Alone

Fruits
Eat melon alone,
other fruits only with each other

Proteins ——————— **No** ——————— **Starches**

Proteins		**Starches**
Meat, eggs, poultry, fish,		Bread, grains, pasta,
tofu, seeds, nuts, dairy,		rice, winter squash,
dried beans, and lentils		potatoes (all), corn

OK   OK

Vegetables
All green and non-starchy vegetables
(see Starches, above)

If your busy schedule requires that you eat your fruit breakfast very early in the morning and then you have a late lunch, you may notice that you get lightheaded or irritable sometime in the mid-morning. This may also happen if you are accustomed to having a heavier breakfast. For those who need a mid-morning boost, I have provided recipes for protein drinks, beginning on page 70. You can make your protein drink in the morning and take it with you in a thermos to work. Delicious protein drinks are available in your local health food store. Ready-made almond milk and soy milk, which are also available, are a great substitute for making your own nut and seed milks.

Always be sure to wait two hours after eating your fruit breakfast before you consume the protein drink, to allow time for the fruit to leave your stomach. (Because you will have protein at lunch, the timing between your mid-morning protein drink and your lunch is not as critical.)

In the mid-afternoon, if you feel your energy begin to flag again, have some fresh carrot juice. Carrot juice is very high in natural sugar, so it will raise your blood sugar and help control your craving for sweets. Fresh carrot juice is available at some super-markets and at juice bars and health food stores everywhere. If necessary, stock up on fresh carrot juice, and bring it with you to work.

Allowing for variations in routine, your daily meal schedule will look something like this:

Between 6:00 and 10:00 A.M.: Breakfast
Between 12:00 and 3:00 P.M.: Lunch
Between 5:00 and 8:00 P.M.: Dinner

These meal periods allow the ideal time for the food to pass out of the stomach before you eat different foods at your next meal.

Eating Out in Restaurants

You can dine out in restaurants the entire time on the Rejuvenation Diet, if you wish. Using the simple rules of food combining, you can always choose the proper meals in a restaurant.

Whenever you eat out, you need to make a choice. You are going to have either a protein meal or a starch meal. If you choose a protein meal, then you must exclude starch, and that means excluding bread! Many people find it helpful to ask the waiter not to bring bread to the table. If you are ordering fish or chicken—which is generally served with rice, pasta, or potatoes—ask your waiter to leave off the starch and bring extra vegetables instead. I have never found a restaurant that was not willing to do that. If you choose a starch meal, such as a pasta dish, be sure that it does not include protein or dairy products in the sauce. You might want to ask for a simple tomato sauce or an olive oil and garlic sauce. Often, you will not find a vegetable main dish on the menu, but more and more restaurants will gladly prepare a plate of steamed or sautéed vegetables with a side order of rice, a baked potato, or pasta.

If you eat at a salad bar, remember that you must apply the rules of food combining just as at any other restaurant. Before you make any selections, you must choose between a protein meal and a starch meal. Help yourself to plenty of vegetables, but do not combine a high-protein food such as garbanzo beans with starch crackers or rolls. Stay away from cheeses and other dairy products entirely, and remember not to combine fruits with other foods.

Certain foods in restaurants should be avoided. Prepared salad dressings are often loaded with fats, salt, and preservatives. If you have not brought your own salad dressing with you, ask for olive oil and fresh lemon. Also be careful about ordering soups in restaurants, because they are often loaded with salt and cream. Salt holds fluid in the tissues, and you are trying to continually flush the fluids out of your tissues. Cutting down on your salt consumption helps to speed this process.

Did you know that airlines offer a wide variety of special-order meals, such as fresh fruit plates or vegetable plates? Think ahead, and at the time that you make your reservation, request a special vegetarian meal or some other selection that allows you to follow your food combining rules.

One of my clients, Amy, is a bank manager who had been eating an unhealthy junk-food diet to comfort herself because of emotional problems connected with a failing relationship. When she started her cleansing program, her abdomen was extremely distended, her skin had a yellowish tinge, and she had a strong body odor. Her eyes and her whole body were puffy from water retention. As she changed her diet and started to clean out her system, her skin color changed noticeably. After a couple of months on my program, she had rosy cheeks again, and she even began to change the color scheme of her wardrobe and makeup because her complexion had improved so much. She had previously been very embarrassed about her offensive body odor and had been using a lot of deodorant and perfume to conceal it. As she began to detoxify, her natural scent became fresh and clean.

Although Amy's original purpose had been to clean the toxins out of her system, she also experienced remarkable weight loss. During the second week of the program, she began to notice that she was urinating a great deal and was starting to lose the bloated feeling that had accompanied the water retention. Moreover, as she eliminated the foods from her diet that had been so difficult for her body to digest, her energy began to come back, and she wanted to resume regular exercise. As she stepped up her exercise, of course, she lost more weight.

Amy became a great proponent of food combining. Her management job required her to eat out a lot. She noticed that if she was careful about food combining, she would have high energy all day. If she broke her food combining rules, she would feel lethargic and bloated.

So many of us have been on and off diets all our lives. We binge, binge, binge, then starve, starve, starve. Of course, this never works. By following the simple principles of the Rejuvenation Diet, you can eat delicious food throughout the day and still lose weight. Once your body starts getting rid of the waste that has been clogging your systems of elimination, you will have increased energy, your skin will take on a more youthful appearance and your craving for junk foods will be replaced by a genuine desire to eat clean, healthy foods.

Coffee and Alcohol Strategies

While I do not insist that you abstain from drinking coffee during this program, you will find the benefits greatly enhanced if you cut down or eliminate your caffeine intake. If you want to cut down, ask yourself whether you like coffee because of its taste or because it provides energy. If you drink it for its taste, switch to decaffeinated coffee. Remember, however, that decaf can contain up to 3 percent caffeine and is also acidic, so don't overdo decaf either. If you drink coffee for energy, try green tea or one of the herbal tea blends that is one-half black tea to wean yourself off coffee gradually. If you drink coffee in the morning, be sure to have your Hot Lemon-Water Flush (page 42), beforehand. Also, please drink your coffee black instead of adding dairy products such as milk or cream to it.

If you do not wish to cut out alcohol completely during this program, I recommend that you limit yourself to one glass of wine daily, in the evening. Moderate wine consumption has been shown to protect against heart disease by increasing the blood levels of high-density lipoproteins (HDLs), the beneficial form of cholesterol. In fact, although the French consume much more fat then Americans, they have a lower risk of heart disease. Many attribute this so-called French paradox to their habitual consumption of red wine. Apparently, antioxidant substances in wine exert a protective effect by preventing fatty deposits from building up on the arteries. These antioxidants are called proanthodyns and are thought to be fifty times more powerful than vitamin E. Wine can also aid digestion and is rich in substances that have been shown to suppress bacteria and viruses in the body.

Rejuvenation Foods

The Rejuvenation Diet features simple, fresh, organically raised foods. Make no mistake about it; clean foods are delicious. Today I'm going to show you how to prepare meals that are combined properly and that have no junk in them at all—no preservatives, no additives, no heavy fats, no chemicals. I will introduce some special recipes that will help to stimulate your systems of elimination and nourish every cell in your body to make you feel and look lighter, more youthful, and more energetic.

Fruits and Vegetables

At the very heart of the Rejuvenation Diet are fresh fruits and vegetables. Our bodies are at least 70 percent water, and since fruits and vegetables also are very high in water, they are most perfectly suited to our body composition. The water contained in fruits and vegetables is important for nourishing and cleansing. Water carries the rich cargo of nutrients into the intestines, where they are rapidly absorbed. The water then flushes away the wastes. Of course, you should use organic fruits and vegetables. If you are not able to get organic produce, use the food-cleansing soak described on Sunday: Day 2.

Although I recommend that many vegetables be eaten raw, as in salads, you will also be eating cooked vegetables. The best cooking methods are those in which the vegetables are cooked the least, such as steaming, sautéing in a wok, or microwave cooking. There are many good natural foods cookbooks that provide instructions on these cooking methods.

Vegetables need not be eaten plain to be healthy. The recipes for nourishing Rejuvenation Toppings, beginning on page 65, are a delicious accompaniment for cooked vegetables. Some of these toppings use vegetables as a base and are also suitable for use on starchy foods or protein dishes. Others are based on proteins and make a complete meal with raw or cooked vegetables.

I am emphasizing vegetables in the Rejuvenation Diet because we are focusing on mineralizing the system. Many of the recipes in this book—the broths, teas, protein drinks, and vegetable soups—are extremely high in minerals. Because our soil is so depleted today, it is not necessarily true that people can get all the nutrients they need from their food. This is why I will recommend a program of nutritional supplements later in this chapter.

An excellent way to get minerals into your body is to make mineral-rich vegetable soups. Long a mainstay of the biological clinics in Europe, vegetable broths are very beneficial for anyone on a cleansing, fasting, and alkalinizing program. I am providing you with the recipe for Potassium Broth, a base for delicious, clean vegetable soups and bisques that provide nutrients your body needs to promote cleansing and rejuvenation.

Another source of abundant minerals is sea vegetables. Edible seaweeds have long been a regular part of the diet of coastal peoples such as the Japanese, the Pacific Islanders, and the Irish. Extremely rich in fiber, calcium, iodine and other minerals, and vitamin B12, sea vegetables are a very important food for beautiful hair, skin, and nails and for healthy bones and teeth. The iodine in sea vegetables stimulates the thyroid gland, ensuring proper metabolism and promoting a healthy reproductive system. In traditional Chinese medicine, sea plants are considered warming and are administered for cold conditions such as anemia, poor circulation, and problems with the pancreas or thyroid.

While you may have only eaten seaweed before as a wrapping for sushi, during the vegetarian phase of this program you will enjoy the Hijiki Stir-fry on pages 69-70. You may also add small amounts of dried seaweed to any soup for a flavorful dash of concentrated sea minerals.

COOKBOOKS THAT SUPPORT
THE REJUVENATION DIET

The Book of Whole Meals by Annemarie Colbin (Ballantine)
California Sea Food Cookbook by Isaac Cronin, Jay Harlow, and Paul Johnson (Aris)
Natural Foods Cookbook by Mary Estella (Japan Publications USA)
Ten Talents Vegetarian Natural Foods Cookbook by Frank and Rosalie Hurd
(Ten Talents)
McDougall Health Supporting Cookbook, Vols. I and II, by Mary A. McDougall
(New Century)

Miracle Foods

Some foods provide such marvelous combinations of taste, nutrition, and health benefits that they truly deserve to be called "miracle foods." They are so beneficial that I recommend that you consume them every day during your three-week program.

Garlic and Onions

Garlic has long been valued for its healing properties. In World War II, it was used against typhus and dysentery, and its germ-killing and immune-strengthening actions have been widely documented by modern researchers. Garlic is very helpful against yeast and fungus infections. The active ingredient in garlic is the volatile oil allicin, which gives garlic its unmistakable smell, and which is able to kill harmful bacteria without hurting your body's naturally friendly bacteria.

Garlic is rich in selenium, a powerful antiaging nutrient, and has been shown to be helpful in controlling high blood pressure, heart disease, intestinal problems, liver disorders, and sinus conditions. Recent medical research has shown that garlic is very powerful in reducing cholesterol and triglyceride levels in the blood. By reducing the stickiness of platelets, it prevents blood from clotting, thereby helping to protect against heart attacks. As a demonstration of garlic's life-extending powers, a study in India of people more than one hundred years old found that the only common factor they shared was that they all consumed large quantities of this aromatic bulb.

Garlic is best eaten raw. You can dice it or crush it and add it to vegetable salads, soups, or any cooked dish. Raw garlic produces a stronger odor than cooked garlic. Chewing some fresh parsley will help to mask the garlic odor on your breath. Garlic capsules are also available, but read the labeling to make sure that they contain the active ingredient allicin.

Onions belong to the same plant family as garlic, and like garlic, onions help to bring down cholesterol levels and to prevent the clumping together of platelets. These two vegetables, especially eaten together raw, help to prevent the accumulation of unwelcome fats in the arteries, which can lead to heart attacks and strokes.

Lecithin

A derivative of soybeans, lecithin can be purchased as a supplement in granular form at health food stores. Lecithin contains acetylcholine, which helps to remove lactic-acid wastes from the body, making the joints and muscles more flexible. It flushes fat out of the liver and prevents its accumulation in the bloodstream. Lecithin washes wastes away from the nerve cells and improves the reflexes.

Sprouts

Sprouted seeds, whole grains, and legumes are among the healthiest foods you can eat. They are a perfect example of a living food that carries nutrients in the most beneficial form directly to your cells.

The sprouting of seeds for food was recorded in China as far back as 3000 B.C. Sprouts are extremely high in the purest forms of protein, and they contain cholesterol-reducing lecithin. Sprouts are rich in enzymes that trigger increased activity in your digestive system. Sprouts are also full of vitamins and minerals and are extremely low in calories.

The produce sections of supermarkets and health food stores will often have different kinds of sprouts available. However, in places where it may be difficult to get fresh or organically grown food, growing your own sprouts at home is a simple way to guarantee a source of clean, living food.

Alfalfa seeds are the easiest to begin with, but you can use other seeds or grains such as lentils, mung beans, rye, yellow soy, wheat, sunflower, and radish.

Sprouting Seeds at Home—Try to find alfalfa seeds prepared especially for sprouting. These are becoming increasingly common in health food stores. Otherwise, buy food-quality seeds.

Place two tablespoons of alfalfa seeds in a one-quart glass jar with a screened lid. These jars are generally sold in health food stores and hardware stores. Fill the jar with purified water and cap it. Let the seeds soak overnight. Pour the water off in the morning. Add fresh purified water and pour it off again to rinse the seeds.

Place the jar upside down and slightly tilted, so it can drain. Keep it in a dark place or cover with a towel. Rinse the seeds twice a day, in the morning before you leave for work and in the evening when you get home, by filling the jar with water through the screened lid, then pouring it out. After two or three days, the sprouts will be ready for eating.

You can use this same procedure for sprouting other seeds and grains. However, use only one tablespoon of the larger seeds, such as sunflower seeds, in a quart-sized jar.

The Super Salad on pages 62-63 is a great way of making sure you get all the miracle foods I have discussed, as well as other nutritious ingredients.

Green Superfoods

Many Japanese studies have measured the benefits of green superfoods, such as spirulina, chlorella, and blue-green algae, and have found them to be effective against a series of viruses, including HIV, flu, mumps, measles, and herpes. Both scientific documentation and reliable anecdotal reports also indicate that these green superfoods are also effective in helping to reduce the symptoms of numerous types of cancers, diabetes, arthritis, hepatitis, bacterial infections, low blood sugar, peptic ulcers, and anemia.

Five million Japanese use these medicinal algaes everyday; they are even more popular than vitamin C. They contain 60 percent protein, including all of the essential amino acids, as well as high levels of beta-carotene and chlorophyll. In fact, many researchers attribute the multiple health benefits of these green superfoods to their high chlorophyll content.

They are also considered a first-string detoxifying agent, capable of removing alcohol from the liver and heavy metals and chemicals from the body's tissues. They can also absorb toxins from the intestines and help relieve chronic constipation.

Look for chlorella and other green superfoods such as blue-green algae and spirulina in your local health food store.

Soy Foods

The history of the soybean began more than five thousand years ago in Eastern Asia. The ancient ancestors of this legume, which grew wild, were harvested by early Chinese farmers. Soybeans arrived in the United States in the early 1800s and have been growing in popularity ever since.

More than fifteen million Americans now eat soy foods, such as tofu, soy milk, miso, and tempeh. Research from around the world indicates that scientists have barely scratched the surface of what this incredible food can do in the prevention and treatment of many diseases. Studies suggest that eating soy products may help prevent and treat high cholesterol, some cancers, diabetes, osteoporosis, and symptoms of menopause.

A recent study at Children's Hospital in Cincinnati indicates that soy seems to exert a protective effect against breast cancer through its ability to lower women's estrogen levels. In fact, Asian women generally ingest more soy foods than Western women and have four to five times less incidence of breast cancer rates than their Western counterparts. In another study performed at the University of Alabama, soybeans were added to the diets of rodents. The number of breast tumors decreased by about 50 percent.

Genestein, the specific phytochemical found in soy, may actually block estrogen's ability to begin malignant changes in breast tissue. Soy phytochemicals have also been shown to convert leukemia cells back into normal cells and to fight colon and rectal cancer. In fact, the incidence of these cancers declined 40 percent in men who consumed tofu five to seven times weekly.

Soybeans are high in fiber, low in fat and calories, and high in protein. They supply all eight of the essential amino acids and are equivalent in quality to the protein found in meat and dairy products. For these reasons and more, I recommend that we follow the lead of traditional cultures in the Far East, which use many soy products daily. I have provided you with a recipe for miso sea soup on page 70 and for delicious tofu toppings for your vegetables on pages 67-68.

Miso—Miso is a fermented soybean paste that is consumed daily by the Japanese. It was first discovered in China more than 2500 years ago and then brought to Japan. This highly nutritious food is so much a part of Japanese daily life that the average household has 365 different recipes for miso soup.

Miso is available in a variety of types, with different colors and flavors to suit different uses and tastes. It is an excellent seasoning in soups, sauces, stews, and marinades. It is very easy to digest and actually supports the digestion of other foods. A great source of vitamin B12 and protein, it should be used generously by vegetarians.

The Japanese consider miso an excellent restorative and a perfect pick-me-up after a hard day's work. It is even used as a hangover remedy.

Whole Grains

Whole, unprocessed grains are an excellent choice for your starchy meals. They contain important nutrients that processing has removed from much of the food in the American diet, including B vitamins, vitamin E, and bran fiber, which helps to cleanse the walls of your intestines.

While you are practicing proper food combining on the Rejuvenation Diet, you have an excellent opportunity to experiment with some new grains. Remember, however, that grains are starchy foods and should not be combined with animal protein.

Many grain cookbooks are now appearing in bookstores, as more and more people recognize the benefits of these wholesome foods. There are four grains that I find to be especially healthful and delicious.

Buckwheat

Buckwheat is the staple grain in Russia, where it is made into a porridge called kasha. Russian scientists attribute the life-extending and rejuvenating properties of buckwheat to the fact that it contains rutin, a bioflavonoid, which helps to keep blood pressure down. Buckwheat contains complete, high-quality vegetable proteins and many vitamins; it is especially rich in the minerals manganese, magnesium, and potassium. Because the proteins in buckwheat are a natural component of the grain, your digestive system supplies the proper enzymes in the right order to make use of this vegetable protein, as long as it is not improperly combined with other proteins, such as meats.

Millet

The staple grain throughout much of the Near and Far East and Africa, millet has been eaten by human beings longer than any other grain. The ancient Greeks and before them the Egyptians recognized its high nutritional value. Millet is a complete protein food, containing all the essential amino acids, and is thus comparable to meat or milk in its protein value. It is extremely rich in vitamins and minerals, especially calcium, magnesium, and trace elements such as molybdenum. It alkalinizes the system, unlike most grains, and hence is nonfattening, since alkalis tend to dissolve fat and counteract its accumulation in the body. Millet is also extremely tasty.

Quinoa

Native to the Andes Mountains, quinoa (pronounced *keen-wa*) has been a staple food for thousands of years. Health-conscious American visitors, impressed by the extremely high nutritional value of quinoa, have recently brought this grain back to the United States and are now cultivating it in the Colorado Rockies. You can find it in many health food stores, along with recipes for preparing it. Quinoa has a higher protein content than any other grain and an interesting, nut-like flavor. It is more expensive than other grains, because it is still relatively rare.

Barley

Praised for its strengthening and invigorating properties, barley was eaten by the Roman gladiators and is used extensively today in many parts of the world, particularly the Middle East. Its fiber, known as beta glucans and also found in oats, helps to lower blood cholesterol, prevent constipation, and improve bowel function in general. Barley, a great nourisher of the nerve cells, also helps to calcify the bones. The most beneficial forms of barley are the least processed, such as whole-grain barley, barley grits, and barley flakes, all available in health food stores. Barley is also the base for Rejuvelac, a fermented beauty drink that I will introduce on Wednesday: Day 5.

Protein Foods

Even our more conservative dietary establishment has recognized that Americans eat much more protein than their bodies require. Too much protein in the diet creates toxic nitrogen by-products that place an extra burden on the kidneys. Studies also show that populations that eat high animal-protein diets run a greatly increased risk of developing cancer.

The Rejuvenation Diet provides a fully adequate supply of protein every day this week, although you may be eating less protein than you are accustomed to. As a result, you may notice a lighter feeling and an overall improvement in your digestion. In particular, I want to emphasize reducing your consumption of animal protein during this program. As you begin to add foods back in Week 3, we will discuss the individual metabolic variations that may help you decide just how much animal protein to eat regularly.

In any event, I do not recommend red meats during the 21-Day Program, so when you do buy flesh foods, please select chicken or fish. Range-fed chicken is the best choice for chicken, and deep-water ocean fish come from a less polluted part of the ocean. For your fish or chicken meals, select a simple cooking method, such as broiling, grilling, or steaming. Avoid cooking methods that use fats.

Another option for your protein meals is tofu, which is made from soybeans. The cookbooks listed in this chapter contain recipes for tofu main dishes. On pages 67 and 68, I have given some recipes for tofu toppings that make a satisfying protein accompaniment to raw or cooked vegetables.

As you select your protein meals for the week, try to select a different source of protein every day. You can consider each kind of fish as a different type of protein. Rotate your selections so that you are not eating the same protein more than once every four days. This will reduce the stress on your digestive system.

I advocate a restriction of dairy products on the Rejuvenation Diet. During the three-week program, you should consume no milk and no cheese at all. Many people have a hard time digesting milk, while cheese congests the system and dehydrates the body, which makes it one of the most constipating foods. Later on, when you have completed the program, you should consider cheese as an infrequent high-fat treat, not a dietary staple.

Except for a small amount of butter, the only other dairy food I would recommend at all is yogurt. Yogurt is easier to assimilate than other dairy products, because the fermentation process has broken down the milk sugar. I suggest that you not eat yogurt too often—no more than every fourth day. For those who enjoy an occasional yogurt dish, I have given you a recipe for a yogurt topping on page 68 and for a yogurt-enriched beet borscht on pages 59-60.

Many people are reluctant to cut down on their intake of dairy products, because they are afraid they will not get enough calcium. There are many sources of calcium besides dairy products, including raw sesame seeds; raw nuts; corn tortillas; leafy greens such as kale, broccoli, mustard, watercress, and parsley; and sea vegetables, especially dulse and kelp. Also, most people benefit from calcium supplements, no matter what foods they eat.

Nuts and seeds are alternative sources of protein that can be made into satisfying and nourishing protein drinks. Such drinks are an important part of your three-week program. There are several recipes on pages 71 to 73.

Fats

Many people believe that if you want to lose weight and prevent heart disease, you cannot eat any fat at all. The truth is that some good fats are essential to your health and beauty. To maximize your health, prevent the effects of aging, and flush the fat out of your body, you need a daily supply of these good fats, known as omega-3 and omega-6 oils, or EPAs and GLAs.

Often my clients come to me for help after years of intermittently starving their bodies on low calorie, very low fat diets. Among their complaints, they mention dry hair and skin, weak and brittle nails, as well as problems of elimination. By adding the essential GLA and EPA oils to their diet, we are able to reverse these problems to restore healthy, glowing skin, shiny hair, and strong nails.

GLAs and EPAs are necessary for the manufacture of prostaglandin, hormone-like compounds that regulate all your bodily functions at the molecular level. Every cell in your body needs a daily supply of these essential fats in order to produce the all-important prostaglandin.

The omega-3 fats, or EPAs, are polyunsaturated oils, for which the richest source is oily cold-water fish, such as herring, salmon, mackerel, cod, sardines, rainbow trout, and halibut. The EPA in the diet of Eskimos prevents them from having heart disease, despite a diet composed almost entirely of animal protein and fat. Other societies that consume large quantities of fish have also been found to have a low incidence of heart disease, confirming the protective value of the EPAs.

EPA makes the blood platelets less sticky, helping the blood to flow more freely and preventing clots in the heart and blood vessels. It helps to bring down blood-fat levels and may also help reduce the stiffness and aching of arthritis. You can supply some of your EPA requirement by eating cold-water fish two or three times a week. EPA is also available in supplement form at pharmacies and health food stores.

The omega-6 polyunsaturated oils, or GLAs, are even more important than the EPAs for protecting the heart and cardiovascular system, the immune system, and the skin. GLAs help flush fats out of the body, and when GLA and EPA are taken together, the production of health-promoting prostaglandin is maximized.

Unrefined vegetable oils, especially safflower and flax oils, contain the raw material for the GLA that the body needs. Evening primrose and borage seed oils are naturally high in GLA, and other high-GLA oils include sunflower, corn, soy, and sesame. Always be sure that the safflower, flax, or other high-GLA oils you buy are cold-pressed and unrefined.

On the Rejuvenation Diet, I recommend that you use two tablespoons of safflower or flax seed oil each day, to ensure that you get the required amount of fat-flushing GLAs. I recommend one tablespoon of flax seed oil in your protein drink as well as salad dressings based on safflower and sesame oil, both excellent sources of GLAs. Use these dressings regularly on your salads to promote healthy hair, skin, and nails and to provide the antiaging benefits of a clean and clear circulatory and cardiovascular system.

Heat changes polyunsaturated oils, creating free radicals—substances that age your body prematurely. For this reason, when you use oil for cooking, never use safflower or flax seed oils. Use olive oil instead, since it can stand higher temperatures. Recent research has shown that olive oil in the diet selectively reduces levels of LDL, the dangerous form of blood cholesterol, while keeping the beneficial form, or HDL, intact. This may explain why Mediterranean peoples such as the Greeks and Italians, who use olive oil as a staple in their diet, have half the mortality rate from heart disease that Americans do. Olive oil contains monounsaturated fat, as do avocados and nuts. Another recently discovered monounsaturated oil is canola oil, which can also be used in cooking. While you should still be careful not to consume too much fat, you may enjoy these delicious foods in moderation without fear of damaging your heart and arteries.

For cooking, you may also use a little butter, but definitely avoid margarine, because it is made of oils that have been chemically altered through hydrogenation, producing toxic substances.

Supplements

During the 21-Day Program, I would like you to fortify yourself with the extra protection of a simple combination of supplements. You will find the Daily Supplement Schedule on pages 90-91.

While I certainly believe that you should get as much nutrition as possible from your food, it is a fact of modern life that there are some nutrients that you are not going to be able to get enough of. Also, until you have completed this cleansing program, it is likely that you are not absorbing all the nutrients that you are eating, since your digestive system is probably not yet functioning up to par. A goal of this program is to make your absorption of nutrients more efficient, but even with improved efficiency I recommend supplementation.

Nutritional supplements can help reverse the aging process by stimulating the body's own ability to repair and maintain its organs and cells. Supplementation can also assist us in our fight against genetic predisposition. We are born with a unique genetic code and a tendency to certain types of physical and mental functioning. That genetic inheritance has a lot to say about how quickly we age and how long we live. However, the timing on this genetic clock is subject to an enormous variation depending on how we actually live. Antiaging supplementation addresses this issue by maximizing the basic building blocks within each of our cells, preventing damage to and increasing repair of our DNA. Supplementation can help us to escape our genetic destinies, at least to some extent.

I am often asked why it is necessary to take supplements if you eat a healthy diet. I realize that taking supplements can be expensive and time-consuming and that, for some, it represents a dependency on pharmaceutical-type products. Unfortunately, our soil is depleted of valuable minerals; thus, our foods, even healthy ones, are not as nourishing as they once were. Additionally, our absorption and digestion become less efficient as we age.

There is abundant evidence that regular use of certain vitamins and minerals reduces the risk of cancer and heart disease, retards aging, and protects against toxic injury. For example, it is recommended that 400–800 units of vitamin E daily will reduce the risk of atherosclerosis and more. Yet, it is just not possible to get those quantities from dietary sources. Recent studies confirm that selenium protects against heart disease and cancer, but it is just not possible to get enough selenium from dietary sources, because of our depleted soil.

As you can see, it may be possible through diet alone to get enough of these and other nutrients to satisfy our minimal needs. However, if we want to achieve optimal health, longevity, and true well-being, nutritional supplementation is not only encouraged but substantiated by research.

Antioxidants

In preventive nutrition, antioxidants are perhaps the single most important class of supplements. These vitamins, minerals, and enzymes help protect our body from the formation of free radicals. Free radicals are atoms that can cause damage to our cells, impairing our immune systems and leading to infections and degenerative diseases. In fact, many age-related health issues are directly linked to free radical buildup. The free radicals may be formed by external factors, such as overexposure to radiation, toxic chemicals, and sun, but they are also created internally through the action of metabolic processes, such as eating, digesting, and breathing. Simply the process of life itself creates free radicals.

Given the body's wisdom, naturally-occurring enzymes act as free radical scavengers and attempt to keep them in check. In today's environment, the scavenger enzymes should be supported by a diet and supplement program rich in antioxidants such as beta-carotene, vitamins C and E, GLA, selenium, and zinc. These are also scavengers that assist the body in destroying free radicals.

Life in the twenty-first century requires antioxidant supplementation for almost everyone. Antioxidants can prevent and even repair free radical damage. The publication *Cancer Research* reports on a Scottish study of fifty men, half of them cigarette smokers. This study proved that nutritional supplementation with antioxidants such as vitamins C, E, and beta-carotene for up to twenty weeks had a highly significant moderating effect on DNA damage done by free radicals. In particular, the antioxidants were able to stop the spread of cancer caused by the generation of free radicals. In an Italian study, the dietary habits of 2,500 women, aged 20–74, with breast cancer, were compared to 2,600 women without cancer. Researchers found that the women with cancer had significantly lower intakes of antioxidants and calcium than the cancer-free women. Lower intakes of riboflavin, iron, and potassium were also observed in the women with breast cancer, according to the *International Journal of Cancer.*

ANTIOXIDANT VITAMINS AND MINERALS

Vitamin E is an immune stimulant that neutralizes free radicals against the effects of aging. It protects against blood clots and heart disease.

Selenium protects the body from free radical damage and works best in conjunction with vitamin E.

Vitamin C protects against infections, radiation, and environmental pollutants. It is essential to the formation of new collagen tissue and supports the body against stress.

Beta-carotene is a powerful anti-infective, which supports the immune system, protects against environmental pollutants, and slows the aging process.

Pycnogenol is a highly active bioflavonoid extract from pine bark. It is fifty times stronger than vitamin E and twenty times stronger than vitamin C.

Co-enzyme Q-10 is essential to cellular energy. It has a long history of effectiveness in boosting immunity, increasing cardiac strength, and overcoming periodontal disease.

Germanium is a potent antioxidant mineral, which detoxifies and blocks free radicals.

Ginkgo biloba has been used in both Europe and Asia to combat the effects of aging. It protects the cells from free radical damage and reduces blood cell clumping. It increases blood circulation to the brain and has been used in the treatment of Alzheimer's.

SOD is an antioxidant enzyme that helps to scavenge and neutralize free radicals.

Wheat-germ oil is rich in B vitamins, proteins, vitamin E, and iron. One tablespoon will provide the antioxidant equivalent of an oxygen tent for 30 minutes.

Octacosanol is derived from wheat germ; it will counteract fatigue and increase oxygenation during exercise and active sports.

Gamma linoleic acid (GLA) is obtained from evening primrose, black currant, and borage seed oils. It energizes the cells, insulates the nerve fibers, and helps regulate hormonal and metabolic functions.

GREEN TEA

Green tea has been widely consumed in Asia since antiquity. In fact, five thousand years ago, the Chinese discovered that green tea had antibacterial qualities and used it to purify their drinking water. Since that time, it has been used for detoxification, to treat fatigue, and to combat colds and flu. It is also known to promote digestion, soothe the nervous system, stabilize blood fats, and lower blood pressure.

Recent research has shown that green tea, when taken internally, may have protective effects against cancer due to its high antioxidant properties. Japanese research has shown that people who drink strong green tea daily have a low incidence of stomach, skin, and lung cancers. Both black and oolong tea contain some of the same preventive compounds, but green tea contains the highest levels. The National Cancer Institute also reports that green tea provides a protective effect against esophageal cancer. Researchers are also studying green tea as a protection from radiation, oral cancer, arthritis, and rheumatism.

Green tea differs from black tea primarily in that it is not produced by fermentation. In the production of black tea, one or more of the tea plant's intrinsic healing ingredients is lost during the fermentation process. There are many types of green tea, including Bancha, Hojika, and Kukicha. The varieties vary in their caffeine content. Green tea is the only caffeinated beverage that does not affect my sleep cycle.

Perhaps less well publicized are green tea's healing powers when applied topically to the skin. The polyphenols in green tea play the primary role in maintaining healthy body tissues. One of them is an antioxidant twenty times stronger than vitamin E. It seems to protect skin cells from free radical damage and the cancers that are commonly initiated by such environmental factors as UV light exposure and pollutants. In combination with the xanthines in tea, these polyphenols help create anti-inflammatory and anti-irritancy effects. The xanthines have also been shown to reduce the appearance of cellulite.

Minerals

I also suggest that you include liquid minerals, an extract of key minerals suspended in liquid form in an ionic state. Few people understand the importance of minerals, the basic element of every object on earth. Minerals act as co-vitamins and co-enzymes, that is, they actually make it possible for many vitamins and enzymes to function.

Dr. Linus Pauling, winner of two Nobel Prizes, once said that every sickness, disease, and ailment can be traced to a mineral deficiency. These mineral deficiencies are even more likely to occur than vitamin deficiencies. Even with a balanced diet, most of us are still deficient in minerals. Unfortunately, our absorption of minerals declines with age, yet stress and pollution have raised our basic requirements. The twenty or so minerals available in today's foods or the twelve to fourteen minerals available in most supplements are no doubt helpful, but there were actually seventy-five to eighty minerals available before soils were depleted due to wind and rain erosion and centuries of unwise farming practices.

When plants grow, they draw minerals from the soil. Yet the mineral content of plants has been severely reduced over the years. The growing and harvesting of crops on the same fields for the last hundred or so years, combined with ongoing wind and rain erosion, has left our soils greatly deficient in both major and trace minerals. Thus, our foods are deficient as well. To obtain all the minerals we need, we must supplement. Liquid minerals are easy to use and are available in most health food stores.

DAILY SUPPLEMENT SCHEDULE

For all of the above reasons, I recommend that you fortify yourself with the extra protection of a simple combination of supplements. Always take your supplements with meals. If you take your supplements on an empty stomach or wash them down with only water or juice, chances are they will not be absorbed and used very efficiently by your body. Taking your supplements with food also prevents the possibility of stomach upset.

Be aware of getting your daily requirement of the beneficial GLA and EPA oils. Simple safflower oil in your salad dressing can help cover your need for GLA. You can also take safflower oil capsules. To provide your EPA, you can supplement the fish in your diet by taking EPA capsules, derived from fish oil. I discuss more about these and other "good fats" in the Fats subsection.

Even though you will be absorbing nutrients from your food more efficiently on the 21-Day Program, I recommend this daily supplement program for additional nutritional insurance. You may want to make a copy of this schedule and keep it where you can refer to it easily.

- Multivitamin Supplement: Take a good, high-potency multivitamin supplement with one or more meals daily. There are many liquid and powdered combinations available.

cont'd.

- Antioxidant Supplement: Take a good, high-potency antioxidant supplement with at least one meal daily.

- Vitamin C Plus Bioflavonoids: Take a 1,000-milligram tablet with at least one meal daily and at bedtime. Delicious chewable "C's" are available in most health food stores.

- Vitamin E Plus Selenium (preferably in dry form): Take one 400 IU capsule of vitamin E with selenium at one or more meals daily.

- Calcium/Magnesium: Divide a total dose of 1,000 to 1,200 milligrams of calcium and 400 milligrams of magnesium among your meals and/or at bed.

- GLA: Take two 90-milligram capsules with each lunch and dinner that does not include a GLA-oil salad dressing.

- EPA: Take one 1,000-milligram EPA capsule with each lunch and dinner that does not include a serving of fish.

- Lecithin: Take one 1,200-milligram capsule of lecithin with each lunch and dinner that does not include a tablespoon of granulated lecithin sprinkled on salad or added to other food.

- Enzymes: Take two multiphase digestive enzymes with each meal heavier than simple fruits and vegetables.

Minimum Daily Requirement

It is always a good idea to rest from your supplement program from time to time. I often do not take supplements on the weekends or occasionally will skip a week. So please don't be too hard on yourself if you forget to take, or don't feel like taking, your optimum supplements.

ALOE VERA

Aloe vera has been used successfully for thousands of years to treat a wide range of maladies. It is most often used as a salve to heal wounds and sunburn, and it is also a great moisturizer. Alexander the Great used aloe to treat his soldiers' wounds and reportedly conquered an island off the coast of Africa to preserve a sufficient supply. Cleopatra used it as a moisturizer.

Current research suggests that beyond healing the epidermis, aloe is also useful for soothing internal tissue and healing many digestive and gastrointestinal problems. Dr. Ivan Danhof is studying the use of aloe in treating inflammatory bowel problems, including Chrohn's disease and colitis. He has found that aloe has potent internal healing powers. It lines the gastrointestinal tract and remains for forty-eight hours or more.

Aloe is also getting lots of study for its potential for treating cancer and AIDS. It is already being successfully used in veterinary applications, including the treatment of feline leukemia. According to Carrington Labs, aloe appears to have antiviral and immune-boosting properties and has reduced the dosage of AZT required for patients with HIV/AIDS.

I recommend a freeze-dried aloe vera product called Manaloe. No other aloe product on the market today is as potent as this capsulized product. Each bottle of sixty capsules contains the equivalent of two liters of fresh aloe juice.

Keep your eye on aloe research. If aloe were discovered today, it just might be declared the wonder drug of the century!

SHOPPING LIST AND INVENTORY:
WEEK ONE

This weekend's shopping list includes all breakfasts and special beverages, all ingredients needed to make Potassium Broth, and all ingredients for beauty treatments. Remember that there are many ready-made products available at your local health food store that will make this program both easier to follow and less expensive. However, I am giving you a complete list of herbs and essential oils should you wish to follow the 21-Day Program recipes as provided. The choice is yours.

cont'd.

Please check your daily schedules and refer to the indicated recipes so that you can buy the fresh ingredients and staples you will need for lunches and dinners you prepare at home. Please keep in mind that I encourage you to make individual adjustments in the meal plan based on your available preparation time, likes and dislikes, and social engagements. For example, you will still get great results if you substitute the Potassium Broth or Bisque for any of the other vegetable soup and bisque meals. If you wish to substitute ready-made almond milk or soy milk in your protein drink recipes, please add them to your shopping list. If you never plan to make the drinks from scratch, you may omit the almonds, sesame seeds, and sunflower seeds. Delicious, ready-made protein drinks available in many health food stores and juice bars would be acceptable as an occasional substitution.

The Equipment Inventory lists equipment you will need this week. Purchase or borrow any listed items that you do not already have.

Nuts, Grains, and Cereals

Almonds, ½ pound
Barley, 3 pounds
Millet, 2 pounds
Oatmeal, 1 pound

Vegetable Oils (cold-pressed only)

Almond oil, 8 ounces
Olive oil, 16 ounces
Peanut oil, 8 ounces

*Beverages and
Miscellaneous Foods*

Apple juice, organic, 32 ounces,
    or pure maple syrup, 8 ounces
Milk, 1 quart
Water, bottled if you do not have
    a water purifier, 3 gallons
Yogurt, plain, low fat, ½ pint

*Fruits and Vegetables
(organic, if possible)*

Apples, 4
Beets, with tops, 2 bunches
Cantaloupe, 1
Carrots, with tops, 16
Celery, 2 bunches
Cucumber, 1
Garlic, 6 bulbs
Lemons, 4
Onions, 4
Orange, 1
Papaya, very ripe, 1
Parsley, 1 bunch
Pineapple, very ripe, 1
Potatoes, baking, 4
Raspberries, 1 pint basket,
    or blueberries, 1 pint basket
Strawberries, 1 pint basket
Summer squash, 3
Zucchini, 4

cont'd.

Herbs, Supplements,
and Health-Care Items

Aloe vera juice, 1 quart
Body brush, vegetable bristle, 1
Body soap, nonchemical
Castor oil, 8 ounces
Dried Herbs:
    alfalfa, dried, 2 ounces
    cayenne pepper, 2 ounces
    mustard powder, 4 ounces
    oat straw, dried, 2 ounces
    peppermint leaves, dried,
        4 ounces
    sage, dried, 2 ounces
Epsom salts, two 4-pound boxes
Essential Oils: basil, chamomile,
    clary sage, eucalyptus, laven-
    der, marjoram, orange, pepper-
    mint, rose (or blended rose),
    rose geranium, rosemary,
    sandalwood, tincture of
    benzoin, tolu balsam
Hydrogen peroxide, 3 percent
    solution, 1 small bottle
Loofa mitt, 1
NaPCA moisturizing spray
Sea-algae shower gel
Sea salt, 9 pounds
Sea sponge, soft, 1

Supplements:

co-enzyme Q-10, 20 milligrams,
    20 tablets

Supplements con't.

Emergen-C, 36 packets, *or*
    powdered vitamin C
    (ascorbic acid), 1 bottle
vitamin E, 400 IU plus selenium,
    dry form, 60 tablets
germanium, powdered or
    sublingual form, 1 gram
ginkgo-leaf extract, 40 mil-
    ligrams, 20 tablets
lecithin, granulated, 1 pound, *or*
lecithin supplement,
    1,200 milligrams, 380 capsules
minerals, liquid, 1 quart
multivitamin supplement,
    1 month's supply
omega-3 (EPA) oil supplement,
    1,000 milligrams, 20 capsules
omega-6 (GLA) oil supplement,
    90 milligrams, 20 capsules
wheat-germ oil, 4 ounces
witch hazel, 1 small bottle

Equipment Inventory

Blender
Coffee grinder or seed mill
Journal, blank
Mini-trampoline
Slant board
Tape recorder
Tub or bucket, small,
    for foot soaks
Vaporizer *or*
    electric frying pan

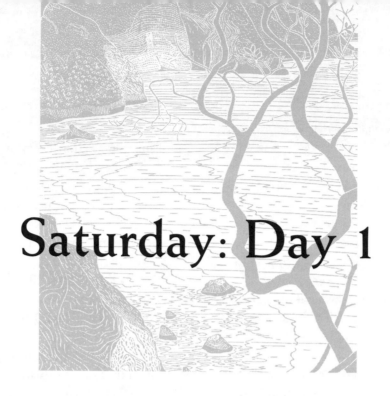

Saturday: Day 1

Afternoon Activity: Clean out your kitchen (page 105). Review the Rejuvenation Shopping List and Inventory: Week One (pages 101 to 103), Schedules for Days 1 through 7, and the Rejuvenation Program Recipes (pages 42 to 73). If you have decided to alter the meal plan in any way, make the necessary adjustments to your shopping list. Go shopping and store food.

Evening Activity: Stress Reduction Evening: Yoga Stress Releasers (pages 109 to 111); follow with Stress Reduction Bath (page 101).

Creating Your Cleansing Environment

Today's activities are designed to set the scene and the mood for your 21-Day Program. Before you go shopping, please look around your home—particularly your bathroom— and think about what you can do to make it a more peaceful, nurturing, fun place to spend time in. You are embarking on a special program of taking care of yourself—a program just for you. Perhaps this is a good time to buy some fluffy new towels to enrich the experience of the wonderful baths, soaks, and steams that I will be showing you. You may want to buy colorful new sheets, or perhaps you would like to select some music, incense, or candles to create a meditative, peaceful atmosphere.

Now, go into your kitchen, open the cupboards, and remove all the things that will not be included in the 21-Day Program. Please remove the refined sugar, sugar syrups (except pure maple syrup), white flour, artificial creamers and sweeteners, candy, cookies, cakes, muffins, processed and canned foods, jams and jellies, raisins and other dried fruits, packaged cereals (except oatmeal), canned meats, bread, and crackers. If you plan to stop drinking coffee or alcohol during this program, get rid of them, too, although I am not insisting that you break your habits entirely.

I am not saying that you must never eat any of these foods again. If you decide to keep some of these items, simply pack them away in a box. If you are sharing your kitchen with your family or a friend, clear out a shelf in your cupboard and in your refrigerator for your own special foods.

Now, look in your refrigerator. Get rid of all the dairy products—cheese, milk, sour cream, and sweetened yogurts. You may keep a little butter if you wish, and you will be using plain yogurt for a facial this week. Clean out the processed meats, red meats, sodas, and diet sodas. Remember, I am not saying that you must never eat cheese again or never eat another lamb chop. The 21-Day Program will teach you how to incorporate such foods into your lifelong diet, but for the next three weeks I want you to start with a clean slate and reeducate yourself. Now, pack up all these things and donate them to a worthy cause or store them away out of sight. Your kitchen is now clean and clear.

Please review the entire shopping list, so you will know what kinds of foods, supplies, and equipment you will need. Some of the items on the shopping list may sound strange to you. Trust me; they will all be explained and enjoyed as we go through the program together.

You will probably need to visit more than one store to complete your shopping. Many supermarkets now have health-food sections, and you may be able to find many of the items there. If you have a health food store in your area, you will likely find the organically grown fruits and vegetables that I recommend available there. Seeds, nuts, grains, and herbs will probably be available in bulk at the health food store, too.

As you go through the various recipes for herbal teas, internal flushes, and aromatherapy baths, please keep in mind that there are high-quality, ready-made alternatives for most of these combination recipes available at your local health food store. These excellent options will save you time and money. I am providing you with the complete recipe, so you have the knowledge; I also am providing you with the alternative, so you can make a choice. You will get great results either way.

I am assuming that you already have a number of kitchen appliances, such as a blender or a coffee grinder. All such items needed for this program are listed under Equipment Inventory on the shopping list.

When you return from shopping today, be sure to store your food properly. Keep your oils in their glass bottles in a cool, dark place. Grains, seeds, and nuts should be stored in airtight glass (or less desirably, plastic) containers. Seaweed can be stored as it comes, in its package. Herbs should be stored in airtight containers, preferably glass ones. Tofu should be removed from the water it is packed in and rinsed with fresh purified water every day. Store fruits and vegetables as you would normally do; tomorrow I will show you a Cleansing Soak for fruits and vegetables that will not only remove contaminants from any nonorganic produce, but will also increase its storage life.

Stress Reduction

Before you begin to cleanse your system of toxins, I want you to take this evening to cleanse your mind and body of stress and tension. The more relaxed and positive you are as you begin your 21-Day Program, the more benefit you will derive from it.

Prepare a quiet, pleasant place for your evening activities. These activities are a very important part of my 21-Day Program. If you wish, put on some quiet music, light some candles, or burn some incense.

The Quality of Your Sleep

I want you to take some time to think about the quality of your sleep. If you have trouble falling asleep, wake up in the middle of the night and have difficulty getting back to sleep, or awaken earlier than you would like, you suffer from insomnia. A good night's sleep is crucial to recovering from stress. In fact, much research today indicates that many of us are actually sleep deprived. We know that feeling of deprivation when getting up several times nightly to feed a newborn or to care for a sick child. A shortened attention span, the loss of physical strength, emotional vulnerability, and difficulty in responding to unfamiliar situations are all common symptoms of sleep deprivation.

Sleep is a restorative process, which serves to replenish us both physiologically and psychologically. As an essential part of the daily human cycle, sleep is a determining factor in the state of one's health. Some people may need only four or five hours of sleep, while others may need eight or nine hours. I encourage you to discover your own personal rhythm and to give yourself the gift of enough rest. Many emotional and physical problems will simply disappear when you are properly rested, and you will awaken looking forward to the day.

I encourage you to use bathing or other stress-releasing evening activities I will be teaching you throughout your 21-Day Program to ease yourself into sleep. Before getting out of bed in the morning, practice some of the deep breathing and stretching practices we will discuss, as well.

If necessary, please consider taking one of the many natural herbal or amino acid supplements for better sleep rather than taking conventional pharmaceuticals. Many sleeping pills can lead to even more dangerous health risks and dependencies. They can alter the brain wave patterns of sleep and thereby prevent a normal sleep cycle. Although they may work initially, sleeping pills lose their effectiveness after a few weeks and can cause many side effects, such as withdrawal symptoms, a hangover effect, alteration of memory, and depression. Perhaps the most serious side effect is that sleep can actually worsen upon discontinuation of the drug.

If you have trouble falling asleep at night or wake up in the middle of the night and find it difficult to get back to sleep, please consider your caffeine intake as a causative factor. Remember, coffee, black teas, many colas, and chocolate all contain high amounts of caffeine and may be preventing you from a good night's sleep. You may be aware that you cannot ingest caffeine after dinner without interfering with your sleep; but some of us have very sensitive nervous systems and find that caffeine past noon will affect our rest. Some, like myself, are so sensitive that even one cup of black tea in the morning will cause sleep irregularities. Before resorting to sleeping pills, experiment with your caffeine intake. What works for your friends may not work for you.

Intolerance to certain foods, eating excessively, the intake of drugs and alcohol, and emotional factors such as depression, anxiety, fear, and excitement may also be affecting the quality of your sleep. External circumstances, such as a noisy sleeping room or an electric blanket, may also be affecting your sleep. Many natural health practitioners are suggesting that your own unique electromagnetic field may be disturbed by the electric coils of a blanket.

I encourage you to experiment with several of the natural remedies available in your health food store and pharmacy. My personal favorite is melatonin. According to research from Rhinebeck Medical Center in New York, your body's supply of melatonin measurably declines as you age; the elderly produce only about half as much as children. Two to three milligrams of melatonin before bed will not only ease insomnia, but may also strengthen the immune system, ease PMS symptoms, and help prevent memory loss and hardening of the arteries.

I also get tremendous results from the herb Kava. It acts as a sedative and a muscle relaxant and is used to promote sleep. In several studies that compared Kava to popular tranquilizers, Kava seemed to enhance memory while the tranquilizers impaired it. Kava also reduced symptoms such as palpitations, chest pain, headache, and dizziness. Kava has been used in the Pacific Islands as both a traditional remedy and ceremonial intoxicant for thousands of years. Unlike pharmaceutical alternatives, it is not habit-forming, does not lose its effectiveness over time, and has a remarkable absence of side effects.

The quality of your sleep reflects the quality of your waking state. By learning to have a more relaxed, vital, and joyful daytime life, you will also enjoy a more pleasant, restful, and beneficial sleep. In fact, as you incorporate some of the dietary recommendations and detox techniques I recommend throughout the book, you'll find it easier to fall asleep and will awaken feeling more refreshed and positive.

NATURAL SLEEP REMEDIES

Take a cup of "sleepytime" tea before bed. Many selections are available in the health food store. They will contain one or more of the following herbs: chamomile, catnip, lemon balm, St. John's Wort, and hops.

Take a single or combination herbal extract or capsule which has been formulated for sleep. These remedies will contain one of more or the following herbs: valerian, skullcap, passion flower, kava, hops, and wild lettuce leaf.

Take your calcium-magnesium supplements before bed. If you tend to awaken in the middle of the night, take an extra 500 milligrams of magnesium.

Take the amino acid gaba in conjunction with inositol, niacin, vitamin B6, and magnesium. Many "amino relaxer" products are available in the health food store. Take another in the middle of the night if you awaken and find it difficult to get back to sleep.

Try the homeopathic remedy Calms Forte in conjunction with any of the above options.

Take 3 milligrams of melatonin on a temporary basis to reset your biological clock.

Yoga Stress Releasers

You may want to use a special mat or carpet for the following exercise, as is traditional in yoga. Before you begin this exercise, you may wish to read it slowly into a tape recorder. Then you can play it back, instructing yourself, without breaking your concentration to refer to the book.

Lie quietly on your back on the floor, with your arms at your sides and your heels lightly touching. Relax for a moment with your eyes closed and breathe normally. Now raise your hands and feet straight up in the air. Hold them that way for a few moments and then begin to shake your arms and legs, your hands and feet. Shake them vigorously, feeling them loosen up, shaking out all the stress. Let go of all the tension in your muscles. Let your hands and feet flop back and forth at the ends of your arms and legs. Continue this shaking for a few minutes, then return your arms and legs to the resting position and feel the effects of releasing the tension.

Next, in the lying position, I want you to go through each part of your body, tensing and releasing. This exercise is designed to let you experience the greatest tension you can feel, before you release it and let it go. Lie quietly with your eyes closed, breathing gently. Now, bring your attention to your feet. Breathe in through the nostrils, and tense both feet, as tense as you can get them. When you feel the greatest tension you are capable of feeling, breathe out through pursed lips, and as you release your breath, release the tension from your feet. Relax and breathe normally for a moment, feeling the effects of this release.

Now, as you inhale, begin to tense again, not only the feet but also the calves. Tense as much as you can, and as you release your breath, let go of the tension, first from the calves and then the feet. Feel the tension not just in the muscles, but also in the nerves, the blood vessels, and even the bones.

Again breathe in through the nostrils, tense the feet and the calves, then add the thighs and hips. As you release your breath through pursed lips, release the tension downward, from the hips and thighs to the calves and feet. Relax for a moment and enjoy the feeling of releasing the tension.

Now breathe in again, and tense upward from the feet to the thighs and hips, and now add the abdominal section and lower back. Feel the internal abdominal organs tensing and contracting, so that you are completely tensed from the waist down. As you release your breath, first let go in the abdomen. Feel the abdominal organs relax, then release the tension downward, ending with the feet. Each time, release more deeply than the time before. On the next inhalation, tense upward to the abdomen, then add the upper torso, the chest, back, and spine. Feel everything completely and evenly tightened and tense. Release your breath, and let go of the tension first in the chest, down the spine, into the abdomen, and down to the feet.

Breathe in, tense from the feet up through the upper torso, and now make a fist with your hands, tensing up the arms into the shoulders. As you exhale, release the arms and hands, moving down all the way to the feet.

Finally, breathe in, and tense from the feet upward to the chest, arms, and hands, and now tense the face, head, and brain. Feel even the sensory organs tight and tense. Every organ and every cell of your body should now be as tense as you can get it. Hold the tension for a moment, and then as you release your breath, first let go of the tension in the head and face, down through the neck, the shoulders, the arms and hands, all the way down to the feet. Let all the tension melt away.

As you inhale, repeat this last full-body tensing once more, all the way up into your face and brain, feeling every cell in your body tensed, and now, as you exhale, release from the top down, until every part of your body is relaxed.

Now, as you lie relaxed, take a gentle breath in, and as you release that breath, feel yourself melting into the floor, with no tension anywhere in your body. Breathe normally, and just lie there for a few minutes, feeling completely relaxed.

As you do this exercise, notice any parts of your body where it seems harder to release the tension. Learning to recognize tension in your body is the first step toward learning to let it go.

As you soak in your Stress Reduction Bath tonight, take the time to appreciate the changes you have made in your home to create a rejuvenating environment. Inhale the soothing fragrances of the oils, knowing that you are already enjoying the benefits of your program. Twenty-one days from now, you will be more relaxed, cleaner, lighter, lovelier, and filled with youthful energy and optimism.

STRESS REDUCTION BATH

Stress puts a tremendous strain on both the nervous system and the immune system, and it can produce a state of mental and physical exhaustion. As the aromatic fumes of the essential oils in the Stress Reduction Bath envelop you, they will help to strengthen and revive your nervous system. At the same time, they will relax your body and soothe away your anxieties.

> *6 drops basil essential oil*
> *6 drops rosemary essential oil*
> *6 drops chamomile essential oil*

Add the essential oils to a hot bath. Lie back in the water and inhale the wonderful fragrance. Soak for twenty minutes, allowing the water to cool and bring your body back to normal temperature. Dry off vigorously with a coarse towel, wrap yourself in a warm robe, and prepare for a good night's sleep.

Sunday: Day 2

Morning Cleansing: Warm shower. Scrub with a loofa mitt, using a gentle non-soap cleanser. Follow with fifteen seconds of cool water.

Food and Beverage Preparation: Prepare and drink Hot Lemon-Water Flush (page 42). Prepare Inner Beauty Herbal Tea (pages 42-43) and drink one cup at a time throughout the day between meals. Prepare Hydrating Drink (pages 43-44) and drink it throughout the day between meals. Use Cleansing Soak for Produce for any nonorganic fruits and vegetables (page 116). Prepare Potassium Broth (pages 44-45).

Dinner: Nonprotein dinner: Potassium Broth (pages 44-45), as much as you want. Combine with pasta or potatoes and salad or vegetables.

Exercise: Take a brisk walk for thirty minutes. Pay attention to your surroundings and your breathing.

Evening Activity: Review your Goals Contract (page 32). Complete Toxicity Symptom Checklist (pages 117 to 118). Follow with Inspiration Bath (page 118).

Cleansing for Optimal Health

Good morning! I hope you have awakened with a new resolve and a sense of anticipation as you look forward to the next three weeks. You will be doing an intensive make-over of your body, your thoughts, and your lifestyle, cleansing and nurturing yourself both within and without.

There is no better way to initiate the cleansing process than to begin to flush your body with the beverages that will be an integral part of this week's program. Start out the morning with your first daily Hot Lemon-Water Flush, prepare a pot of Inner Beauty Herbal Tea to drink throughout the day, and you are on your way to cleaner, healthier cells and tissues. Today you will also begin to use the special Hydrating Drink that I recommend as an enhanced form of drinking water to sip throughout the day. While you are in the kitchen this morning, I will show you how to cleanse any nonorganic produce you purchased yesterday, to rid it of toxins and contaminants so that all your meals will be rejuvenating. Then make your first batch of mineral-rich Potassium Broth, which will be the base for many of the meals during the program. Be sure to use purified water for all the recipes I give you. When you eliminate the chemicals and other contaminants in tap water, you begin to lighten the load of toxins in your body.

After your Hot Lemon-Water Flush, have whatever you want for breakfast. To speed along the cleansing process, you may choose to restrict your morning meal to nothing but fresh fruit. Eat whatever you want for lunch today, but I suggest that you begin to establish the habit of eating protein and vegetables for your mid-day meal. This evening, have some of the delicious Potassium Broth that you will be making this morning. Have it along with a salad, steamed vegetables, pasta, potatoes—any vegetables or starchy foods. But please do not eat any meat, eggs, tofu, fish, chicken, cheese, or other protein foods this evening. Eating lightly today and drinking plenty of the special beverages I will be introducing you to will help prepare your body for the Rejuvenation Diet that you will begin tomorrow morning.

Your daily walks are an essential part of the 21-Day Program. Try to find a place close to nature where you can walk, even if you must drive or take a bus there. Open yourself up to your surroundings. Pay attention to your breathing, and allow yourself to be refreshed by the sights, sounds, and smells of the outdoors.

Toxicity in Our Environment

Each year we are exposed to literally thousands of toxic chemicals and pollutants in our air, food, and water. This overexposure is often in the news. For example, this past Thanksgiving I heard my favorite radio "green grocer" giving advice on which fruits and vegetables were safe to feast on, or free of dangerous contaminants. A couple of days later I heard that many thousands of people had gotten ill in one of our major metropolitan areas from drinking polluted tap water. Recently, school children in another major city had to be rushed to the hospital due to overexposure to chlorine in a public pool.

We are all too familiar with the problems from air pollution, including asthma, bronchitis, sinus headaches, and fatigue. Now research is beginning to link the chemicals in the food chain to many illnesses. Rates of breast cancer in Long Island communities have drawn national attention in the past few years; they are as much as 6 percent higher than the rest of the country. Some believe that the increase is nothing more than better detection; but many women and their doctors fear that the rates are due to the indiscriminate use, in years gone by, of DDT and other pesticides on the island's once-vast potato fields.

Researchers at the World Resources Institute in Washington, D.C., argue that environmental pollutants are causing an increase in some cancers. For example, pesticides used on crops and lawns can behave in the body like hormones, increasing estrogen or blocking testosterone, and may be partially responsible for an increase in infertility, as well as hormone-related breast, testicular, and prostate cancers.

Women in the San Francisco Bay Area have the world's highest rate of breast cancer (104 cases per 100,000 women). The International Agency for Research on Cancer reports that this is double that of Europe and five times higher than that of Japan. Two-thirds of the women have no known risk factors, and experts are querying whether exposure to radiation, pesticides, and chlorine-based chemicals may be contributing factors. California leads the United States with 17,800 new breast cancer cases and 4,400 mortalities every year. With 258 sites, it also tops the list of America's toxic waste sites. This is nearly one hundred more than second-place Alaska and two hundred more than third-place Maryland.

In addition to the assault on our food, water, and air supply by this environmental pollution, we deliberately add contaminants known to be deadly, such as artificial hormones, antibiotics, preservatives, and colorings. Because the body is not designed to metabolize these man-made compounds, many of them are stored as toxic waste.

In fact, as a result of the petrochemical revolution, toxins have accumulated in the human system faster than they can be eliminated. We are all carrying around, in varying degrees, the residues of legal and illegal drugs, industrial chemicals, pesticides, and food additives. These pollutants manifest themselves in a variety of symptoms, including decreased immune function, hormone imbalance, psychological disturbances, and cancer.

Throughout my years of practice as a health educator, I have learned that many health problems are caused by the accumulation of toxic waste in the body. Obviously, the healthy human body can handle certain levels of toxins; our concern is with the excessive intake of toxins or a reduction of elimination. Toxicity occurs when we ingest more than we can utilize and eliminate and seems to increase as we age. Many of our chronic diseases and dilemmas result from this systemic congestion.

Detoxification helps to rid our bodies of these chemicals and pollutants and stimulates a return to optimum health.

We all know that our bodies require nourishment—food, water, and oxygen—and much emphasis is placed on putting the right things into your body. It is equally important for waste to leave your body efficiently.

The key to maintaining a constant cleansing process in your body is fresh, pure water, an essential component of every cell in the body. When you constantly flush your organs of elimination with water, your body remains clear of waste and is able to make the best possible use of your food and oxygen.

When you consume food, your digestive system breaks it down, uses what it needs, and then eliminates the waste, not only through the intestines, but throughout the body. You breathe in oxygen through the lungs and exhale waste carbon dioxide. Your bloodstream and lymph system carry nutrients to the cells and carry away cellular waste. Your skin eliminates waste through sweat and the shedding of dead cells. The water you drink and absorb from your food carries away waste products in solution to be eliminated through the kidneys.

If any of these systems of elimination are clogged up by waste, the whole system begins to back up. Not only does the waste create a toxic condition, but your body is also unable to properly use the new nutrients that are taken in. If the plumbing in your house were to become plugged up and the garbage collectors were to go on strike, you would no longer be able to dispose of the waste that is produced in the course of the day, and soon your home would be unfit to live in. Your body works in much the same way, and your outer beauty and vitality are affected.

The bottom line is that toxins and toxic wastes that remain in the body are harmful in two ways: First, they initiate chemical reactions that ultimately produce free radicals, known to age and deteriorate the body. Second, the body's defense mechanisms surround the toxins with fluids and fats in an attempt to render them harmless. These globules of protected toxins form the basis of the lumps we know as cellulite and the condition we think of as water retention. To rid yourself of toxins, you simply need to cleanse the body at the level of the organs, blood, and lymphatic system. It's much easier than it sounds.

CLEANSING SOAK FOR FRUITS AND VEGETABLES

You may not be able to purchase organically grown produce. Don't worry, you can remove harmful contaminants from your fruits and vegetables by using the following cleansing soak. This soak not only purifies your produce, it also helps it to stay fresh longer.

Travelers and American families stationed abroad have traditionally used a chlorine bleach soak to cleanse fruits and vegetables of sprays, bacteria, viruses, parasites, and toxic metals. A more recent idea is the hydrogen-peroxide soak. Hydrogen peroxide is a common antiseptic that many people use as an external germ killer. Dentists recommend hydrogen-peroxide solution for cleansing teeth and controlling gum disease.

If you have a water purifier, use purified water for this soak; if not, you may use tap water.

¼ cup of 3 percent hydrogen peroxide (drugstore variety)
2 gallons of water (about a dishpan full)

Fill a dishpan or other container with the water and add the hydrogen peroxide. Soak thin-skinned fruits (berries, peaches, apricots) or leafy vegetables in this cleansing bath for fifteen minutes. Soak thick-skinned fruits (apples, citrus) or fibrous, thick-skinned, or root vegetables for thirty minutes. It is okay to combine fruits and vegetables of the same type.

Remove the fruits and vegetables from the cleansing bath and let them stand in clear purified water for ten minutes. Then drain them, dry them thoroughly, and store in the usual manner.

Toxicity Symptom Checklist

Many different conditions can be indications of toxicity in the system. Complete the Toxicity Symptom Checklist to evaluate your present toxicity level. Put today's date at the top of the first column (Day 2), and then score yourself for each of the symptoms listed according to the following scale:

0 = absent   *2 = moderate*

1 = mild   *3 = severe*

Add up your scores for a total toxicity score for today's date. After you have finished the 21-Day Program, you will notice a marked drop in your toxicity level. Retest yourself at the end of this program (on Day 21), again three months later (on Day 21 + 90 days), and then at three-month intervals as you continue to incorporate your new lifestyle practices into your daily routine.

Symptom	(Day 2) Date:	(Day 21) Date:	(Day 21 + 90 days) Date:
Overweight or underweight	____	____	____
Abdominal pain, tenderness, or cramping	____	____	____
Protruding abdomen	____	____	____
Heartburn	____	____	____
Gas, burping, or flatulence	____	____	____
Bad breath	____	____	____
Coated tongue	____	____	____
Offensive body odor	____	____	____
Skin blemishes or sallow complexion	____	____	____
Dark circles under the eyes	____	____	____
Facial puffiness	____	____	____
Fluid retention or bloating	____	____	____
Dry or brittle hair	____	____	____
Brittle nails	____	____	____
Low back pain	____	____	____
Premenstrual tension	____	____	____

Premenstrual or menstrual discomfort (e.g., sore breasts, bloating)	____	____	____
Sore joints	____	____	____
Reduced sexual desire	____	____	____
Headaches	____	____	____
Fatigue	____	____	____
Depression	____	____	____
Irritability or anxiety	____	____	____
Low energy	____	____	____
Total Toxicity Score:	☐	☐	☐

As you relax in your bath tonight, congratulate yourself. You are making a major commitment to becoming the very best you can be. This evening's review of your goals is a first positive step toward cleansing and nourishing your body, mind, and emotions. Without thinking in detail about your specific goals, let the aromatic fumes of the essential oils subtly influence your mood. Absorb the wonderful combination of fragrances through all your senses. Tomorrow you will wake up full of anticipation and optimism, as you start on the Rejuvenation Diet. The diet will immediately begin to give you an energetic, buoyant feeling, freeing your potential for creativity and loving self-expression.

INSPIRATION BATH

The essential oils in the inspiration bath work together to create a euphoric, self-nurturing mood that will help you affirm your resolve to take better care of yourself. Eventually, you will come to associate these scents with feelings of self-love and well-being. Essence of rose is traditionally associated with love.

Lavender essential oil
Clary sage essential oil
Rose essential oil (or blended rose oil)

To a hot bath, add six drops of each of the essential oils. Relax and inhale the fumes, allowing them to put you in a dreamy mood. Soak for twenty minutes as the water gradually cools. Dry yourself with a coarse towel and prepare for bed.

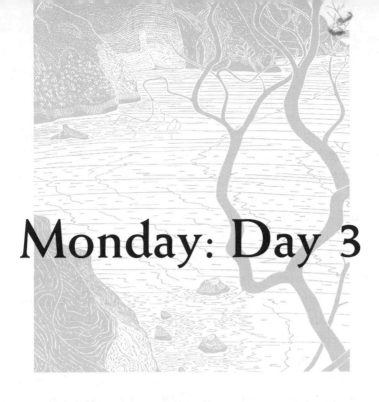

Monday: Day 3

On Awakening: One 8-ounce glass of Hot Lemon-Water Flush (page 42). Prepare your Inner Beauty Herbal Tea (pages 42-43); drink one cup at a time between meals throughout the day.

Morning Cleansing: Using a loofa mitt, scrub the entire body using a non-soap cleanser such as Seaweed Shower Gel, while showering with hot water. End with thirty seconds of cold water.

Breakfast: Fresh Apple Breakfast (pages 53-54).

Mid-morning Snack: Optional protein drink—Sesame Seed Milk (page 71).

Lunch: Fish, chicken, or tofu with steamed or raw vegetables.

Dinner: Yam Delight (pages 58-59); Super Salad (pages 62-63) with Fat-Loss Dressing of your choice (pages 63 to 65).

Exercise: Precede exercise with Ionic Cocktail (page 46). Then take a walk for thirty minutes. Maintain a brisk, steady pace, paying attention to your surroundings and your breathing.

Evening Activity: Cucumber Cleansing Facial (page 137). Remove facial and apply the Yogurt Toning Mask (page 136), which is kept on during the Tranquility Bath (page 137).

The Holistic Perspective

My cleansing program deals with your body as a whole system. This holistic view is somewhat different from the general medical perspective. Western medicine tends to focus on a specific disease or symptom in a specific part of the body, as if it were isolated from the whole. From the holistic point of view, what goes on in one part of the body is connected to what happens in every other part of the body. The holistic approach looks at what goes on in your mind and your spirit as well as in your body, and recognizes that all these aspects of your being influence and reflect one another.

Rather than looking at health as the absence of disease, the holistic approach defines health in terms of a positive model of wellness. The wellness model goes beyond the absence of symptoms to encourage a high level of functioning on the physical, mental, and spiritual planes. I define wellness as a creative process of growth and change, where we take responsibility for using our bodies, minds, and emotions in a constructive way and recognize our connection to a larger community of beings. Such self-responsibility and caring are the ultimate goals of my program. I do not promise you any "magic bullet" to eliminate isolated symptoms. Rather, I offer you a holistic approach to bring out the very best in your physical functioning, your mind, emotions, and spirit.

Nourishing Your Whole Self

Everyone knows that your emotions have great impact on the efficiency of your digestive processes. The best way to eat is in pleasant, calm surroundings. Put yourself in a relaxed mood, with no distractions such as television or a book. Before you begin eating, take a few deep breaths to calm and center yourself. You can then truly appreciate your meal. Eating your food consciously not only helps digestion, but it also prevents overeating, since you taste and appreciate every bite.

From childhood on, our social lives tend to center almost entirely around food. When Grandmother comes to visit, she brings the kids cookies; when you are good, you are rewarded with an ice-cream cone; when you go out on a date, you often go to a nice restaurant. Under these circumstances, it is easy to develop the habit of using food as a form of emotional fulfillment. It is also easy to believe that refusing food that is offered when you are not hungry or that you prefer not to eat might be interpreted as refusing the love that motivated the offer.

Like so many people, I have been dealing with food addiction for most of my life. In my family, I learned very early to equate food with love. While on the one hand, food was treated as an expression of love and family togetherness, on the other hand, my mother often encouraged me to lose weight. When I was a schoolgirl, my lunch bag would be full of celery, carrot sticks, and cottage cheese, while all my friends would have nice-looking sandwiches and cookies for dessert. I developed the habit of sneaking out to buy hamburgers, French fries, and milkshakes to express my rebellion.

As I began my quest for better health, I knew I had to get rid of my obsessive feelings about food. Realizing that I was using food for emotional nurturance as well as physical nourishment, I began to look for other things that were nurturing for me. Getting a massage, talking with a close friend, going to the movies, or walking by the ocean are some of the things that now provide the emotional support I used to seek in food. I look for uplifting options when I am upset or burned out or bored, and instead of turning to food, I can choose one of these other outlets to gratify myself.

Radiant Skin

Your skin is the mirror of your health. When you are well nourished, adequately exercised, and free of toxins and wastes, your skin will be smooth, unblemished, and youthful looking—it will glow with an inner radiance. Your hair and nails, which are an extension of the skin, will be strong and healthy as well.

Did you know that the skin is your body's largest organ? Wrapped around you at a thickness of only one-twentieth of an inch, your skin weighs about six pounds. This thin layer of tissue performs several very important functions. It serves as a protective covering, keeping your body fluids in and harmful materials out. The skin regulates body temperature through a network of blood vessels just below the surface, which expand or contract to control how much blood is brought to the surface to be cooled by evaporating sweat. Your sense of touch—pain, pressure, light touch, warmth, and cold—depends on specialized nerve endings in the epidermis near the skin surface.

An often-overlooked function of the skin is its vital role as an organ of elimination. About one-third of the body's impurities are excreted through the skin—more than one pound of wastes each day! Your sweat glands not only regulate body temperature, but they also function like miniature kidneys that cleanse the system of impurities.

In fact, sweat has almost the same chemical makeup as urine, and if the pores are choked with dead cells and uric acid, wastes will remain in the body, forcing the other organs of elimination to work harder. Many of these toxins and wastes end up lodged in the skin tissues, producing a mottled or sallow appearance.

The traditional Chinese medical system recognizes the relationship between the skin and other organs. By looking at the skin on certain areas of the body, Chinese doctors are able to determine the functional performance of the inner organs. This makes sense when you consider that improperly functioning internal organs will cause additional toxins to appear in the skin.

Your skin is constantly renewing itself. It actually consists of four layers. At the bottom is the basal, or growing, layer, where basal cells divide to produce new cells. These new cells displace the older ones, pushing them upward through a clear cell layer and a granular layer, until they finally reach the outer, keratin layer. It takes about three to four weeks for the cells beginning at the basal layer to end up on the surface. As the cells mature, they produce granular material that eventually causes the cells to consolidate into a thick, tough outer keratin layer. Finally, the cells in this protective outer layer slough off, carrying away large molecules of waste material with them.

We sometimes forget that the skin not only moves wastes from the inside out, but is also capable of absorbing substances directly into the body. This fact was brought dramatically home to me when I observed the effects of progesterone cream that one of the doctors I work with was giving to his patients for premenstrual stress (PMS). Applying just a little of this hormone cream to the skin often produced a remarkable improvement in the emotional ups and downs and other symptoms that are so common a few days before your period.

This absorptive power of the skin is now being employed as a way of administering medicines. Special skin patches, called derms, deliver estrogen for menopausal problems, scopolamine for motion sickness, and nitroglycerin for cardiovascular pain. Scientists are experimenting with derms for controlling diabetes, weight loss, fertility, and nicotine withdrawal.

If beneficial substances can be so readily administered through the skin, then harmful substances can also enter our bodies in the same way. When you put on perfume, cosmetics, deodorants, or insect repellents, remember that it is not just the surface of the skin that you are affecting. The British medical journal *Lancet* recently reported toxic physical and mental symptoms, especially in children, from the application of

PROGESTERONE CREAM

Some of the most promising research being done today demonstrates how natural progesterone helps build bone back even in older women, thus reversing some osteoporosis. Natural progesterone, made from the popular wild yam herb, can also restore or prevent the occurrence of vaginal dryness, a common complaint among menopausal women. According to extensive research in England, it can also reduce many symptoms associated with PMS, especially mood swings, depression, bloating, and breast tenderness

A cream containing 3 percent natural progesterone is sold over the counter in many pharmacies and health food stores. You may be surprised that a cream applied to the skin can be so effective. Remember, many medicines are administered through the skin, such as estrogen, nicotine, and nitroglycerin.

Wild yam contains the precursors that help the body with hormonal balance. It may be a safer, more natural way to rejuvenate the system than hormone replacement therapy. I will elaborate on wild yam in particular and hormonal balance in general on Tuesday: Day 18.

insect repellent on the skin. Try to use skin-care products that contain pure and natural, recognizable ingredients.

Today's schedule will focus on cleansing and beautifying your skin from within and without by promoting its eliminative functions. I will help you to clear it of the toxins and waste materials that produce blemishes, dry patches, furrows and wrinkles, fatty cellulite deposits, and unhealthy coloration. You will also learn how to stimulate the lymph system, which carries impurities and toxins away from the cells and out of the body.

Beauty Beyond Skin Deep

Now that you understand how your skin cells reproduce and move from the basal layer to the surface, you can see how quickly you can improve your complexion. In fact, at the end of the 21-Day Program, most of your facial skin will be new. The quality of your skin depends on the quality of the raw materials from which the skin cells are made. This means that your complexion is a direct reflection of the quality of your diet.

The best diet for your skin is the Rejuvenation Diet, emphasizing fluid-rich fresh fruits and vegetables with nutrients that maintain your body's ideal acid-alkali balance, so important to a glowing complexion. Eating right eliminates harmful saturated fats and ensures an adequate supply of GLA and EPA oils, which nourish the skin and protect the heart. A healthy, youthful skin requires large doses of the vitamins and minerals in the supplement program you began on Monday.

Vitamin A is essential for forming healthy cells in the basal layer and helps to enhance the skin's moisture level. A vitamin-D supplement nourishes dry skin, especially during the winter months, when it is not as readily manufactured by the body in response to exposure to sunlight. Vitamin C is an age retardant, preventing the oxidative processes that produce wrinkling of the skin and hardening of the collagen in connective tissue. Minerals that promote skin health include calcium, magnesium, zinc, manganese, and potassium.

FOREVER YOUNG

There really does exist a product from Sweden that rebuilds collagen and elastin! It is a totally natural compound, which, when taken orally, has a rather miraculous effect on the quality of aging and sun-damaged skin. It contains natural protein and carbohydrate structures from a marine source—vitamins and minerals of the same composition as the skin tissues.

The European research has been performed by dermatologists, biochemists, gerontologists, and physiologists. After three months of daily ingestion of the product, skin thickness improved by 82 percent and skin elasticity improved by 25 percent. Significant improvements were also noticed regarding wrinkles, sun spots, dry skin, hair, and nails. All women participating in the study had wrinkles before the study began. After the treatment period, 50 percent of them had no signs of wrinkles and the rest had just minor signs.

I personally have been taking it for about two years and have experienced dramatic changes in my skin tone and elasticity. Many wrinkles have virtually disappeared and my neck is no longer sagging! I have recommended Forever Young to many hundreds of clients and friends, and those results have been duplicated with everyone who has remained on the product for ninety days or more.

Skin-nourishing vitamins and minerals are often helpful when applied topically as well. Vitamin E cream or ointment, and vitamin A and D ointment, are very useful in preventing and correcting dry skin. One of the B vitamins, PABA, has been found to be the best topical protection against dangerous ultraviolet rays in sunlight, a principal cause of wrinkling. Some people, however, have an allergic reaction to PABA, so choose your sunscreen carefully.

Please remember that smoking, too, dries and ages the skin. If you are a smoker who has set quitting as one of your goals in this program, this is a good way to strengthen your resolve.

To counteract the unavoidable effects of aging on the skin, I recommend the twice-daily use of the natural moisturizer NaPCA. NaPCA, the sodium salt of pyrrolidone carboxylic acid, is the most important natural moisturizer found in the skin. Your body manufactures NaPCA from glutamic acid, one of the amino acids that make up proteins. As skin ages, its NaPCA content decreases, so that older skin contains only half the amount found in younger skin. It is water, not oil, that keeps your skin soft and supple. NaPCA draws moisture out of the air to keep the skin hydrated and plump, helping it retain the natural resiliency of youth.

NaPCA is one of the most exciting new natural products in skin care. It is available in health food stores in the form of a spray concentrate, often combined with aloe vera. Use it twice a day to spray your face. After bathing, you can spray your entire body. NaPCA is a wonderful moisturizer under makeup. Rather than a cosmetic cover-up, it is a natural way of correcting a deficiency that occurs with aging of the skin.

I spray my hair with NaPCA before I go to bed. In the morning, my hair looks shinier, fuller, and healthier.

You must drink at least eight glasses of purified water each day to properly nourish your skin. Some of this water will be supplied in herbal teas and beverages such as your morning Hot Lemon-Water Flush, your pre-exercise Ionic Cocktail, and the skin-food drink Rejuvelac. The rest should be provided by the Hydrating Drink I mentioned on Sunday: Day 2. For the sake of your complexion, avoid caffeine beverages, limit or eliminate alcohol use, and stay away from diet sodas full of chemicals and caffeine.

Constipation Is Your Complexion's Worst Enemy

When your colon is clogged with waste material, your body tries to eliminate toxins through the skin. Even if your skin is functioning properly, these waste materials end up deposited in the pores and tissues. Many women, as they get older, think they need to use more makeup because their skin color has changed and their complexion has become blotchy.

Many of my clients initially decide to go on a cleansing program because they are having skin problems. Often they have tried everything, including antibiotics prescribed by a dermatologist. Not only do their skin problems not clear up satisfactorily, but many have undesirable side effects from the drugs.

Sarah is such a client of mine. She was referred to me by a skin-care specialist. When I first saw her, she had terrible acne, from her jawline all the way down to the bottom of her neck! Sarah had just lived through a stressful two years filled with some major lifestyle changes. Following her father's death, she had taken over the family business, and her own personal care had assumed very low priority. Once her business affairs were in order, she took a look at herself and realized something needed to be done. Sarah had always had some slight problems with her skin, but nothing like the massive acne that she had now.

It took us more than a year of proper diet and an internal cleansing program, in conjunction with her regular skin-care treatments, to clear her skin of acne. For Sarah, her complexion problem was a warning sign that something was the matter. The condition of her skin is her barometer to tell her when to pay more attention to her diet, her stress management, and her systems of elimination. We all have warning signs in our bodies, and for many of us, the first changes occur in the skin. When you have a sudden breakout, your body is trying to tell you that something beneath the surface needs to be corrected.

The cleansing process is not always easy. You should be aware that you may experience minor symptoms and reactions as your cleansing progresses, and the skin is one of the most common places for cleansing reactions to show up. Do not panic if you notice a new pimple or two as your stored wastes are eliminated through the skin. Your body is detoxifying and cleansing itself.

One of the most pleasurable parts of the rejuvenation program is the variety of techniques to beautify your skin through bathing, dry skin rubs, and fume baths. These procedures are easy, relaxing, and enjoyable ways to take care of yourself while indulging your senses. The results are worth it: a vibrant complexion, an energized body, and a relaxed state of mind.

Dry Skin Rubs

Before I introduce you to the cleansing and revitalizing powers of baths and herbal steams, let me begin by showing how to stimulate your skin's eliminative functions with dry skin rubs.

Dry Brush Massage

Dry brush massage has many benefits. It removes the dead layers of skin and opens the pores, promotes blood circulation and lymph flow to help your body excrete toxins, stimulates the hormone-and-oil-producing glands in the skin, and invigorates the nervous system by stimulating the nerve endings. Stimulation by dry massage can help enhance immune-system function, promote muscle tone, and help break down the accumulations of fat and toxic waste known as cellulite. Regular dry brushing will accomplish these functions and also improve your overall complexion and make you look younger and feel better all over.

The only equipment you will need is a stiff bath-type brush with natural vegetable bristles. The brush should be at least the size of the palm of your hand, and should have a long handle so that you can reach all parts of your body. Avoid nylon or other synthetic bristles, because they are sharp and may damage the skin.

Begin at the soles of your feet and brush vigorously in a circular motion, moving upward gradually to massage every part of your body. Use as much pressure as you can stand, remembering that different parts of the body have different degrees of sensitivity. After brushing the feet and legs, move upward to the abdomen, then brush the hands and arms inward toward the chest. Brush down from the neck, down the back, and up from the abdomen toward the chest. Brush until your skin is rosy and glowing—about five minutes.

Remember that the brush is removing toxins and pore-clogging dead cells from the surface of your skin. Keep your brush clean by washing it periodically with soap and water and drying it in the sun or a warm place. Do not brush irritated skin, and do not brush the sensitive skin of your face.

The best time for a dry brush massage is when you wake up in the morning. Follow the massage with an invigorating shower or bath. Some people prefer a dry brush massage after bathing. During the 21-Day Program, you will be experimenting with several variations, so you can choose the one you like best.

Sea Salt Scrub

Another excellent method for stimulating the eliminative function of your skin is the Sea Salt Scrub. Use 100 percent sea salt, widely available at grocery and health food stores. Place four or five generous handfuls of salt in a plastic container. In another container, put a little water, about a quart, as hot as you can stand. This will open your pores. Sitting or standing in a dry bathtub, take a soft sea sponge, dip it into the container of hot water, and wet down one part of your body at a time—your arm from the wrist to the elbow, for example. Then rub in the dry sea salt with your hand. If it is too abrasive, you can add a little water to the container of salt to make a paste, if you wish. Rub the salt on your skin with circular motions. Proceed to cover your whole body with the salt, from your feet up the legs, from your hands up the arms, and from your neck down toward the chest. Use a long-handled brush to rub the sea salt onto your back. Scrub with circular strokes until your body has a pink, healthy, warm glow.

Now, relax (as best you can) for about ten minutes. You will begin to feel your body tingle pleasantly. As the salt dries, it is drawing the toxins out of your skin. Rinse off in a warm shower, followed by a thirty-second cold splash. If your skin is very reactive, it may flush pink for a day or so. Avoid getting salt on the mucous membranes.

Friction Air Bath

Exposure to fresh air is very beneficial for the skin. It promotes all the skin's normal functions and aids the cleansing process. An air bath, combined with a dry skin rub, is wonderfully invigorating and promotes a clear, healthy complexion.

You may give yourself an air bath after any bath or shower. Before drying off as usual, when the weather permits, wrap yourself in a towel, go outside, and let yourself dry naturally in the fresh air. Even if you aren't wet, you may simply go outdoors, completely naked, and expose your skin to the air. If you do not have access to a private place outdoors, or during bad weather, you can take your air bath indoors with the windows open.

After your air bath, warm yourself by rubbing your skin with a rough towel or doing a dry brush rub to rid the skin of excreted waste material. You may do the dry rub inside or outdoors, depending on the weather.

Whenever you have the time, try this combination of bathing, air bath, and dry skin rub to provide a complete workout for your skin.

Rejuvenating Baths

What can be more relaxing after a long, busy day than to soak in a fragrant, cleansing bath? Many people tend to cleanse themselves in a very utilitarian way—they jump in the shower, soap themselves down, rinse off, and hop out. But a bath can do so much more. It is a way to gently unwind, soothe tire muscles, open your pores, and draw wastes and toxins out through your skin. The time you take for a leisurely bath is precious personal time well invested in your health, beauty, and inner peace.

Bathing has always been a treasured ritual of personal hygiene, healing and relaxation—from the great public baths of Rome to the elegant bath ceremonies of the Orient, the sacred healing water rituals of ancient Greece, or the fashionable European spas. Your bathroom can be a sanctuary, a private retreat from the hustle and bustle of the world outside. As you luxuriate in the fragrant aromatic essences, the healing mineral salts, and the stimulating and relaxing effects of a daily water ritual, you will come to appreciate how bathing can be a way of cleansing your body of waste and your mind of stressful thought.

Different bath temperatures have different effects on the system. Hot water is very enervating. It is a great natural tranquilizer and muscle relaxant, and many people find a hot bath just before bedtime a perfect cure for insomnia. Warm baths are very pleasant, refreshing, and relaxing. Because you can stay in warm water for a long time, it helps to maximize the cleansing and healing effects of the salts or oils that you add to your bath. Cold baths are very stimulating. You may shudder at the thought of a cold bath or shower, but as your body becomes accustomed to brief exposures to cold water, you will begin to realize its benefits.

I remember when I was a girl, my mother always told me I should end my showers with cold water. Really, it was very sound folk wisdom. A cold shower might actually be considered as close to a cure-all as any other use of water I will suggest in this book. It rejuvenates the entire system, enhancing circulation, increasing muscle tone, and activating the nervous system. It stimulates the endocrine glands, improves digestion, and speeds up metabolism, and if used regularly, it can increase resistance to infections and colds.

Throughout the program, I will be stressing hot baths for specific reasons, but I want to encourage you to use warm, cool, and even cold baths and showers just as often. The temperature of your bath will be determined partly by the time of day. A hot bath at night can be very relaxing and help you fall asleep, while a cold shower in the morning can help to wake up your entire system.

It is not wise to use hot water too often. Hot baths tend to dry out the skin, because they draw the body's natural oils out of the skin. You may think that by adding oil to your bath you are putting oil into your skin, but bath oils simply rise to the surface of the water and do not add moisture to the skin. To protect your skin before taking a hot bath, oil your entire body before getting into the water. If you have dry skin, use almond oil, castor oil, olive oil, or peanut oil. If you have normal to oily skin and you take a lot of hot baths, use safflower oil, sesame oil, or sunflower oil.

I recommend that you always splash your body with cold water following a hot or warm bath or shower. After being exposed to hot water, your skin is quite sensitive to cold, because the pores are open. A cold splash invigorates the system by reducing excess body heat, closing the pores, and preventing the oils from seeping out. If you cannot bear the thought of standing under a cold shower, sponge yourself off with cold water. Over time, your body will get accustomed to the temperature change, and you will begin to relish a cold splash. Incidentally, you will also find that a cold sponging or a quick cold shower after a hot bath at night does not interfere with sleep, but helps you to relax even more.

One of the most invigorating kinds of showers is a contrast of alternating hot and cold. This stimulates all the body functions, especially the glandular system. It revitalizes skin function and improves circulation. Always be sure to finish a contrast shower with cold water. To prevent chilling afterward, wrap in a bath towel or do a dry skin rub to warm yourself.

Before a long, luxurious bath, it is a good idea to take a quick shower first, as is the Japanese custom, to get the day's grime off your body. When cleansing your skin, please avoid commercial deodorant soaps, because they are very drying. Many delightful moisturizing soaps are available in health food stores and body-care shops, such as those made with an olive oil or glycerin base, or with other beneficial oils. Many people use Ivory soap because it does not contain a lot of chemicals. Review the labels on soaps; remember that your skin has absorptive qualities.

While you should not expose your skin to harmful chemicals, bathing does offer an opportunity to beautify your skin and delight your senses with the aromatic essences of plants. The art and science of using natural plant essences for healing and beauty is known as aromatherapy. Although it was given that name during the present century, the use of plant essences dates back to prehistory. From the Orient to Europe and the New World, from ancient times to modern, aromatic flowers, barks, and leaves have been prized for their healing, preservative, and beautifying powers. It was not until the Middle Ages that the great Arab physician Avicenna discovered the method of distilling the pure essential oils from plants. Herbal remedies and essential oils were an important part of medicine in the Middle Ages and the Renaissance, but gradually, with the birth of modern pharmacology, these natural substances were displaced by their more powerful synthetic forms. Now, essential oils are being rediscovered by practitioners of aromatherapy and herbal medicine as we seek gentler, lasting methods of healing and rejuvenation.

CURATIVE PROPERTIES OF ESSENTIAL OILS

This table will help you to customize your daily bath to benefit from the rejuvenating effects of these natural essences.

Antidepressant: Bergamot, chamomile, clary sage, geranium, jasmine, lavender, oranges, rose, sandalwood, ylang ylang

Antiseptic: Bergamot, eucalyptus, juniper, lavender, rosemary, sandalwood

Aphrodisiac: Clary sage, rose, sandalwood, ylang ylang

Detoxifying: Fennel, garlic, juniper, rose

Diuretic: Benzoin, chamomile, cedarwood, cypress, fennel, frankincense, geranium, juniper, rosemary, sandalwood

Expectorant: Benzoin, bergamot, eucalyptus, marjoram, myrrh, sandalwood

Hypnotic: Chamomile, lavender, marjoram, ylang ylang

Moisturizer: Carrot oil

Pain Relief: Bergamot, chamomile, lavender, marjoram, rosemary

Sedative: Benzoin, bergamot, clary sage, frankincense, juniper, lavender, marjoram, rose, sandalwood

Stimulant: Black pepper, eucalyptus, geranium, rosemary

Essential oils are very readily absorbed by the skin, and inhaling their fragrance in steam also has an effect on both the mind and the body. Adding the beneficial effects of essential oils to the healing properties of water offers a very wide range of possibilities for relaxation, rejuvenation, invigoration, and beautification. Today you will learn how to use essential oils to revitalize and moisturize the skin, stimulate the systems of elimination, and influence your mental and emotional states. I will be giving you recipes for baths and steams and other uses of essential oils throughout my program. You may wish to refer to the table Curative Properties of Essential Oils to customize the recipes to suit your own physical or emotional requirements.

Whether it is a hot soak, a fume bath, a sauna, steam room, or mud bath, the benefits of bathing are essentially the same. Bathing opens the pores and pulls the waste-laden sweat out of the system, promoting the function of your skin as an organ of elimination and restoring its youthful, glowing color and smooth, clear texture. Minerals and herbs added to your bath amplify the healing, cleansing, and beautifying properties of water. The following bath preparations will get you started in discovering the pleasures of bathing.

Epsom Salts Soak

Epsom salts, or magnesium sulfate, are an age-old favorite for hot soaks. Epsom salts are available in pharmacies, supermarkets, and health food stores. During this soak, you will be submerged in the water as deeply as possible, so your natural cooling mechanisms will not be operating. Holding the heat in the body promotes the detoxifying and drawing properties of the Epsom salts.

Pour two whole pounds of Epsom salts into a hot bath, as hot and deep as you can stand. (Cover the outflow in your bathtub if you want to raise the water to a higher level.) Soak for twenty minutes, then get out, wrap yourself in a towel or blanket, and lie down and continue to sweat. You may want to cover your bed with a plastic drop cloth or other waterproof covering.

The minerals in the Epsom salts, followed by vigorous sweating, really draw the toxins out of your skin. An Epsom salts soak is wonderfully relaxing before bedtime, and it is an important part of the cleansing process during the light diet that will occur on Days 13 and 14.

For a luxurious, skin-soothing fragrance, you may wish to mix a few tablespoons of Hydrating Bath Salts into your soak. Since the purpose of this bath is to overheat the body, I do not recommend a cold sponging or shower afterward.

MAKE YOUR OWN HYDRATING BATH SALTS

Enjoy the mineralizing and cleansing benefits of Epsom salts, the moisturizing effects of castor and carrot oils, and the heady aroma and complexion-enhancing properties of the floral and fruit oils.

4 pound box of Epsom salts

4 ounces castor oil

1 teaspoon orange essential oil

1 teaspoon rose essential oil

1 teaspoon chamomile essential oil

½ teaspoon carrot essential oil

In a small jar, combine the castor oil with the essential oils. Pour the oil mixture over the Epsom salts. Allow the salts to stand for at least twenty-four hours so that the essences are completely absorbed. You will be using your Hydrating Bath Salts throughout the program.

You may keep the Epsom salts in the original box, but I prefer to transfer the Epsom salts to a covered glass jar, so the cardboard box will not absorb the oils. Two handfuls (about one ounce) of the Hydrating Bath Salts added to your bath will be just right.

You may vary this recipe, adding other essential oils from the table on page 131 to produce your own personal combination of scents and healing and cleansing properties. You may also add a packet of concentrated seawater (available in powder form at aquarium stores) to the Epsom salts, to add the benefits of concentrated sea minerals to your bath. You may enjoy these bath salts throughout the year.

Cleopatra's Milk Bath

Milk has a well-deserved reputation for promoting a beautiful complexion when used externally. It is excellent for general skin care and will smooth dry, tired skin. This is the only use of milk that will be recommended during the 21-Day Program!

Simmer half a cup of barley in one quart of water, in a covered pot, for three hours. Prepare a larger quantity if you like, storing the extra barley water in your refrigerator. If you do not have the time to simmer the barley, you can use half a cup of Rejuvelac instead.

Make one-fourth cup of almond meal by grinding whole raw almonds in a coffee grinder or blender. Combine the almond meal with one-fourth cup of oatmeal. Tie the mixture securely in a washcloth or cheesecloth. Fill your bathtub with warm water and add the bag of meal. Add three cups of milk along with half a cup of the cooked liquid from the barley; warm these liquids if necessary, so they will not cool the bath water. Soak in this luxurious bath for twenty to thirty minutes, then finish off with a cold sponging or cold shower. Wrap yourself in a towel and enjoy the feeling of cleanliness and youthfulness that this bath imparts to the skin.

Optimism Bath

Draw a warm bath and add five drops each of the essential oils of rose, rose geranium, lavender, and orange. Soak for at least twenty minutes to calm and heal troubled emotions or stress.

I came across this bath late one night when I was deeply depressed over a broken romance and could not get to sleep. It was too late to call a friend, get a massage, or go to the movies, so I consulted my reference books and came up with this combination of essential oils. I even dabbed a bit of the oil on my temples and also made up the Easy Steam (described on page 135) and let the scented fumes fill the bathroom while I soaked in my bath. My mood improved dramatically.

Rose has an age-old reputation for healing the heart, and is traditionally associated with love. There are many varieties of rose essential oils, usually blended because pure rose oil is so expensive. Lavender is also soothing for the emotions, and orange oil has an antidepressant effect, helping to lift the mood.

Fume Baths

Steam baths, or fume baths, use intense heat to open the pores of the skin and draw the toxins out of the system. By adding various herbal preparations to the steam, you can produce specific cleansing, healing, and beautifying effects. At the Inner Beauty Institute, my clients sit in a steam cabinet with essential oils. You may want to take advantage of the steam bath in a local health club or gym, but you can also enjoy the benefits of a fume bath by making your own at home.

Aromatic Fume Bath

Prepare a steaming unit, using an electric vaporizer, a partially covered electric frying pan, or an old electric coffeepot or tea kettle. Half-fill the container with water to make the steam, plug it in (using an extension cord if necessary), and place it in an empty, dry bathtub or shower. (Be certain the tub or shower is dry to avoid electric shock.) Place a chair or stool over the steaming apparatus, and sit down carefully. Drape a "tent" around you, made out of a large blanket or shower curtain. Leave an opening for your head, draping a bath towel around your neck to keep the steam in, or you may prefer to keep your head inside the tent. Sit inside the tent, which will fill rapidly with steam, for about twenty minutes. Be sure to wrap up in a towel afterward to prevent chilling.

For healing and beautifying benefits, there are a variety of herbal preparations that you can add to your fume bath. Witch hazel is wonderfully detoxifying and cleansing. Add tincture of witch hazel, widely available in pharmacies, to your steaming device before you turn it on. The witch hazel should constitute one-fourth of the total liquid volume. You can also use a healing essential oil, consulting the table on page 131 to guide your selection. Some of my favorites are lavender, excellent for relieving headaches, menstrual cramps, stress, and skin eruptions; chamomile, to relax away tension and induce sleepiness; and sandalwood, a great skin moisturizer and meditation enhancer. Add six to eight drops of essential oil on top of the water in the steaming unit.

Easy Steam

For a quick fume bath that requires little preparation, try this variation as an accompaniment to a tub bath.

Put some water in an electric frying pan or vaporizer and plug it into your bathroom outlet. If you choose to use a frying pan, place it on a dry surface near the tub. Add some almond oil to the water, as well as a few drops of essential oils that you have chosen for your bath. The almond oil adds to the moisturizing benefits of the steam, imparts a delightful fragrance, and serves as a carrier for the essential oils. Prepare a hot bath, adding the aromatic oils of your choice. Keep the bathroom door closed, sit in your bath, and let the scented steam fill the room.

While you stretch out in your tub or sit in your fume bath, relax and visualize the toxins leaving your skin. Feel your sweat glands and pores opening to expel impurities. Close your eyes and picture the dead cells gently floating off the surface of your skin. Picture the minerals or herbal aromas flowing in, cleansing and nourishing your skin, making it smooth and clear.

Breathe deeply and inhale the marvelous scent that rises in the steam around you. The relaxed, pleasant mood that this fume bath produces is an important part of my program for youthful, beautiful skin. Stress can take a toll on your complexion, and relaxation can help to smooth out the frown lines and wrinkles and promote the flow of nourishing blood and oxygen into the tissues.

During the 21-Day Program, you will discover that relaxing baths, besides all their other health benefits, are a wonderful source of emotional support. Tonight's Tranquility Bath will provide an opportunity for you to lie back and reflect on what kinds of things nurture you. At the same time, the Cucumber Cleansing Facial and the Yogurt Toning Mask will show you that many foods can be beneficial outside the body as well as inside. Put a full glass of cool water near the tub to sip while you bathe.

As you lie in your bath, think about the things that nurture you. Before going to bed tonight, write in your journal. List the things that you know give you physical and emotional comfort—perhaps puttering in your garden, listening to music, or curling up with a pot of peppermint tea and a good book. In the days ahead, as you go through this program, you will probably discover some new activities that you can add to your list. Keep this list up-to-date; it is a catalog of resources for those times that you might be tempted to turn to food for emotional gratification.

YOGURT TONING MASK

The Yogurt Toning Mask is a rejuvenating beauty treatment that takes only seconds to apply. You will feel its deep cleansing effect as it penetrates the pores to remove obstructing wastes. When used regularly, yogurt facials refine and smooth the texture of the skin.

Combine one-half cup of plain yogurt with a little fresh lemon juice. Apply it to your face and keep it on while you bathe, about twenty minutes. The mask will tighten and dry on your face.

The tingly, cooling sensation of the yogurt contrasts refreshingly with the heat of your bath. After your bath, remove the mask with splashes of cold water.

CUCUMBER CLEANSING FACIAL

Cucumber juice is a great natural treatment for the complexion. It helps to soften hardened skin, soothes sunburn, and gently bleaches dark spots and freckles. It has an astringent effect that will leave your face feeling wonderfully cleansed and refreshed.

Apply thin slices of fresh cucumber to your face. Cover the cucumber slices with a washcloth dipped in very hot water and wrung out. Let the facial stay on for fifteen minutes, then remove the cucumber slices, splash your face with cold water, and pat dry.

A cucumber facial is one of the beauty treatments that you could spend a lot of money for in a salon, but that you can easily do at home.

TRANQUILITY BATH

Hot water is very enervating. Combined with the aromatic oils in this Tranquility Bath, it will help to calm and relax you after a busy day. Lavender and chamomile oils soothe away tension, lift the mood, and prepare you for sleep. Marjoram oil has an antispasmodic effect on tight, stressed-out muscles and deepens the relaxation provided by the other oils.

Draw a hot bath and then add each of the following essential oils:

7 drops of lavender essential oil
10 drops chamomile essential oil
5 drops of marjoram essential oil

Lie back and feel the fumes penetrate your lungs and your skin. After your bath, douse yourself with a cool-to-cold sponge to close the pores and send the heat back to the center of your body. You will find this cool sponging very relaxing. Don't worry; it will not wake you up.

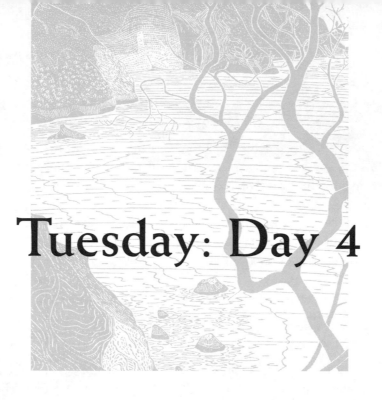

Tuesday: Day 4

On Awakening: One 8-ounce glass of Hot Lemon-Water Flush (page 42). Prepare
Inner Beauty Herbal Tea (pages 42-43); drink throughout the day between meals.

Morning Cleansing: Alternating Hot and Cold Shower—begin with three to five minutes of hot water; switch to ten to fifteen seconds of cold water. Repeat three
times, ending with cold water. Dry briskly with a coarse towel.

Breakfast: Sliced Fresh Pineapple (page 54).

Mid-morning Snack: Optional Protein Drink—Almond Milk (page 71).

Lunch: Fish, chicken, or tofu with steamed or raw vegetables.

Dinner: Squash Bisque (pages 57-58); Super Salad (pages 62-63) with Fat-Loss
Dressing of your choice (pages 63 to 65).

Exercise: Precede exercise with Ionic Cocktail (page 46). Wake-Up Shake-Up (page
148), followed by brisk walking for thirty minutes using Meditative Walking
Breath (page 151).

Evening Activity: Antigravity Tone-Up (pages 152-153), followed by Deep Heat
Bath (page 155).

Brisk-paced Walking

A central feature of your 21-Day Program is an invigorating daily walk outdoors. Walking is a natural function of the human body. It provides all the benefits of other forms of vigorous exercise. It is easy, it requires no special equipment, and, as you will see for yourself, it is enjoyable.

Doing exercise that you enjoy is a key to your success on the 21-Day Program. I remember that when I was younger, exercise was practically my whole life. I spent much of my time dancing, swimming, riding my bicycle, and enjoying the exuberant energy and freedom of youth. I never thought of these activities as work; they were my greatest source of pleasure. As I grew older and became busy with my studies and my career, I became more sedentary. For years I got very little exercise. I was lucky that I was able to maintain the tone I had developed when I was younger because I was getting regular massage.

Finally, as I neared thirty, my health and appearance became more important concerns for me, and I realized I needed to set up an exercise program. I tried jogging and exercise classes, but somehow they seemed more a chore than a pleasure. When I injured my knee while running, my doctor suggested I take up swimming. Suddenly, I rediscovered the joy I had felt as a young swimmer, when exercise was so natural for me. I got myself a new bicycle, and I still ride it to my office whenever possible. In addition, I started walking regularly and continued swimming once a week. I began to realize that all the activities I had enjoyed years ago were exercise, and I simply put them back into my life.

Walking has become an essential part of my lifestyle. Living in the lovely town of Sausalito, California, I have endless opportunities for walks in nature, enjoying the views and the fresh air along San Francisco Bay. An early morning walk, with a stop for tea at my favorite cafe, is one of my most treasured rituals.

Of course, it takes some discipline to develop a daily practice of aerobic activity, which takes walking one step further. People who exercise regularly can tell you that it makes them feel great, and years of medical research have verified the benefits. Exercise has powerful psychological effects. It alleviates anxiety, elevates the mood, and produces an enhanced sense of well-being. Exercise also promotes the inner and outer cleansing that is the goal of this program. The increased intake of oxygen during exercise accelerates the burning of wastes that otherwise accumulate in the tissues and joints. Brisk movement promotes the circulation of blood, carrying nutrients to the tissues and removing toxins, and it stimulates the flow of lymph to carry away debris. Increased perspiration during exercise eliminates wastes through the skin. Exercise also stimulates the function of the internal organs and intestines, promoting better digestion and elimination.

Inner Cleansing through Exercise

Active people who walk as part of their regular work are much less likely to suffer from heart disease, high blood pressure, and other afflictions of our high-tech lifestyle. Exercise helps to control cholesterol levels, preventing the formation of plaque deposits in the arteries. Physical activity, especially exercise that makes the bones bear the body's weight, such as walking, also helps to build up the mineral content in the bones, protecting against osteoporosis, the loss of bone mass that has become such a problem among older people, especially women.

Brisk walking is one of the most important keys to maintaining a youthful appearance. It promotes clear skin and healthy color, and it is a crucial factor in weight control. People who do one hour of energetic walking each day can generally eat just about anything they want without gaining weight. Not only does the walking itself burn calories and body fat, it also helps to decrease appetite.

Scientists who have studied the legendary isolated groups of people who remain healthy into their eighties and nineties and longer, have found that regular exercise is one of the key factors contributing to longevity. The Hunza of Pakistan and the Vilcabamba of Ecuador, for example, walk up and down their native mountains as part of their daily activity. Exercise also promotes longevity by enhancing one's sense of well-being. And this positive mental state is another of the important keys to a healthy and vital long life.

Recent research into longevity has proven the common-sense notion that active people live longer and are healthier than sedentary ones. The good news about exercise is that it does not have to be strenuous to improve cardiovascular function. Studies have shown that people who walk briskly for half an hour six days a week have similar mortality rates to those who run forty or fifty miles a week.

Research has also brought to light many other interesting findings about exercise. For example, if you want to lose weight, dieting alone may not do it. Scientists at Boston University found that after two months, those who both dieted and exercised had lost twenty-seven pounds while those using dieting alone had shed twenty-three pounds, both respectable weight losses. But the exercisers had not regained a single pound eighteen months after the study ended, while those that only dieted had.

It has been documented that people can obtain longevity benefits from such exercises as walking at four to five miles per hour for forty-five minutes five times a week, playing one hour of singles tennis three days a week, cycling for one hour four times a week or practicing yoga three times weekly. The *Journal of the American Medical Association* lists brisk walking, cycling, swimming, calisthenics, racket sports, golf (if you pull your cart or carry your clubs), housecleaning, and raking leaves as some of the options for moderate-intensity physical activities.

Researchers at the Harvard School of Public Health studied the activity levels of 13,000 men aged twenty through eighty and found that those men with the highest cardio-respiratory fitness level are four times less likely to develop prostate cancer than those with one-half that level. Vigorous regular exercise is also a proven preventive measure against adult-onset diabetes. In a study of 87,000 female nurses, those who exercised vigorously once a week had 37 percent lower risk of developing diabetes. Similarly, in a study involving 21,000 male physicians, once weekly exercise resulted in a 30 percent lower diabetes risk.

These are only a few of the many examples that exist in research from around the world that validates the concept that some form of regular exercise is your best guarantee of a longer, healthier life.

OXYGEN CONSUMPTION DURING EXERCISE
(Expressed as calories burned per minute)

Activity	Weight in Pounds			
	100–119	120–144	145–174	175–200
Bicycling				
leisurely	3.16	3.58	4.25	4.66
moderate	5.41	6.16	7.33	7.91
brisk	8.58	9.75	11.50	12.66

Dancing				
aerobic	5.83	6.58	7.83	8.58
rock	3.25	3.75	4.41	4.91
Gardening				
weeding & digging	5.08	5.75	6.83	7.50
Jogging				
5.5 mph	8.58	9.75	11.50	12.66
6.5 mph	8.90	10.20	12.00	13.20
8.0 mph	10.40	11.90	14.10	15.50
9.0 mph	12.00	13.80	16.20	17.80
Sexual Intercourse				
active partner	3.91	4.50	5.25	5.83
Skiing				
downhill	7.75	8.83	10.41	11.50
cross-country (moderate)	9.16	10.41	12.25	13.33
cross-country (brisk)	13.08	14.83	17.58	19.33
Stair-Climbing				
normal	5.90	6.70	7.90	8.80
rapid	8.70	14.80	17.60	19.30
Swimming				
leisurely	3.91	4.50	5.25	5.83
moderate	7.83	8.91	10.50	11.58
brisk	11.00	12.50	14.75	16.25
Tennis				
singles	7.83	8.91	10.50	11.58
doubles	5.58	6.33	7.50	8.25
Walking				
leisurely	2.40	2.80	3.30	3.60
moderate	3.90	4.50	5.30	5.80
brisk	4.50	5.20	6.10	6.80

Nutrients Support Your Exercise Program

To derive the greatest benefit from brisk walking, you must provide your body with the proper nutrients to supply energy and build new cells. Especially important is the mineral potassium, which is often deficient in our sodium-laden diet. Potassium supports proper muscle tone. Remember, the heart and intestines have muscle tissue.

Low tissue-potassium levels can lead to muscle spasm and fatigue; such muscle problems are frequently an underlying cause of low-back discomfort and even constipation.

Today's dinner menu features a Squash Bisque based on my recipe for mineral-rich Potassium Broth—one of the essential liquid foods of the Rejuvenation Diet. Potassium Broth provides important minerals to help keep your cells and muscles properly nourished as you go in and out of the fast in the second and third weeks of the program.

Because you perspire during vigorous activity, your body needs extra fluid to support an exercise program. I recommend drinking plenty of fluids before and after exercise, but not during the actual exercise period. For a walk of one-half hour, there's no need to carry water with you. Drink the Ionic Cocktail just before exercising each day, for a powerful cleansing and rejuvenating effect.

GARCINIA

There are many weight loss products on the market today. The pharmaceutical varieties often have dangerous side effects. Many of the "natural" products contain the herb Ma Huang, which is known to have unfavorable side effects as well. The safest product I have found is an extract of the herb Garcinia cambogia. The berry of this plant has been used in culinary practices in Thailand and India for hundreds of years, where it is called the "Malabar Tamarind."

It has become the subject of much scientific interest in America due to its high concentration of a unique active constituent called hydroxycitrate, or HCA. HCA has been found to inhibit the building and storage of fat tissue in the body. It appears to stop the fat produced from excess caloric intake or beyond the fuel needs of the body from being stored. This has particular benefit for those people over forty or fifty who find that, due to the metabolic changes that often accompany age, they simply cannot eat as much as they are accustomed to eating without gaining weight.

There are many products containing Garcinia on the market today. Check your local health food store.

Making Your Workout Work for You

A strong heart and healthy lungs are central to any cleansing and fitness program. The stronger your heart is, the less work it will have to do to pump blood, nutrients, and oxygen to all the tissues in your body. When your heart is in good condition, it beats harder but less frequently.

The best kind of exercise to keep your heart and lungs in top condition is aerobic, which means "with oxygen." Through continuous, vigorous movements of the large muscles, you are speeding up your heartbeat and breathing more deeply, sending a richer supply of oxygen to nourish your tissues.

When you are exercising aerobically, you will feel your heart beating faster, and your breathing will speed up. As your body heats up, your skin becomes moist, and after a while you begin to feel exhilarated. After an aerobic workout, you will feel a glow and a sense of well-being that will last for hours.

Brisk walking allows you to enjoy the well-publicized benefits of aerobic exercise in a way that is safe and gentle to your bones, joints, and muscles. I know many joggers who have injured their feet, ankles, knees, or backs with the high impact and stress of their chosen sport. If you truly enjoy jogging, then keep it up, but please be sure always to do warm-up exercises before you jog, and cool-down activities afterward, to minimize the chance of injury. In addition, try to jog on dirt trails or on sand, since jogging on cement or asphalt jars the lower body.

Other forms of exercise besides walking also provide safe aerobic conditioning. Swimming is a wonderful alternative, which we will explore on Thursday: Day 6. Many people like bicycling and find it a much better way to get around than in their cars. Dancing is a lively activity that you can do in public places, in aerobics classes, or at home by simply putting on some of your favorite music. Skiing, especially cross-country skiing, provides an excellent workout, if you have access to snow and equipment. The main criterion is that you select an exercise that you enjoy, because that is the best guarantee that you will keep it up. Vary your choice of exercise to suit your mood, your schedule, or the season.

Use the Oxygen Consumption During Exercise chart on pages 141 and 142 to compare the relative strenuousness of various popular forms of exercise. The figures represent calories burned, but were actually determined by measuring the amount of oxygen consumed—that is, how aerobic the exercise is.

As you get in better shape, you will need to exercise more vigorously to derive the same benefits. That is the time to add more exertion to your workout. It always takes effort to enjoy the rewards of exercise, but you will soon learn that such exertion can be very worthwhile.

The experience of one of my clients, Monica, is a good example of the dramatic benefits of stepping up the challenge of an exercise program. I had been working with Monica on a cleansing and weight-loss program for about five months. She had been losing weight steadily and was looking radiant from the cleansing, but she had got to the point where the weight just wasn't coming off quickly enough. Every time she came in, I would ask her whether she had been exercising, and she would say yes. Finally, I asked what kind of exercise she had been doing, and she told me she had been taking a nice, leisurely walk for about forty-five minutes every day. "That may have been enough a few months ago," I said, "but now you need to include more aerobic activity in your walk." I encouraged her to push herself just beyond her comfort level, that point where she wanted to stop. Since Monica lived in San Francisco, she began walking briskly up and down the hills, instead of on level ground. When she came in two weeks later, I was amazed at how much weight she had lost. She was spending the same amount of time on her exercise, but because she was getting more aerobic activity from hill-walking, she had given her metabolism a boost, and the weight was coming off very quickly again.

Just as important as committing yourself to a daily exercise program is developing an exercise attitude. Get into the habit of walking to work or to the store. If you use public transportation, get off a few blocks away from your destination and walk the rest of the way. Use stairs instead of elevators or escalators. When you feel groggy or bored, take a short, brisk walk instead of a snack or a cup of coffee. By making exercise a natural, joyful part of your life, you will guarantee yourself added years of vibrant beauty and good health.

Building a Lifetime Walking Habit

It's never too late to take up some form of exercise. The benefits of physical activity are as great for a ninety-year-old as for a twenty-year-old. Even someone who has always been sedentary will improve his or her health almost immediately upon beginning an exercise program.

The hardest part of any exercise program is actually getting started. Since it takes about three weeks to establish a new habit, your 21-Day Program is an ideal beginning. As you begin to feel the elation and increased vigor that are immediate benefits of regular brisk walking, you will become more and more motivated to keep it up.

Eventually, when you experience the long-term benefits, you will most likely be a life-long walker.

On Sunday's questionnaire, you established your goals and constructed your exercise schedule. Begin an Exercise Log in your journal and use it each day to record your daily workout. Over the course of your three-week program, you will see an improvement in your stamina and conditioning, as indicated by an increase in the speed, distance, or time you record in your Exercise Log. Just as I encouraged Monica to push herself beyond the point of wanting to stop, I encourage you to do the same, just a bit farther each day! I recommend about one-half hour of brisk walking every day. If you have been telling yourself up until now that you just don't have the time to spend on regular exercise, get up a half-hour earlier, and do your walking then. At the end of your exercise period, ask yourself if it was worth it. Your sense of well-being and the glow in your body will tell you that it was.

Since walking is such a safe activity, most people will be able to begin their walking program immediately. If you are over forty-five and are not now exercising regularly, you should consult a physician before beginning any exercise program. If you have high blood pressure, heart disease, or other problems requiring medical attention, no matter what your age, you should also check with your doctor. Most likely you will get an enthusiastic go-ahead.

One of the nicest things about walking is that you don't need any special equipment. Of course, you do need to wear comfortable, sturdy shoes, but please don't fall victim to the notion that you must have a different pair of shoes for every activity. Running shoes, lightweight hiking boots, or tennis shoes are fine. Specially designed walking shoes are heavier than running shoes but lighter than regular shoes, making it easier to lift your feet. Whatever shoes you wear, make sure they are a comfortable fit, leaving enough room to wiggle your toes, and flexible enough to allow for normal walking motion. The shoes should allow your feet to breathe; leather, canvas, or nylon mesh, or combinations of these, are suitable materials. The shoes should have thick, flexible soles to absorb shock and cushioned insoles to help prevent blisters. Wear cotton socks to allow your feet to breathe and perspire freely.

When you walk, wear comfortable, loose-fitting clothing of natural fibers so your skin can breathe, too. You may want to layer your clothing so you can remove the outer layer as you warm up. If you are walking on sunny days, wear a hat to protect your face from harmful ultraviolet rays, and do use a sunblock, even when it is overcast.

To allow your arms to swing freely when you walk, you may want to use a waist pack or a small day pack if you need to carry anything with you.

Part of the fun of walking is the opportunity it provides to be out in nature. America's great naturalist Henry David Thoreau wrote, "I think that I cannot preserve my health and spirits unless I spend four hours a day at least—and it is commonly more than that—sauntering through the woods and over the hills and fields, absolutely free from all worldly engagements." Today's busy lifestyles do not permit most of us to walk for four hours a day in nature, but you can experience some of the same benefits on shorter walks if you select a route that exposes you to plenty of fresh air, greenery, or water.

Take a moment now to think about the opportunities for walking in your community. Do you live near an ocean, a river, a reservoir, or a lake? The air near running water or breaking waves is rich in negative ions, which increase your alertness and sense of optimism. Perhaps there are woods or open fields near your home. Every city has parks. You might select a route that takes you from your home to the nearest park, through the park and back. Another possibility would be to drive or bike to a park, do your walking there, and then ride back. Or take a bus to some distant location close to nature and walk home. Choose a route that allows you to walk two to three miles. Even if you don't walk that far at first, you will eventually build up to that distance.

It is a fact of modern life that many of us live in crowded, noisy urban areas. If you simply cannot get away from city streets and sidewalks, I suggest that you use a portable cassette player and listen to your favorite music. Try to avoid streets where traffic produces smoggy air.

People differ in their preferences about when to do their walking. In general, the best time to exercise is before eating. Brisk walking before meals produces a rise in blood sugar that will decrease your appetite and boost your metabolic rate. Many people find that going for a walk first thing in the morning gives them a burst of energy and a positive mental attitude that carries them through the day. Others find that vigorous exercise after a day of work helps them to unwind and relax. Some people prefer to use a portion of their lunchtime for a brisk walk to help break up the stress of the workday. Whatever time of day you choose, remember that your exercise period is a gift to yourself, a time to enjoy the pleasure of movement and being out of doors—to free yourself, like Thoreau, from "all worldly engagements."

Warming Up and Cooling Down

Even for low-impact exercise like walking, it is important to do warm-up exercises before you begin. Warming up prepares your body by stimulating the flow of blood and oxygen to the heart. It warms the muscles so they become more elastic and are less likely to be injured. Here are two warm-ups you may use throughout my program before your daily exercise. Other activities will be introduced throughout the program. Each warm-up is a series of movements and stretches, many of which are based on yoga. The postures of hatha yoga are scientifically designed to promote rejuvenation and regeneration by stimulating and regulating the endocrine glands that govern the aging process. These are not calisthenics. Do not move quickly from one part of the activity to the next, but take the time to relax after each phase and feel its benefits.

Wake-Up Shake-Up

This is a favorite moving meditation of mine. It is a great way to warm up the muscles, enhance your body awareness, and release emotional tension.

Stand relaxed with your feet apart and parallel to each other. Imagine that the balls of your feet are glued to the floor. Begin to wake up your body by slowly and rhythmically lifting your heels, one foot and then the other, while keeping the balls of your feet on the floor. Imagine you are walking without lifting your feet. After lifting alternate heels for a while, begin to include your legs. Keep the balls of your feet in place on the floor with your knees slightly bent, pretending you are walking but keeping your feet in place. Next, rhythmically move to include your knees. Now, begin to shake your legs all the way from the ankles to the hips, with the balls of your feet still planted on the floor. Wake up the whole bottom of your body. Shake your legs and your buttocks, gradually moving the shaking all the way up your body. Shake your shoulders, arms, and hands. Loosen up, shaking all over. Stop, relax for a moment, and feel the effects throughout your entire being.

Now, raise your arms over your head. Stretch from the waist up, and feel the pull from the waist down. Allow your body to hang for a minute or so. Breathe in as you raise your arms above your head, then slowly and gently exhale, bending down toward the floor, keeping your knees loose and relaxed. Breathe rhythmically throughout this exercise. Do not hold your breath. After you have awakened your whole body with this shake and stretch, begin your day's exercise.

Dancer's Warm-Up

These isolated movements of different body parts are warm-ups from an Afro-Haitian dance class that I attended for years, and many of them have their roots in yoga. Dancers know that they have to warm up every part of the body before they can do any more strenuous dance routines. Warm-up activity is probably 50 percent of every dance class. You may wish to read this routine into your tape recorder so you can play it back before your daily walks.

Begin with neck rolls. Bring your left ear down to your left shoulder, roll your neck all the way to the back, over to the right shoulder, and then down so your chin touches your chest. Keep the neck moving, using a continuous, smooth, rolling movement. Repeat five times, then reverse direction and roll your neck five times in the opposite direction. Breathe in as you roll your neck back, and breathe out as you roll your neck forward.

Next, do shoulder rolls. Rotate your left shoulder backward five times, then forward five times. Repeat for the right shoulder. Then roll both shoulders together, five times backward and five times forward. Continue the breathing pattern you established with the neck rolls.

Follow with a spinal twist. Stand relaxed with your feet apart at about shoulder width. Keep your lower body in position and twist from the waist up, bringing your torso all the way around to the left, as if you are trying to touch the back of your waist with your right hand. Twist all the way around, looking as far behind you as you can over your left shoulder. Now, holding this position, turn your head around and look as far as you can to the right to provide a full-body stretch. Return to a relaxed center position and reverse direction, twisting your torso to the right. Repeat each direction five times. Breathe in as you move to the left, and breathe out as you twist to the right.

With your feet still apart at shoulder distance, extend your arms in front of you at shoulder level and do some gentle knee bends. Move slowly, avoiding any bouncing movements. Don't be alarmed if your knees creak. Repeat five times, breathing out as you lower yourself and in as you rise.

Now, lift one foot at a time and rotate the ankle, twisting each foot clockwise and then counterclockwise, wiggling your toes and tightening and releasing the arches of your feet. Repeat five times for each foot, maintaining your breathing pattern as you go.

End with a good upward stretch. Breathe in, extending your arms over your head. Breathe out and bend down to touch the floor. Relax and hang for a few moments, breathing normally.

In addition to warming up, allow time at the end of your daily exercise for cool-down activity. Without gentle movement at the end of a workout, the blood remains pooled out in the arms and legs; as a result, you may experience dizziness and nausea. An easy way to cool down after walking or running is to slacken your pace to a slow walk for about five minutes.

Walking-Enhancement Techniques

It may seem unnecessary to have instructions for such a natural activity as walking, but the more aware you are of your body and your surroundings, the more benefit you will derive from your daily walks. Join me now, as I guide you through an easy, enjoyable walk that will give you a mental lift, condition your muscles, and carry oxygen to all the cells of your body.

Before you begin walking, take a moment to pay attention to posture. Nothing can age your appearance more quickly than poor body alignment. Your spine is one of the most important parts of your body; when it is not properly aligned, your internal organs cannot work as effectively.

For a quick posture check, imagine you are balancing a heavy basket on your head. Pull up, and feel your spine straighten.

Now, begin with five minutes of slow, gentle walking. Swing your arms freely at your sides, use a heel-to-toe gait, and keep your posture in mind. Gradually increase your pace until you are walking briskly. Swing your arms quite strongly at right angles, back and forward, to stimulate the flow of lymph. For most adults, a pace of three to four miles per hour will provide the same aerobic conditioning benefits as jogging or other vigorous activities. Notice how your breathing and heartbeat speed up.

Keep up your rapid aerobic pace for twelve to fifteen minutes, and preferably longer. At the end of the brisk walking period, return to a slow pace for five minutes to allow your body to cool down.

As you walk, pay attention to your breathing and establish a comfortable rhythm. Count along with the beat of each step, practicing the following breathing patterns as part of your regular walking exercise.

Meditative Walking Breath

Breathing patterns derived from yoga can help to bring your body, mind, and spirit into harmony as you walk. Nothing helps you center yourself better than focusing on your breath.

Breathe in through both nostrils to the count of four paces. Hold your breath in for a count of four, then breathe out through pursed lips to a count of four. Repeat the cycle; in to four, hold for four, and out to four, as you walk along briskly. This 4-4-4 breath is wonderfully invigorating.

As you breathe, be aware of your surroundings. Feel the cool, clean air enter your lungs. Notice the fresh, natural smells around you, the aroma of trees or water. Breathing in to the count of four, inhale the sights, smells, and sounds of nature. Open your hands and feel the green of the trees, the blue of the sky, the warmth of the sun. Then, for the next four paces, hold your breath and feel the glow throughout your body, the warmth and tingle in your arms and legs. With each step, be aware of the movement of the bones and muscles in your feet. Now, breathe out on the next four paces, and as you breathe out, release all the negative thoughts that flit through your mind. Let go of your anxieties and worries, and feel the toxins being released from your body, the waste products being expelled through your breath and sweat. Breathe in to the count of four and focus on positive thoughts: peace, harmony, joy, well-being. Find the words that seem best for you, and breathe them in with each inhalation. Hold for the count of four and feel the glow. Exhale to the count of four and release, relax, and be at peace with yourself.

Once you have mastered the 4-4-4 breath, vary your breathing pattern by inhaling to the count of six, holding the breath in for three, exhaling for six counts, and holding the breath out for three, with the lungs empty of air. Then repeat the 6-3-6-3 pattern. This breathing pattern helps dispel tension and anxiety whenever you feel it creeping up on you during the day. Use it regularly on your walks, or at any other time you want to relax and unwind.

A further variation you can try is an 8-4-8-4 breath, inhaling for eight counts, holding the breath for four, exhaling for eight, and holding the breath out for four. I find this pattern even more calming than the 6-3-6-3. Besides using it with walking, try it when you are upset or are having difficulty getting to sleep.

If you regularly practice these breathing patterns and the sensory awareness that goes with them, they will become a habit. You will be inhaling peace, serenity, and joy and exhaling all your worries whenever you walk.

At the end of your daily walk, be aware of how you feel. Ask yourself, do I feel less tired than when I started? Am I in a better mood? Do I feel more relaxed? Each time you check in with your mind and body at the end of an exercise period and recognize the positive benefits, you are giving yourself additional reinforcement for the next workout.

Resistance Toning for Supple Muscles

Aerobic activity is not the only form of exercise you need. Especially if one of your goals on this program is to lose weight, you will benefit from the toning that comes from resistance training, or using your muscles against the force of gravity. I work out regularly with small dumbbells at home to strengthen and tone my upper body. The free weights let me make adjustments in muscle motion angles that are not possible with exercise machines.

Besides the muscle toning that resistance training provides, it also helps to send oxygen-bearing blood into parts of the body that are difficult to reach with other forms of exercise. Resistance training encourages you to work with your breath to put oxygen deep into the tissues. It also provides an opportunity to direct your full attention to the specific part of the body that you want to strengthen and fill with oxygen.

Antigravity Tone-Up

The slant board has long been a beauty secret of health-conscious people. It works by reversing the effects of gravity. The aging process causes the skin, facial features, and internal organs to droop. When you lie with your head below your feet, the effects of gravity are reversed, and all the organs are in a relaxed, suspended position. Blood flows to the face, neck, and head, bringing nutrients and oxygen to the brain and facial tissues and improving the complexion. The antigravity position on the slant board relieves sinus problems and eyestrain and helps to eliminate wrinkles. It improves circulation throughout the body, and it is very helpful for anyone with distressed organs. A few minutes on a slant board in the antigravity position provide a quick pick-me-up, revitalizing your brain cells and restoring your energy. (If you have high blood pressure or other medical problems, check with your doctor before using a slant board. Except for specific cautions, daily use of a slant board will generally help any health problem.)

If you don't have a slant board, you can make your own by covering a board with padding and securely tacking it down. The board should be longer than you are tall and at least as wide as your body when your arms are at your side. Rest the slant board on a stable surface so it is at an angle of twenty to forty-five degrees, then lie on it with your feet up and your head down. If you cannot find a board the right size, try improvising with an ironing board so you can begin to experience the benefits of the Antigravity Tone-Up.

The following activities will help to improve both your strength and your appearance. Again, you may wish to read these exercises into your tape recorder and create a routine for repetitions.

Beauty Exercise

Lying on your back on the slant board, exhale all the breath from your lungs. Touch your lower waist with your fingertips while exhaling, and see how small you can get your waist to be. Keeping your lungs deflated, draw your chest toward your chin, tensing the abdominal muscles at the same time. Draw your waist in, as small as you can. Pull everything in and up inside. Then relax and breathe normally. This is another exercise derived from yoga. It will help slim your waist and get rid of fatty deposits around your middle. Repeat the exercise ten times, then relax in a resting pose on the slant board, in the antigravity position.

Alternate Knee Lifts

These knee lifts will begin to tone and strengthen your abdominal muscles in preparation for more challenging exercises later. Bring one knee up to the chest, inhaling as you do so. As you exhale, straighten and lower that leg and simultaneously bring the other bent knee up. Keep the toes pointed and the straightened legs parallel to the slant board; you are not trying to pedal high in the air. Breathe in as you lift one knee, and out as you lift the other, maintaining a brisk pace. Start by doing ten lifts for each knee, increasing gradually over time until you can do thirty. After the exercise, relax in the resting position.

Palming

Finish your Antigravity Tone-Up with this pleasant facial muscle relaxer and eye revitalizer. Rub your palms together until you feel the heat. Then cup your hands over your closed eyes, crossing your fingertips over your forehead. Be sure to cover your eyes completely, so no light would get in even if your eyes were open. Feel the heat going into your closed eyes and the relaxation spreading to all the muscles of your face. Let go of the tension in your jaw, lips, and cheeks, and let the relaxation spread down to your neck and throat, out to your shoulders, and down your arms. Relax your back, chest, rib cage, abdomen, hips, and thighs, your lower legs, feet, and hands. Often tension accumulates in the eyes. As you release this tension, you not only renew and beautify your eyes but allow the relaxation to spread to every part of your body. Stay with this at least five minutes.

Exercise for Life

Research has shown that people who continue their exercise program for twenty weeks are likely to continue exercising all their lives. At that point, their self-esteem improves dramatically, and exercise then becomes self-reinforcing. Do not hesitate to try variations in your exercise activities to keep up your interest and motivation. Above all, remember always to do exercise that you enjoy.

Over time, you will need to exercise more vigorously to enjoy the same health benefits, since your muscles will become stronger and will not have to work as hard. To make your exercise more challenging, try walking briskly uphill, or hold your arms out at a ninety-degree angle and pump them energetically as you walk. Alternate between skipping five minutes, then walking five minutes, marching five minutes, swinging your arms briskly at your sides with your posture straight and tall, then walking five minutes. You may also alternate five minutes of walking with five minutes of jogging, if you wish, but be sure you are well warmed up before you begin to jog.

Just as you vary your exercise activities, vary the setting. Find several different routes that you enjoy. Change your activity as the seasons change, or try walking before dawn, after sunset, or in the rain, for a different sensory experience. If you usually walk alone, try walking with a partner or form a walking group to give each other mutual support. If you have a dog, it will be delighted to romp along with you at your fastest pace. If you have children, get them to establish a walking habit with you. They may not be able to keep up with your rapid aerobic pace or to walk as long as you do, so you might spend half an hour doing brisk walking at one time during the day and then join your kids for another short walk later. Walking with children in nature is a wonderful opportunity for learning. Talk about what you see. Point out and name the trees, birds, and flowers. They will probably have something to teach you, too.

As you restore your tired muscles in your hot bath tonight, close your eyes and feel the penetrating, healing power of the herbal essences. Think of the walk you took today. As you breathe in, recall the smells you noticed around you, the freshness of outdoors. Feel the air once again on your face, the fresh breeze or the warm sun. Hold your breath in to the count of four, and once again feel the tingle in your arms and legs as you walked briskly along. As you exhale to the count of four, release, relax, and know that your diet, exercise, and cleansing program is speeding toxins out of your body. Breathe in feelings of peace, joy, and well-being. Hold your breath and feel your aliveness and youthful vitality. Breathe out, and release negative thoughts: How am I going to stay with this for twenty-one days? What if it rains? What if I get hungry? Breathe out your resistances and anxiety, clearing your mind for cleansing, rejuvenating, revitalizing sleep. Remember, you don't have to do this program perfectly to get great results. Do the best that you can, and know that you are improving your body, mind, and spirit with each day!

DEEP-HEAT BATH

Draw a very hot bath, then add each of the following essential oils:

10 drops eucalyptus essential oil
8 drops rosemary essential oil
5 drops sandalwood essential oil

The hot water helps to relax your muscles, and these essential oils are all beneficial for soothing your body after exercise. Eucalyptus oil is good for aching joints and muscles, and for skin problems and chapped skin. It is also used as an antiseptic inhalant, and the vapor helps clear the respiratory passages. Rosemary oil is a nervous-system stimulant. It is used as a tonic for the heart and to enhance liver functions. Hot compresses of rosemary oil are used for the aches and pains of rheumatism. Sandalwood oil cleanses and moisturizes the skin. Its lovely aroma is used in India to induce a meditative state.

Soak in this bath for twenty minutes, inhale the fumes, and feel them clearing your mind and your breathing passages, allowing the essential oils to work their magic.

Wednesday: Day 5

SCHEDULE

On Awakening: One 8-ounce glass of Hot Lemon-Water Flush (page 42). Prepare Inner Beauty Herbal Tea (pages 42-43); drink throughout the day between meals. Prepare Rejuvelac (page 47).

Morning Cleansing: Dry Brush Massage (page 127). Follow with a hot shower, finishing with a thirty-second cold splash.

Breakfast: Papaya Complexion Breakfast (pages 54-55).

Mid-morning Snack: Optional Protein Drink—Sunflower Seed Milk (page 72).

Lunch: Fish, chicken, or tofu with steamed or raw vegetables.

Dinner: Cauliflower Bisque (page 58). Super Salad (pages 62-63) with Fat-Loss Dressing of your choice (pages 63 to 65).

Exercise: Precede exercise with Ionic Cocktail (page 46). Dancer's Warm-Up (page 149), followed by Rebounding Workout (page 160) for ten to twenty minutes, or walking for twenty to thirty minutes.

Evening Activity: "Hot Foot" Soak (page 161), followed by Lower-Body Lymphatic Massage (pages 162 and 163). Drink one cup Rejuvelac (page 47).

Lymph: The Hidden Ocean Within

As you relax in your cleansing and beautifying baths, remember that the interior of your body is also bathed in fluid. Much of this "inner ocean" is lymphatic fluid. Probably the only occasion you have had to be aware of your lymph system is when you had a sore throat or other infection, and felt enlarged lymph nodes in your neck or armpit or groin. These little pea-shaped organs are part of a network of delicate vessels throughout your body that transport the lymphatic fluid.

Lymph is a clear or milky fluid that originates in the blood capillaries, leaking out into the spaces between the cells. Inside the cells, fluids serve to transport nourishment and carry away wastes. Each cell is surrounded by a permeable membrane that allows materials to pass through to the outside. The fluid that bathes the outside of the cells is the lymph. Waste materials pass out of the cells, and out of the bloodstream through the capillary walls, and are eventually picked up by the lymph vessels. After traveling a short distance, these lymph vessels enter lymph nodes. The major lymph nodes are concentrated in the groin, armpits, neck, chest, and abdomen. Within specialized compartments in the lymph nodes are found different white cells, such as lymphocytes and macrophages, which have important functions in the immune system, protecting your body from infection and foreign materials. The lymphocytes circulate throughout the lymph system and attack invading organisms. When your body is fighting an infection, the lymph nodes become swollen near the site of the infection, as the bacteria are carried to the nodes, where they are engulfed and gobbled up by the macrophages. The lymph nodes also contain webbed areas that filter the lymph, removing foreign materials. After the lymph has been filtered, it leaves the lymph node, carrying the freshly cleaned lymph out the other side. The lymph vessels have valves, which allow the fluid to flow in only one direction, toward the heart. The lymph flow rejoins the bloodstream at the base of the neck, where the largest lymphatic collecting vessel, the thoracic duct, empties its lymph into the internal jugular vein to mix with the blood.

Normal lymph is a watery fluid, and it must remain at the proper consistency in order to move readily through its vessels. Certain kinds of debris and toxic materials cause the lymph to become thick or mucoid-like in consistency.

As you might expect, the lymph system has a direct impact on the appearance and condition of your skin. When the lymph system becomes clogged, it is not able to carry the impurities away as readily for excretion, placing a burden on the other organs of elimination, so, many of the waste products end up being trapped or excreted by the skin. Similarly, cellulite deposits tend to form when toxins carried by stagnant lymph get lodged in fatty accumulations just beneath the skin.

Keeping Your Lymph Clean and Clear

Every aspect of my program is designed to promote the proper functioning of your lymphatic system. Let's begin by looking again at the food you eat.

You may have heard some discussion of so-called "mucus-forming" foods. This term is something of a misnomer. Clear, slippery mucus is a normal secretion of the mucous membranes. The sticky mucoid material that can clog up the lymph system is not produced by the mucous membranes; rather, it is an accumulation of incompletely broken-down nutrients and waste products that tend to thicken the lymph and make it harder for it to move through the body and cleanse the tissues. Foods vary greatly in their tendency to form mucoid material, with foods high in protein and fat having the greatest mucoid-forming power. The diet in your 21-Day Program emphasizes non-mucoid-forming foods, such as vegetables and fruits.

MUCOID-FORMING ACTIVITY OF FOODS

The foods here are listed in order of the intensity of their mucoid-forming properties. Note that meats and dairy products are very high, while grains and sprouts are low-mucoid-forming.

HIGH MUCOID-FORMING FOODS

Dairy Products: pasteurized or raw cow's or goat's milk, butter, cheese, cream, yogurt, kefir, whey

Flesh Foods: Meat, fish, eggs

Soybeans: Soybeans and soy products such as tofu, tempeh, miso, soy milk

Other Legumes: Dry beans, lentils, dry peas

Buckwheat: Grain, flour, cereal

Other Grains: Wheat, rice, rye, barley, oats, millet

Seeds and Nuts: Sunflower, sesame, pumpkin seeds; all nuts

Sprouts: The longer the sprouting time, the lower the mucoid-forming activity. Bean and pea sprouts are totally non-mucoid-forming after three to four days' sprouting time; grains, buckwheat, and soy are non-mucoid-forming after six days.

Honey: Mucoid-forming activity depends on source of honey; all honeys are low in mucoid-forming activity except for eucalyptus honey, which is relatively high.

NONMUCOID-FORMING FOODS

Vegetables and Fruits: Completely non-mucoid-forming, except for gas-ripened and sulfured dried fruits, which are high in mucoid-forming activity.

Another factor that influences lymph function is the condition of your colon. When the colon is clear and its walls unlined with waste deposits, the colon wall is able to absorb mucoid material from the lymph for excretion. When you are constipated or the walls of your colon are caked with toxic wastes, mucoid material begins to back up into the lymphatic system. In the second week of this program, you will begin a gentle process of colon cleansing that will help to drain mucoid material out of your lymph system and keep it clear and clean.

Today you will begin to drink the fermented grain drink Rejuvelac, starting to change the balance of the bacteria in your colon to help the cleansing process.

Exercise is another very important factor in keeping your lymph clear. Whereas your blood is moved through the body by the pumping action of your heart, the lymph system depends on the contraction of the muscles surrounding the vessels to keep it moving along. Muscular contractions increase pressure within the system, causing the valves to close; when pressure decreases, the valves open and the lymph flows. When the body is not moving, the lymph in the arms, legs, and head does not move measurably.

With activity, drainage of the lymph system increases tenfold. Some kinds of exercise are better than others for moving the lymph through the system. All vigorous exercise, such as brisk walking with strongly swinging arms, is beneficial in moving the lymph.

REBOUNDING WORKOUT

One of the best forms of exercise for stimulating the lymph system is rebounding on a mini-trampoline. Rebounding stimulates lymphatic circulation because it produces a change in the body's fluid pressure with relatively little muscular effort. At the bottom of each bounce, waste products and toxins are squeezed out from between the cells. When the body rebounds into the air, nutrients pass from the lymph into the cells. At the height of the bounce, the body is weightless, and the lymph begins to flow. As the body descends, the lymphatic fluid flows along, pulling the extracted wastes with it.

Rebounding has all the benefits of aerobic exercise, but it does not jar the skeletal system the way some exercises do. You can buy a reasonably priced mini-trampoline at most sporting goods stores. I highly recommend this piece of equipment as part of your exercise program. There are many different exercises you can do to music or while watching television that make this an easy and pleasurable way to maintain your aerobic conditioning and stimulate and cleanse your lymph system.

Foot Soaks

Foot soaks are an excellent way to stimulate lymphatic function, especially in the lower lymphatic vessels, which tend to get sluggish and clogged because of the effects of gravity. Soaking your feet helps to open the pores and draw the toxins out of the lymph system through the skin. The Romans knew the value of bathing the feet in the waters of their healing springs, and at the great French spas, footbaths were the prescribed treatment for arthritis. The effects of footbaths are aided by specific minerals or herbs added to the water and by the temperature of the water itself.

"Hot Foot" Soak

Mustard has been valued for centuries in both Eastern and Western medicine for its ability to stimulate blood and body-fluid circulation and break up stagnation. Its effects are powerful, so be careful not to use more than the recommended amount of mustard powder. This foot soak will cause you to sweat profusely, as the effects of the mustard promote the expulsion of wastes from your entire system.

In a gallon bucket or small tub, dissolve three tablespoons of mustard powder in very hot water, as hot as you can stand. Soak your feet for twenty minutes. Mustard powder is a powerful rubefacient, causing the skin to redden as it dilates the blood vessels near the surface of the skin, bringing more blood to the area. It also draws lymph to the surface, helping to flush it of toxins and waste materials. Miraculously, mustard foot soaks have been used successfully to relieve the pain of earache, tooth abscess, and sinusitis by drawing the body fluids to the surface of the feet.

Father Kneipp's Foot Bath

Father Kneipp was one of the modern pioneers in the therapeutic uses of water. This hot-and-cold contrast footbath is considered an excellent treatment for colds, sinusitis, headaches, poor circulation, neuritis, and congested abdominal organs. Try it the next time you are feeling congestion or sluggishness anywhere in your body.

Fill one small tub or gallon bucket with hot water and a second tub with cold water. The water in each tub should be eight to twelve inches deep. Place your feet in the hot tub for three to five minutes, then switch to the cold tub for thirty seconds. Repeat this procedure twice.

As with any alternating hot-and-cold bath or shower, this footbath is very invigorating. You will find it wakes up your whole body and leaves you feeling energized.

Lymphatic Massage

After your foot soak, an excellent way to continue lymphatic stimulation is through massage. You have already learned how to do dry brush massaging. Skin brushing is one of the best ways known to stimulate the expulsion of mucoid material and other obstructions from the lymphatic system and to correct inflammations of the lymph nodes. Skin brushing works hand in hand with colon cleansing to keep the lymphatic system clear. Now, I am going to show you how to do a lymphatic massage, to stimulate lymph flow in your lower body. Remember that the lymph flows toward the heart—up from the feet and down from the head.

THE LYMPH NODES

Lower-Body Lymphatic Massage

Massage one leg at a time. Using one or two hands, begin by massaging at the base of each toe and between the toes. Massage gently in a circular motion; imagine yourself loosening the toxins and debris from all the tiny lymph vessels between your toes.

After you have gently massaged the base of each toe, stroke upward with both hands, drawing the lymph up and toward the ankles with a gentle, feathery, upward stroking motion. Move up to the ankle; gently massage in a circular motion all around the ankle, and then lightly stroke upward, drawing the lymph up the calf until you get to the knee.

Massage with both hands all around the knee, over the lymph nodes behind the knee, and around the kneecap, in circular motions. Use light pressure; this is the best way to stimulate the lymph. Remember that the lymph vessels are close to the surface of the skin.

Draw the lymph up along the thighs, using the fingertips or the palms of the hands. At the back of the thigh, massage gently at the base of the buttock, in a gentle circular motion; this is one of the areas where the toxic waste of cellulite tends to accumulate.

Stroke upward, along the thigh, and bring it all around and back into the groin. After you have completed one leg, work on the other leg.

In the groin area, work on both sides at once. Stroke upward and diagonally across the groin area with the flat of the hand on each side, moving the hands toward each other so they come together over the abdomen. Repeat this upward stroking all along the groin area; there are many lymph nodes in this area.

As you stroke gently upward and into the abdominal area, picture all the debris and waste being moved along, to be absorbed and eliminated through your colon.

When you do a lymphatic massage, you may notice that some areas react painfully to pressure. Most people, for example, if they press hard between their breasts, will feel a very sensitive spot. This is one of the areas where lymph congestion can produce tenderness. If you find such a sensitive spot, do not be afraid to touch it; continue to gently massage it with a light, circular motion, and then with a feathery touch move it onward—up from the legs, down from the head. As you progress in your rejuvenation program, you will notice that there is less and less lymphatic congestion and that you have fewer sensitive spots.

Spend about ten minutes on the lymphatic massage. Proper lymphatic functioning produces clear, glowing skin, and, because lymph is a vital part of your immune system, it helps to promote your resistance to disease.

As you fall asleep tonight, imagine the lymph flowing freely beneath your skin, carrying away wastes and toxins. Know that even as you sleep, your program of diet, exercise, cleansing, and massage is promoting the growth of clean, clear new cells in the bottom layer of your skin, building the foundation for a fresh, youthful complexion.

Thursday: Day 6

On Awakening: One 8-ounce glass of Hot Lemon-Water Flush (page 42). Prepare Inner Beauty Herbal Tea (pages 42-43); drink throughout the day between meals. Prepare and use Cleansing Inhalant (pages 168-169).

Morning Cleansing: Hot shower followed by Friction Air Bath (page 128).

Breakfast: Berry Breakfast (page 55).

Mid-morning Snack: Optional Protein Drink—Sesame Seed Milk (page 71).

Lunch: Fish, chicken, or tofu with steamed or raw vegetables.

Dinner: High-Iron Salad (page 63); steamed mixed vegetables with Tofu-Miso Topping (page 68).

Exercise: Precede exercise with Oxygenation Cocktail (page 47). Dancer's Warm-Up (page 149), followed by Yogic Swimming (pages 171 and 172) for twelve to twenty minutes, or brisk walking for thirty minutes.

Evening Activity: Use Cleansing Inhalant (pages 168 and 169); follow with Three-Part Breathing (pages 172-173), Complete Breath (pages 173 and 174), and Alternate-Hemisphere Breathing (pages 174 and 175). Take the Sea-Mineral Bath (page 176). Drink one cup Rejuvelac (page 47).

Youthful Breathing

Breathing is the only bodily function that can be both consciously controlled and automatic. Our intelligent marine friends, the whales and dolphins, must take every breath consciously, and therefore can sleep for only a few moments at a time. We humans, however, allow the muscles that control breathing to breathe for us as we go about our business, letting our bodies automatically adjust our intake of air, depending on our level of activity or our emotions.

Beyond automatic breathing, we also have the opportunity to regulate our own breath, and by so doing to establish a connection between our conscious and unconscious functions. We can use our breath to change our energy level or our mood. In fact, taking control of your breath is a very important step toward taking control of your health and self-awareness.

Today I am going to show you how to establish a new, conscious breathing habit that is basic to my cleansing and rejuvenation program. When practiced daily, youthful breathing will give you a glowing appearance, greater vitality, and increased alertness.

Rejuvenation through Breath

Because the aging process takes place within the individual cells of the body, staying youthful depends on maintaining cellular health. Two critical factors in preventing aging are the oxygenation and detoxification of the cells. Proper breathing is essential to both these functions.

Oxygen is our most vital nutrient. We can live without food for weeks and without water for days, but without air we can live only a few minutes. Oxygen nourishes the cells and burns the waste that would otherwise accumulate in them. The more oxygen we deliver to the cells, the more our tissues can be cleansed and rejuvenated with each breath.

Your lungs are like two bunches of grapes, except that the grapes are microscopic air chambers called alveoli. Tiny blood capillaries surround the walls of these alveolar air spaces like a fine net. The oxygen in the air you breathe is transferred across the thin walls of the alveoli into the blood, which turns bright red as the blood picks up oxygen. The blood then returns to the heart, which pumps it via the arteries to the body's cells. The oxygen passes into the cells, where it combines with sugar or fat to give off the heat energy that powers our life processes. The by-products of this oxidation are carbon dioxide and water. The carbon dioxide passes out of the cells into the blood, which is now dark and bluish, to be carried back to the lungs. Here the carbon dioxide passes out of the alveoli into the air and is breathed out along with some of the water. The remaining water is carried away to be eliminated by the kidneys.

Within the red blood cells are molecules of hemoglobin, an iron-containing protein that is able to pick up life-giving oxygen, carry it to the cells, and then release it. Therefore, the body's supply of oxygen depends on an adequate supply of iron in your diet. Today's dinner menu features a High-Iron Salad made of iron-rich vegetables, which help to maintain your hemoglobin, ensuring an adequate supply of oxygen to the cells and imparting a rosy glow to your complexion.

LUNGS AND AIR PASSAGES

On Monday you began to drink an Ionic Cocktail before your exercises. Today's Oxygenation Cocktail amplifies that recipe by adding powerful nutrients that help to deliver oxygen to all the cells of the body.

The elimination of waste through the breath is as important as the intake of oxygen. Classical Chinese medical theory recognized this cleansing function of the lungs thousands of years ago when it classified the lungs, the skin, and the colon as a single organ system. All these organs of elimination remove toxins from the body. In fact, your skin actually breathes, too. It performs about one-seventh of the body's total respiration, absorbing oxygen and eliminating carbon dioxide along with other impurities.

Give your skin a chance to breathe by wearing clothes made of natural fabrics. Wear loose clothing at home so that the air can circulate around your body. Whenever possible, take "air baths," wearing nothing at all, so that your skin can really do its job. The Friction Air Bath I described on Monday: Day 3 is a pleasant addition to any bath or shower. Today, if the weather permits, include this invigorating skin treatment in your schedule.

If you are a smoker, or have been in the past, you will be encouraged to know that proper breathing of fresh, clean air will help to restore your lungs to their best possible condition. If one of the goals you have set for yourself is to quit smoking or cut down, correct breathing can be a powerful tool to help you carry out your resolution.

I was a smoker myself at one time. When I finally decided to quit, whenever I wanted a cigarette I would take a deep breath, which helped me relax. When I paused to take a breath, I would also notice that the desire for a cigarette was really prompted by some emotion that I was suppressing. Breathing helped me become aware of these underlying emotions, so I could deal with them. To combat the urge to smoke, I would also take a walk by the ocean, where I would do deep breathing for about a half-hour. The negative ions at the seashore and the salt air helped me overcome my craving for tobacco.

Of course, cigarette smoke is not the only pollutant that injures your lungs and ages your appearance. Our environment is filled with smog and other toxic substances that produce free radicals that damage all the cells of the body. To enjoy the full anti-aging benefits of youthful breathing, make use of your daily brisk walks to fill your lungs with plenty of clean air. Whenever you can, visit the seashore or the countryside to revitalize your lungs, rejuvenate your cells, and lift your spirits.

Even if you have decided to remain a smoker, or if you have bronchial asthma or sinus problems, you can still clear your lungs of congestion by using a cleansing inhalant based on essential oils. On Monday: Day 3, you learned to use essential oils to cleanse and beautify your skin and to influence your mood, by relaxing in fragrant herbal steams and baths. Such external treatments are one form of aromatherapy, or the use of natural aromatic plant essences. Essential oils can also be used internally, by inhaling their fumes, for their healing properties. Do not be deceived by the lovely fragrances of these plant essences. They can have potent medicinal properties and must be treated with caution when used in inhalants.

A prepared herbal inhalant that is my personal favorite is Inspirol, a product based on the formulas of Edgar Cayce, the renowned twentieth-century psychic who formulated natural remedies for all kinds of physical dysfunctioning. It is quite stimulating energetically and as an expectorant. This product has assisted many of my clients in quitting smoking. Instead of inhaling a cigarette, they inhale a dose of Inspirol! You may also make your own Cleansing Inhalant, which you will be using throughout the 21-Day Program.

TIPS FOR CUTTING DOWN ON SMOKING

Smokers can benefit from many elements of the 21-Day Program in their efforts to reduce their tobacco consumption. Exercise is not only healthful in itself, it also helps smokers to cut down. Research has shown that a brief period of brisk walking actually reduces the craving for the next cigarette.

A good herbal alternative to tobacco is to get a bag of licorice root, available in health food stores, and chew or suck on a piece of root whenever you feel the urge to smoke. Many of my clients have been able to quit smoking this way. Licorice is very high in natural sugar and helps to even out irregularities in blood sugar levels produced by smoking. It is also a mild stimulant.

Cleansing Inhalant

The regular use of this Cleansing Inhalant is a pleasant way to keep breathing passages clear. Its fragrant fumes exert a stimulating and decongesting action on the lungs and provide a healthful alternative to tobacco for smokers.

In a small wide-mouthed glass jar, preferably of dark glass, combine the following:

20 drops eucalyptus essential oil　　　*10 drops lavender essential oil*
15 drops chamomile essential oil　　　*5 drops rosemary essential oil*
15 drops tolu balsam essential oil　　　*5 drops peppermint essential oil*
15 drops tincture of benzoin

To use the Cleansing Inhalant, shake the tightly closed jar, remove the top and inhale the fumes cautiously through your mouth. Hold your breath for about twenty seconds and exhale through pursed lips. Then inhale the fumes cautiously through one nostril, hold twenty seconds, and exhale through both nostrils. Repeat for the other nostril. You will feel this fragrant inhalant open the breathing passages that have been clogged and congested.

Not only does this combination of essential oils draw the phlegm out of the lungs, but other properties of the oils also calm the emotions, stimulate the mind, and lift the mood. All the oils used in aromatherapy have multiple effects. Consult the chart on Curative Properties of Essential Oils on page 131 to review some of the benefits of the oils in this Cleansing Inhalant.

Keep your Cleansing Inhalant in plain sight in your bathroom, in the kitchen, or wherever you will remember to use it several times during the day. Use it in the morning on arising, just before you go out walking, before you do your breathing exercises, and whenever you have a minute during the day. It is a wonderful aid in clearing your breathing passages and helping to maximize the benefits of your new practice of youthful breathing.

Balloon Breathing

After using the Cleansing Inhalant, you will benefit from Balloon Breathing. Balloon Breathing increases your ability to cleanse your lungs, your blood, and your cells. It is an enjoyable antiaging practice that you can use at home or during a break at work. Balloon Breathing is used by respiratory therapists to strengthen the lungs of patients with asthma and emphysema. It is also an excellent facial exercise for keeping cheeks firm, eliminating telltale squirrel pouches, and keeping the muscles around the lips elastic.

Perform Balloon Breathing with a large, thick balloon that requires strenuous blowing. Breathe in through your nose to fill your lungs, then blow the air into the balloon, continuing until it is filled. Let the air out of the balloon and then repeat the exercise for a total of five to fifteen minutes, maintaining an awareness of your facial muscles. Balloon Breathing will be a featured activity several times during your program.

Balloon Breathing helps to clean the waste out of the lungs. People with respiratory diseases are taught to exhale through pursed lips for this same reason. Breathing against resistance helps to maintain a higher pressure in the airways, keeping them open longer so more waste can get out, while allowing more oxygen to enter the lungs. This is why I recommend that when you do any breathing exercises you always exhale through pursed lips, as if you were whistling. In fact, whistling is another good way to clear out the breathing passages.

Conscious Breath Control

Your lungs are marvelously designed for taking in nourishing oxygen and eliminating waste, but they are completely passive in their function. They cannot expand and contract without the help of the muscles that surround them. About 80 percent of the work of breathing is done by the diaphragm, a dome-shaped sheet of muscle that divides the rib cage horizontally at about the bottom of the breastbone. It provides the floor on which the lungs and heart sit, and forms an arched dome over the liver and stomach. When the diaphragm contracts, the vertex of its bell shape flattens downward, creating a partial vacuum in the chest cavity to expand the lungs. At the same time, it presses down on the liver, stomach, and intestines, causing the belly to swell and giving the abdominal organs a stimulating massage. When you are resting or sleeping, the diaphragm alone controls breathing, but when you are tense or exercising vigorously, breathing is aided by the muscles between the ribs and in the shoulder girdle.

Breathing a full breath requires pulling the diaphragm as far down as possible to inflate the lungs completely. To exhale fully, you must push your diaphragm up. The more stale air you squeeze out of the lungs, the more toxins you remove from your body, and the more oxygen you can take in during your next refreshing, rejuvenating inhalation.

It requires conscious attention to overcome a habit of shallow breathing. Wearing tight waistbands or constricting undergarments discourages the use of anything but the upper part of the lungs. Proper breathing also requires correct posture. The straighter your spine, the more open your lungs, and the more your internal organs will be held in proper alignment.

Exercise helps to keep the diaphragm muscle toned and to increase the circulatory system's ability to carry oxygen efficiently to all the cells of the body. Vigorous activity and strong breathing help to prevent the deposit of fatty sediment on the linings of the arteries. Swimming is an excellent form of exercise for increasing your awareness of and capacity for proper breathing. If you have access to a pool, you may want to choose swimming as your exercise for today. As you do your exercise, work on developing good breathing habits, supported by proper body alignment. Use your awareness to follow your breath throughout your body.

THE DIAPHRAGM

In yoga, conscious breath control has been developed to a high level of refinement. For more than two thousand years, hatha yoga practitioners have been combining their repertoire of bodily movements with awareness of breath. The breath is equated with prana, the life force.

Breathing exercises derived from hatha yoga will help to bring your awareness and your breath into every part of your body. If you have been a shallow breather all your life, or if you haven't done breathing exercises before, you may find yourself getting a little dizzy. Take it easy; do not overdo it to begin with. These exercises cleanse and purify your whole system, while eliminating toxins and waste through the breath and bringing oxygen to all the cells.

By learning to control breath through these yogic exercises, you can achieve balance throughout your being and direct your consciousness to whatever part of your body needs cleansing, nourishing, and healing. As you continue to practice breathing exercises daily, you will begin to notice an improvement in your concentration. Your mind will become clearer and easier to focus. Apply the combination of breathing, relaxation, and concentration to any problem area in your life; it will bring you great insight and enhanced creativity.

Yogic Swimming

Swimming is one of the best exercises for developing your breathing capacity. It uses all the muscles of the body, and the motion of the arms helps to develop the cartilage between the ribs, aiding in chest expansion. When done correctly, swimming is not strenuous. It has a relaxing effect on the nerves and stimulates circulation. As you glide through the water, all your tissues and organs receive a gentle, invigorating hydro-massage.

The crawl is especially good for deep breathing. Experiment with variations in your breathing pattern. Instead of breathing on every other stroke, so that you always breathe to the same side, try breathing on every third stroke, so that you breathe alternately to the left and the right. This helps to balance your nervous-system function and keeps you more aware of your breathing.

Use your swimming time as an opportunity to experience the relaxing effects of breath. Focus on positive thoughts as you breathe in, and exhale anxiety and stress. Keep your attention on your breath; get into the rhythm of its ebb and flow, and you will move into a blissful state that goes with the peaceful energy of effortless, gliding movement.

Swim continuously for at least twelve minutes to achieve aerobic benefits, with the eventual goal of building up to swimming without stopping for twenty minutes. If you don't swim for the full twenty minutes, enjoy some of your time simply floating, breathing, stretching, and relaxing as your body is supported by the water.

Three-Part Breathing

Three-Part Breathing will help you to become aware of the three segments of the lungs. Most shallow breathers bring air only into the upper lungs. By breathing into the chest, the diaphragm, and the abdomen, you fill your lungs all the way to the bottom of their lower lobes.

Lie flat on your back on the floor. Relax and observe your breathing pattern for a while to become familiar with your natural breathing pattern. Now, place your hands flat on the upper chest and inhale deeply through your nostrils, filling the chest. This is the only part of the breathing apparatus that the average shallow breather uses. Expand your lungs, opening the chest. Feel it expanding not only from back to front as your hands rise with the chest wall, but also out to the sides and into the back. Bring the breath all the way out to the shoulders and all through your chest.

Now, breathe out through pursed lips, feeling the chest deflate. Inhale and exhale very slowly, being fully aware of the way your breath fills and empties your chest. Repeat this process three times.

Now, place the palms of your hands over the diaphragm, just below the rib cage. Your diaphragm lies in the region just below the breasts down to the navel. Now, try to breathe just in the diaphragm area. Breathe in through your nose, but this time don't let the chest expand. Isolate the diaphragm and fill it with breath. As you inhale, feel the lower rib cage expanding, not only to the front but to the sides and back as well.

Diaphragmatic breathing has a positive effect on the emotional center in the solar plexus, bringing a sense of tranquility. Hold your breath comfortably, and then exhale slowly through pursed lips, feeling the diaphragm region deflate. Repeat three times. Don't be discouraged if you cannot do this diaphragmatic breathing right away; you are learning to move a new part of your body. As you practice this exercise during the 21-Day Program, you will improve your ability to isolate and breathe into your diaphragm.

Finally, place your hands over the lower abdomen and inhale just into that section. Do not let your chest or diaphragm expand. Breathe in through your nostrils, and feel the abdominal region expand as you inhale. Keep the expansion as you hold in the breath for a moment, then exhale through pursed lips, slowly and completely, feeling the abdomen deflate. Repeat the abdominal breathing three times.

At the end of this exercise, lie quietly for a few minutes in the resting position, breathing naturally. You will feel the relaxation and clarity spreading through your entire body.

Complete Breath

Now that you have practiced breathing separately in each segment of the lungs, you are ready to coordinate these three phases of breathing into one smooth, continuous, flowing breath. The Complete Breath makes optimal use of your breathing apparatus, allowing the greatest possible intake of oxygen and elimination of carbon dioxide.

Still lying on the floor, breathe in through the nostrils, filling the abdomen first, feeling it expand. Then, on the same inhalation, move the breath up to include the diaphragm and solar plexus. Still inhaling, move the breath into the chest. Now, you are completely filled with breath. Hold your breath and relax for a moment around the held breath. Feel the relaxation spread through your whole body. Now, begin to release the breath through pursed lips. Release from the top all the way down; first, release the breath from the chest, then the diaphragm, and finally the abdomen. Feel the parts of your body deflate as you breathe out.

Relax and breathe normally, taking a nice deep breath. Notice the feelings in the different parts of your body. You may feel your head becoming clearer as the "cob-webs" are gently wafted away by the Complete Breath.

Now, repeat the Complete Breath. Inhale again through the nostrils, filling the abdomen, then the diaphragm, and finally the chest, in a continuous wave-like motion. As it becomes more natural for you, you may want to count. Take in your breath slowly in this wave-like, three-part motion to a count of eight, breathing into your abdomen, diaphragm, and chest. Hold for four, relaxing around the held breath. Then exhale slowly for eight counts, first from the chest, then from the diaphragm, and finally the abdomen.

After just a few of these breaths, you will feel wonderfully relaxed. As you prac-tice, breathe in positive thoughts—peace, harmony, well-being, or whatever words have special meaning for you. As you breathe in, feel the great ocean of life-energy flowing into you, through your abdomen, diaphragm, and chest. As you hold your breath, send this energy to every cell in your body. As you exhale, let go of all the toxins, the worries, and the negative thoughts. Continue this breathing pattern for two to five minutes. The longer you do it, the greater the benefits.

Relaxing in the resting position, allow yourself to breathe normally for a few minutes, and feel the healing, calming effects of the Complete Breath on your body, mind, and emotions. The more you practice the Complete Breath and make it a part of your life, the greater the rejuvenating effect upon your cells.

Alternate-Hemisphere Breathing

Alternate-Hemisphere Breathing, derived from hatha yoga, helps balance all the processes of the body and promotes balanced functioning of the brain.

Sit comfortably with the spine straight. Use a straight-backed chair, or if you sit on the floor, put your back against a wall. Rest the right thumb lightly against the right nostril and the ring and little finger against the left nostril. Before you begin, exhale slowly through both nostrils.

Now, hold the right nostril closed with your right thumb. Slowly and deeply inhale through the left nostril to a count of five. Keeping the right nostril closed, press the left one closed, and hold the air in your lungs for five counts. Now, open the right nostril only and exhale to a count of five.

Without pausing, inhale through the right nostril to a count of five, press the right nostril closed, and hold for five counts. Now, open the left nostril and exhale through it for five counts.

Repeat this cycle ten times to begin with, gradually increasing to twenty as you continue your daily practice. Do not slow down or speed up your breathing, but keep it going at the same slow, regular pace.

Recently, Western research has shown that this ancient breathing technique is a powerful way to control brain function. Scientists at the Salk Institute and the University of California at San Diego have found that we breathe primarily through one nostril for one to three hours, and then switch to the other. When the left nostril is active, the right-brain hemisphere dominates our thinking, and when the right nostril is dominant, the left hemisphere is more active.

Check and see which of your nostrils is clearest at any time during the day. When the right nostril is clear, that is a good time for left-brain activity, such as logical thinking or working with numbers. When your left nostril is clear, that is a good time to do right-brain activities involving intuition, spatial relations, creative and artistic endeavors.

By taking voluntary control of your breathing, you can actually influence your brain activity. If you breathe through the congested nostril, you can switch brain dominance to the opposite hemisphere. So, if you need to do something creative, breathe through the left nostril to stimulate right-brain activity. If you need to balance your checkbook, breathe through your right nostril for a few minutes to stimulate the left brain. You can use the Cleansing Inhalant on pages 168-169 to help clear the air passages and facilitate the switch from one nostril to the other.

Alternate-Hemisphere Breathing is also restful when you have difficulty falling asleep. Try it tonight after your bath, before you retire.

Breathing Away Stress

Breathing is one of your most valuable methods for releasing tension, anxiety, and stress. When you learn to breathe deeply, you begin to release emotional tension that has been trapped in the abdominal area. The solar plexus, a network of nerve fibers in the abdomen, is the emotional center of the physical body. From the solar plexus, nerve impulses control all the abdominal organs and regulate nutrition, assimilation, and growth. Improper, shallow breathing can cause the buildup of nervous tension, because it cuts us off from the feelings centered in the abdomen.

Many of my clients suffer from constipation or sexual problems. We often find that a large part of their difficulty is that they are not breathing in their abdomen. As they direct attention and breath into the abdominal organs, they suddenly bring life to this part of the body.

One client, Melinda, never had orgasms until she learned to breathe correctly. Distraught over a relationship, she had followed a friend's advice and begun attending yoga classes. One day in class, she was sitting on the floor in a yoga posture, with one leg bent in toward the groin and the other leg extended out to the side. As instructed, she leaned over the extended leg, reached out to grasp the ankle, and began to breathe deeply into the pelvis. "You may never have thought of breathing this way," the teacher commented, "but open up the pelvic area with your breath." Suddenly, Melinda began to feel sexual excitement. How could this be happening to her, in this room full of earnest spiritual students? From that moment on, working with her breath, she underwent a sexual awakening. Eventually, she was able to use her breath to encourage full sexual feelings.

Many people unconsciously hold their breath during sex. Are you one of them? With practice, you can learn to use your breath to bring full awareness into your sexual organs. Many sex therapists and bodyworkers are specially trained to work with the breath to help clients achieve sexual satisfaction. Natural birthing techniques also recognize the importance of breath.

Just as breathing helps to expel waste from your body, it is also a powerful way to eliminate negative thoughts. Use your breathing to inhale peace, harmony, and well-being, and to release all your worries and tensions. Whenever you feel anxious or tense, stop for a few moments, take a deep inhalation, breathing in the oxygen, the life-energy, and the positive thoughts that nourish your system, and breathe out, long and slow, to release the tension and anxiety from every part of your body.

As you relax in your Sea-Mineral Bath tonight, briefly review the breathing techniques you learned today. As you inhale, picture the oxygen going into all the cells and tissues of your body, fueling the fires of your life processes and burning away the wastes. Exhale completely, and visualize the toxic carbon dioxide leaving your cells and being expelled by the lungs, clearing the way for the next nourishing intake of air. As you inhale, breathe in positive thoughts of peace and joy; as you exhale, release all your stress and negative thoughts. Remember how we breathe in partnership with the green plants of nature. Experience yourself as part of the great community of living things on this planet, as we share in the exchange of life-energy through our breath.

SEA-MINERAL BATH

Taking a Sea-Mineral Bath is like soaking your body in a warm tropical ocean.

Dissolve three or four pounds of sea salt in a tub of warm to hot water. The temperature of the water has a relaxing effect and helps your body absorb the valuable minerals in the sea salt. Relax and soak for twenty minutes. Remember that the fluids inside your body are in many ways chemically similar to the water of the ocean, so it makes sense that soaking in a bath of sea minerals will help to nourish, cleanse, and rejuvenate the cells in your skin.

Just as saltwater cleanses your skin, salt air opens, refreshes, and cleanses the breathing passages. This is why being at the seashore is so good for your lungs. Try practicing one of my deep-breathing techniques as you relax in your bath.

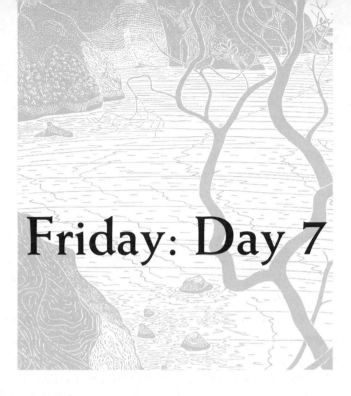

Friday: Day 7

On Awakening: One 8-ounce glass of Hot Lemon-Water Flush (page 42). Prepare Inner Beauty Herbal Tea (pages 42-43); drink throughout the day between meals. Use Cleansing Inhalant (pages 168-169). Pour off today's Rejuvelac (page 47). Drink one cup and save the rest. Prepare another batch for tomorrow.

Morning Cleansing: Morning Cold Splash and Rub (page 185).

Breakfast: Fresh Cantaloupe Breakfast (page 56).

Midmorning Snack: Optional Protein Drink—Almond Milk (page 71).

Lunch: Fish, chicken, or tofu with steamed or raw vegetables.

Dinner: Baked potato with Green Goddess Topping (page 65); sautéed mixed vegetables.

Exercise: Precede exercise with Oxygenation Cocktail (page 47). Warm up with Yoga Self-Massage (page 194-197), follow with thirty minutes of brisk walking.

Evening Activity: Drink one cup of Rejuvelac. Add the remainder to tonight's bath. Antigravity Facial Massage (page 191-192), followed by Warm Soak and Stroke (page 197).

Essential Massage

Massage is a remarkably effective and deeply pleasurable method for moving fresh, rejuvenating fluids into the cells and pushing stale, toxin-laden fluids out. At the same time, massage is also a powerful tool for managing stress, which can age even the best-nourished complexion and mar the look of vitality in even the best-exercised body.

For many people, the idea of massage summons up images of sleazy "massage parlors" or self-indulgent pampering exclusively for the idle rich. Our society still retains many of its puritanical attitudes about the human body, clinging to the belief that anything that feels good cannot really be good for the health or the character.

I would like to dispel such negative, fearful ideas about massage once and for all. For me, massage is an essential part of my health-maintenance program. It is an effective way of releasing the stress that builds up in my daily life, and it is a very important way for me to take care of myself. If I cannot express love for myself and take care of my own body, then how can I love and take care of other people, both professionally and in my personal life?

I am not unique in this attitude. Many successful sports figures, entertainers, business people, and politicians depend on massage to improve their performance, keep them youthful and attractive, and relieve their stress. Lee Iacocca, after his retirement from the Ford Motor Company, continued to receive massages from the company masseur. Members of the U.S. Olympic Team were given massages after competing in their events in Calgary, Canada, and Seoul, Korea. Celebrities such as Bette Midler, Tina Turner, Madonna, Bob Hope, Bruce Springsteen, and Luciano Pavarotti all rely on regular massage to keep them fit, youthful, and able to manage the stress of their hectic public lives.

The use of touch to soothe physical and emotional pain is a built-in response in the human organism. Even animals lick their wounds and groom one another. Massage has a long history in the healing arts. A Chinese medical treatise recorded the use of massage as early as 3000 B.C., and the ancient Hindu literature described its therapeutic value around 1800 B.C. In ancient Greece, Hippocrates, the father of Western medicine, taught that physicians must be experienced in the healing art of rubbing. In Rome, Julius Caesar received daily massages for his neuralgia. During the Middle Ages, massage (and bathing) fell out of favor as the church encouraged a general disdain for "fleshly indulgences." With the rebirth of interest in bodily health during the Renaissance, massage again grew in popularity and began to develop as a science. Many prominent physicians subsequently included massage as part of their repertoire of healing techniques.

In this century, massage has repeatedly come in and out of fashion. During World War I, it was used to treat wounded soldiers. The human-potential movement in the 1970s brought new attention to the healing power of touch. Today, massage is becoming very respectable once again, and competent professional massage therapists are available in ever-increasing numbers.

How Massage Helps to Keep You Young

My rejuvenation program would not be as effective without the catalytic effects of total body massage. Many people think that I look much younger than my years. I attribute much of my youthful appearance and clear complexion to massage. For me, massage has pulled all the other aspects of my self-care program together into a unique, rejuvenating combination. I first started receiving massage when I was doing competitive swimming in grammar school. I noticed that the older, more advanced swimmers were having regular massage, and so I tried it, too. I discovered that if I had a massage after a strenuous workout, I would recover faster, my pre-competition tension would be relieved, and I would be able to swim farther and faster. Later, when I became involved in dance, I used massage to help stretch my muscles and prevent injuries. I then began to study yoga, and noticed that yoga postures served as a sort of self-massage. Like massage, yoga also helped to promote my own body awareness.

Massage is a vital part of staying young. It supports the cleansing and nourishing of the cells by stimulating circulation—of lymph, of blood, and of energy. Massage causes the blood vessels to dilate, so circulation is improved and congestion is relieved. It temporarily raises the red blood cell count, by moving sedentary cells into circulation, thereby increasing the oxygen-carrying capacity of the blood. With increased oxygenation of the cells, the metabolic rate is increased, wastes are broken down more completely, and the calories in food are burned more efficiently. Massage also helps to push the lymph along in its channels, delivering nutrients, hastening the elimination of waste, and keeping the immune system healthy.

Oriental healing systems teach that massage affects an energy system in the body that flows through channels known as meridians. This meridian energy is the basis of the Chinese science of acupuncture, which holds that illness is a result of blockage or stagnation of this energy flow. In acupuncture, sterile needles are inserted into specific points along the meridians to stimulate energy flow. Oriental systems of massage such as acupressure or shiatsu, rather than using needles, simply apply pressure to these very same points to unblock the flow of energy.

Massage helps you to get the greatest possible benefit from your exercise program. By stimulating the circulation of blood and lymph, massage helps to bring fuel— oxygen and nutrients—to the muscles. At the same time, it carries away metabolic waste. Lactic acid, which is produced as a metabolic by-product of exercise, causes muscle soreness and a feeling of fatigue. Massage helps to move this lactic acid out of the muscles, speeding recovery time after strenuous exercise.

Massage also preserves muscle tone. If injury, illness, or an overly demanding schedule force you to be physically inactive for some time, massage can help to compensate for the lack of exercise. I became aware of the toning and conditioning benefits of massage during the years when an increasingly busy professional life caused me to drop exercise from my daily activities. If it weren't for the regular massages I had during this period, I probably would not have maintained the muscle tone that I still enjoy today.

Because it promotes body awareness, massage can also help prevent injuries. So often we tend to disregard the messages from our bodies. We may push ourselves beyond the limit of some part of our body that is tense or sore or weak. Having a regular massage helps you tune in to these problem areas, so you can work with them before they break down or become injured.

If you should happen to be injured, massage also helps to promote rapid healing. It reduces swelling by carrying fluid away from the injured area. It keeps muscle fibers from developing adhesions or fibrosis. Massage has even been shown to speed the healing of fractures by influencing metabolism and encouraging the retention of minerals needed for the bone repair.

For me, the psychological benefits are probably the most important aspect of massage. We live in a society that is starved for touch. It is a perfectly natural thing to touch a child, a friend, or even a stranger to comfort or soothe them. Sometimes a wordless hand on the shoulder, a hug, or a stroke on the back can be the most healing thing we can do for another person. Research at the University of Miami Medical School showed that premature infants who were massaged for fifteen minutes three times a day gained weight 47 percent faster than babies who were left alone in their incubators, as was the usual practice. The massaged infants showed more rapid development of their nervous systems and were able to leave the hospital six days earlier than other premature infants who were not massaged. Skin-to-skin touch is essential for all babies, premature or not. Infants receiving more touch have been shown to have a six-month advantage in their mental development. As a result of such findings, American parents are now learning techniques for massaging their infants—an activity that is a natural part of child care in many other parts of the world.

Adults as well as infants require physical touch. I find that getting a massage is one of the most effective ways to nurture and take care of myself. Many people seek out sexual contacts simply because they need to be touched, and do not realize that they can get touch in other ways as well.

Anita, one of my clients, was typical of such people. A successful artist, she worked alone in her studio, and she lived alone as well. During the time I worked with Anita on a cleansing program, she confided to me that she was having a lot of trouble with her relationships. She would get sexually involved with one man after another, and never seemed to find the love or satisfaction she was looking for. As we talked, it became clear that she was really hungry for touch. I suggested that she try massage, and she discovered that receiving a massage once a week helped her to place sex in the proper perspective and enabled her to be more discriminating in her relationships.

For me, massage is essential for stress management. Stress can have a very aging effect on the appearance, causing furrowing of the brow and worry lines around the mouth and between the eyebrows. I remember one massage therapist who would always point out when I was frowning. I had never realized until then how much tension I was holding in my face. A very important part of stress management is being aware of your stress-warning signals. Being touched by another person helps you to tune into every part of your body and to see where you are holding stress and tension. Over time, such stress held in the body can lead to real physical symptoms. Massage helps call attention to these warning signs before they reach the danger point.

Massage is becoming so widely accepted as a stress reliever today that many major corporations, such as Apple Computer and AT&T, now sponsor regular in-office massages for their employees. In cities across the United States, therapists are providing on-site massages that generally take about fifteen minutes.

Relieving stress through massage will help to keep you on track as you follow the 21-Day Program. Sometimes it is just what is needed to break through old stress patterns and allow your body and mind to experience the dramatic benefits of the sweeping lifestyle changes you are undertaking. A client of mine, a busy executive named Alan, is a perfect example of the hard-driving, Type-A personality. He was having trouble with his digestion, and he was constipated most of the time. Although he denied it initially, it was obvious to me that a great deal of his problem was due to stress. He worked hard at changing his diet, took all the recommended supplements, adhered faithfully to his exercise, and cooperated in the cleansing program, but he was still holding a lot of stress in his body, particularly in his abdominal organs. Finally, I persuaded Alan to set up a series of appointments for massage. For the first time, Alan allowed someone to do something for him, rather than insisting on controlling what was happening to him. With regular weekly massage sessions, Alan finally learned how to let go and relax. He began to respond better to the cleansing program, and he also began to understand what I meant when I suggested he use his exercise period as a time to relax and breathe and open himself up to the beauty of the outdoors, rather than feeling compelled to push himself through a strenuous daily regimen. All the components of his cleansing program began to fall into place once he learned to relax and tune in to the stress signals his body was sending him.

I often find that tension held in the abdomen can be the principal cause of problems with digestion and elimination. Stress can cause clenching of the muscles along the intestinal tract, inhibiting peristalsis and preventing proper digestion and bowel movement. Massage is a great tool for helping people to recognize these muscular holding patterns and learn to release them.

Which Massage Is Right for You?

Essentially, massage can be divided into four main categories: Swedish, Oriental or shiatsu, reflexology, and sports massage. Each type of massage is used for different purposes, and has a different "feel." It is very common for massage therapists to combine elements of different techniques into a more eclectic approach.

My own personal health-maintenance program includes at least one professional massage per week. Every other week, I receive an eclectic bodywork type of massage that works at a very deep tissue level, not only moving the blood and lymph but also producing intense emotional release. On the alternating weeks, I have a Swedish type of massage that helps to keep my lymph moving, relaxes me and relieves my stress, and is wonderfully nurturing. Whenever I am out of balance or feeling emotionally vulnerable, I have an additional Swedish massage during the bodywork week.

Swedish massage, introduced by Peter Ling of Sweden in the nineteenth century, combines traditional techniques brought back from China with a Western understanding of anatomy and physiology. Swedish massage works with the body's muscular and skeletal structure to promote circulation, soothe the nervous system, and promote a feeling of well-being. It consists of long, gliding strokes and a variety of kneading, friction, squeezing, tapping, and shaking movements. Swedish massage is given on a table, with the client partially or completely undressed, since the massage therapist works directly on the bare skin, using oil for lubrication. Because Swedish massage concentrates on promoting circulation of blood and lymph, it is ideally suited to the whole-body cleansing of the 21-Day Program. You will also find it wonderfully relaxing. A less vigorous variant of Swedish massage, known as Esalen massage, uses gentle, rhythmic movements that many people find to be a good introduction to the nurturing, relaxing benefits of massage.

Shiatsu massage, also known as acupressure, is an Oriental technique based on the acupuncture theory of meridian energy. By applying pressure rather than needles to specific points along the meridians, this form of massage is believed to unblock the circulation of the life energy, helping to promote self-healing and prevent illness. Therapists who use these Oriental techniques work with their fingers, hands, elbows, and knees on points along the energy pathways. The deep pressure of shiatsu massage may feel painful when applied to sore, tense muscles; while some people enjoy this intense stimulation, others may find it too much for them. Oriental massage tends to produce an energized feeling rather than relaxation, and is helpful for relieving tension in specific areas of the body. It is usually performed on a mat on the floor, with the client wearing loose, comfortable clothing.

Reflexology is a form of acupressure that concentrates on the feet and sometimes, the hands. It is based on the theory that every organ, muscle, and gland in the body corresponds to a specific area on the feet. By manipulating the appropriate part of the feet, the masseur can relieve tension in the corresponding distant part. I have found, for example, that clients with elimination or digestion problems are able to relax in their abdominal organs when I massage the colon point in the middle of the sole of the foot. Introduced relatively recently, in the early 1900s, reflexology is based on ancient Chinese, Japanese, and Egyptian techniques. You can do this particular kind of massage for yourself, or a massage therapist can give you a reflexology foot or hand massage while you are lying on a table or sitting in a reclining chair. Try massaging your feet as a pleasant, effective way to induce relaxation.

Sports massage is a rapidly growing sub-specialty in the United States today. It caters specifically to serious athletes, but is becoming increasingly popular among amateurs as well. Sports massage consists of a combination of Swedish-massage strokes and pressure-point techniques derived from shiatsu, as well as specific manipulations to prevent injury, improve performance, and aid recovery. If you are actively engaged in a sport that places stress on certain joints or muscles, you may find that sports massage, focused on those parts of your body, can be a valuable part of your training program. Sports massage tends to be brisk, vigorous, and more energizing than a relaxing full-body Swedish massage.

Other forms of massage include Rolfing, which works on deep tissues to release tension patterns stored in the muscles and joints, and provides a release of emotions held in the body. Bodywork techniques such as the Trager and Feldenkreis methods and Polarity therapy use movement and manipulation to balance the body energies and release physical and emotional patterns. These emotional-release forms of massage are really in the realm of psychotherapy. While they can be enormously effective, they are actually beyond the scope of the 21-Day Program, which emphasizes the circulation-enhancing and stress-relieving benefits of massage. If you are accustomed to one of these body techniques, please feel free to continue with it as your massage therapy of choice.

Water Massage

At physical therapy centers and European health spas, massage and treatments with water are an inseparable part of the natural healing programs. While massage was largely ignored in American health spas until recently, the healing effects of hydrotherapy, or water treatment, have always been recognized. The external application of water affects many of the same systems as massage. Like massage, hydrotherapy influences the circulation of the blood, soothes the nervous system, and helps the eliminative function of the skin.

You may be surprised at the powerful effect cold water has as a hydrotherapy treatment. Cold water applied to the skin actually stimulates circulation throughout the system. As with massage, cold-water applications mobilize sluggish blood cells throughout the body, moving them into circulation and temporarily increasing both the red and white blood cell counts. The initial effect of cold-water applications is to chill the skin and drive the blood toward the center of the body, where the body's heat-regulating mechanism then produces a reaction, causing the blood to rush back to the surface, open the pores and capillaries, and release impurities through the skin in the form of perspiration. Today's Morning Cold Splash and Rub is an excellent illustration of how this process works, as is the cold sitz bath, or "youth bath." While the initial effect of these procedures is to produce chilling, a healthy body will rapidly react by producing the opposite effect, and a warm flushing suffuses the parts that have been exposed to the cold water.

A great way to warm up cold feet is to stimulate circulation in them through a reflex reaction to cold. Try walking barefoot in cold dewy grass or on wet stones or even in the snow. Once you feel the flushing reaction, get into a warm place, cover up, and enjoy the tingling heat in your feet and toes.

MORNING COLD SPLASH AND RUB

This Morning Cold Splash is an excellent way to wake yourself up before going for a brisk walk. It promotes the circulation and stimulates the systems of elimination. It is very beneficial if practiced regularly.

Be sure that your body temperature is warm before performing the Morning Cold Splash. Go directly from your warm bed, before early morning chill sets in.

Do the cold splash quickly, so that it doesn't take more than a few minutes. Sit in the empty tub with the stopper in place. Turn on the cold water and use your hands to splash it all over your body, washing first the arms and legs, then the abdomen, then the chest and back. Rub the skin with your hands as you splash water over your body. Use a brush to reach your back if you cannot reach it otherwise.

Leave the tub and dry yourself quickly with a coarse towel. Finish by rubbing with your hands until your skin is dry and smooth and you are glowing from the friction and the reaction to the cold water. At the end of this bath, you should feel warmth and comfort throughout your body.

Evening Youth Bath

The cold sitz bath is often called a "youth bath" because of its rejuvenating effect. It stimulates the organs of elimination and reproduction. Taken just before bedtime, a cold sitz bath will produce a soothing and relaxing effect by drawing the blood away from the head and into the lower abdominal organs.

Be sure your body is warm before taking a cold sitz bath. Fill your bathtub shallowly with six to nine inches of cold water directly from the tap. Cover your shoulders and back with a towel, step into the tub, and, without hesitation, sit down. Keep your feet out of the water by resting them on the end of the tub or on an improvised footrest such as an inverted dishpan, so that only your "sitz" is covered by the water. Count slowly to sixty—the equivalent of one minute. You should notice a strong reaction, with the sensation of cold being followed by a feeling of warmth. Carefully rise from the tub, dry yourself with a coarse towel to warm the skin, then wrap yourself in a towel or robe for warmth, or get into bed and relax.

As you become accustomed to the cold water, you can gradually increase the sitting time, first to a count of 120, or two minutes, and then to 180.

Soothing Hot Seat Bath

The hot sitz bath relaxes and warms the body, especially before bedtime. It relieves pain and inflammation in the pelvic organs and is helpful for rectal problems. Later in the book, I will give a special recipe for a hot sitz bath to relieve menstrual discomfort.

Follow the directions for the cold sitz bath, except use water as hot as you can stand. Sit in the hot sitz bath for ten to fifteen minutes. Dry off with a coarse towel, then wrap yourself in a robe or get into bed to keep warm.

Besides the stimulating and relaxing effects of baths of different temperatures, water can also be used for mechanical stimulation of the skin and circulation in a manner similar to massage. You may be familiar with the wonderfully relaxing effect of a Jacuzzi. If you have a hand-held shower spray in your bathtub, you can use it to direct water at tense, painful areas on your body for a spot hydro-massage. In your yard, you can use a garden hose with the water turned on full strength. For a stimulating leg massage, direct the hose at your feet, ankles, and up the legs, moving toward the center of the body. This garden hydro-massage promotes circulation, tones the tissues, and helps to break down cellulite. When you are at the beach, use the powerful energy of breaking waves to massage your entire body. Stand in the water where the waves can break against painful or tense areas, or lie in the shallow water and let the surf break against you. To soothe your ankles and feet, walk along the water's edge through the foaming surf.

Experiencing Massage

On Sunday: Day 16, at the end of the cleansing phase of this program, you are scheduled to receive a professional massage that helps to promote the cleansing process and give you an added psychological boost. Today is a good time to begin looking for a massage therapist and make your appointment. If possible, arrange for the massage therapist to come to your home, so you can enjoy a relaxing day in your private spa environment.

I recommend a Swedish-type massage because of its great benefits for the circulation of blood and lymph, as well as the wonderful relaxation it induces. If you are very active athletically and tend to have problems in any particular part of your body, you may want to look for a massage therapist who is also familiar with sports massage.

Feel free to schedule additional massages if you wish. The more regularly you receive a massage, the greater are the benefits. Even after one session, however, you should notice a positive difference. You will probably feel marvelously relaxed immediately after your massage, although you may feel a little sluggish the day afterward, as toxins are being mobilized out of your system. To minimize such effects, be sure to drink several glasses of the Hydrating Drink or purified water right after your massage to stimulate lymph flow and carry away the freshly released toxins. Continue to drink water throughout the day, perhaps several glasses more than usual. If you do not feel an immediate improvement after one massage session, you many want to try a different therapist or a different kind of massage the next time.

If you are suffering from any medical problem, check with your physician before you receive a massage. Massage is not advised if you have a fever, an ulcer, cancer, high blood pressure, or a recent fracture or dislocation. If you have varicose veins, an infection, or recently torn tendons, ligaments, or muscles, do not have these sensitive areas massaged, and be sure to call them to the attention of the therapist. Pregnant women and people with heart disease or bone disease should check with their physician before getting a massage.

How to Choose a Massage Therapist

Your massage therapist will be providing a very personal service for you, and you want to be sure you will feel comfortable with the person you select. Begin by asking your friends if they have a favorite massage therapist. A personal referral helps to ensure that the therapist is ethical and experienced. Sometimes, it can be difficult to differentiate the legitimate massage therapist among the listings in the telephone yellow pages or the classified ads in a newspaper. If there is an alternative publication such as *Common Ground* in your area, you will find qualified massage therapists listed there. You can also call the American Massage Therapy Association at 847-864-0123 for referrals to massage therapists in your area.

Some states require a license to practice massage therapy. If your state requires a license, make sure your therapist has one. Ask what kind of training the therapist has had; ideally, select someone who has gone through an extensive formal training program, including the study of anatomy and physiology. Experience is just as important as training. I recommend that you look for a therapist who has been in practice for at least one year.

It is not unusual to feel self-conscious about your body or anxious about what will happen at your first session with a massage therapist. You may feel apprehensive about being naked or about having a stranger touch you. A good massage therapist is sensitive to your feelings and will not push you to do anything that you don't want to. If you are not comfortable removing all your clothes, leave on your underwear. Once you are on the massage table, the therapist will drape you with sheets and towels, both to respect your modesty and to keep your body warm.

At your first meeting, the massage therapist should ask you about your physical condition and your personal needs. You will be asked whether you have any medical problems, are pregnant, on medication, or menstruating, and whether you have had any recent surgery. The answers to these questions will determine what kind of massage you will receive.

Do not hesitate to discuss the cost of the massage when you first call the therapist on the phone. In most parts of the country, rates generally average in the thirty-dollar to fifty-dollar range for a one-hour massage. If there is a massage school in your area, and you are willing to allow a beginner to work on you, call and inquire whether the school offers sessions with apprentices. The rates will be considerably lower.

While I recommend a professional massage on a regular, once-a-week basis, this is more than some people can afford. An alternative is to pay for a professional massage as often as you can and on other weeks call on a friend. You may both need instruction to make the exchange of massage as beneficial as possible. See if massage classes are offered in your area. If you don't have time for a class, some excellent self-teaching materials are available. Exchanging massage with a mate or a friend can be a pleasant and meaningful way to share healing, loving energy. Not only is it wonderful to receive a massage, but it is a very satisfying experience to know how to give one to someone close to you.

Make Your Own Aromatherapy Massage Oil

Massaging the skin with essential oils is an ideal way to get the healing properties of aromatic plant essences into the body. The herbal essences are absorbed even more readily through the skin than through inhalation. Try rubbing some essential oil on the palm of your hand; you should be able to taste it in your mouth in a couple of minutes. The nurturing touch of massage enhances the relaxing, soothing, and stimulating properties of the oils themselves.

You can prepare your own massage oil to use regularly for all the massage activities in this program.

In an eight-ounce container, place the following vegetable oils, which will serve as the base for the essential oils:

3 ounces of olive oil   *3 ounces of peanut oil*
3 ounces of almond oil

Olive oil moisturizes and softens the skin, soothes irritation, and alleviates dryness of cuticles and nails. Almond oil is an excellent moisturizer that imparts its fragrance to many fine cosmetics. Peanut oil is believed to be very beneficial for the joints and is used frequently in natural remedies applied externally for arthritis.

To the base mixture, add essential oils to make your own personalized massage oil formula. A good general-purpose combination is:

12 drops of eucalyptus oil   *15 drops of chamomile oil*
15 drops of lavender oil   *12 drops of rosemary oil*

These essential oils have a pleasant sedative effect, promote circulation, and relax the muscles. To make a mixture more personalized to your taste and needs, consult the chart Curative Properties of Essential Oils, on page 131.

Oil for Varicose Veins

Prepare a small batch of the following special massage oil to help increase circulation and improve the tone of the veins.

1 ounce of olive oil
8 drops of cypress essential oil

Massage with this oil only above the area affected with varicose veins, never below—that is, massage between the varicosities and the heart. Use this oil only for those parts of your body, such as your legs, that have the varicose veins, and use your regular massage oil for the other body areas.

Self-Massage

While nothing can equal the relaxation and sense of being cared for that you derive from receiving a professional massage, you can experience many of the benefits of massage by doing it for yourself. Through self-massage, you can develop a better understanding of your own body. Because you are getting your own feedback, you will know exactly how much pressure to apply without causing pain, and you will discover what feels best to you. Self-massage allows you to tune in to areas where you are holding tension in your body, to relieve aching muscles, and release energy blockages. Whenever you feel tense and under pressure, use these massage techniques, drawn from Swedish and Oriental massage, to relax and nurture yourself.

MASSAGE SELF-INSTRUCTION AIDS

Learn massage techniques by yourself or with a friend. I highly recommend these books:
The Magic of Massage by Ouida West (Hastings)
The Book of Massage by Lucinda Lidell, et al. (Fireside)

Antigravity Facial Massage

Massaging your face on a slant board is particularly beneficial because the antigravity position brings the blood supply to the face, so this massage is beautifying as well as relaxing. You can use the same facial-massage techniques whenever you are under stress. In the privacy of your office, in the bathroom at work, or while commuting by bus, train, or car, you can do a one-minute version of this facial massage for a quick relaxer and youth restorer.

Set up the slant board as described on pages 152-153 for Tuesday: Day 4. Relax for a few minutes in the antigravity position, with your feet above your head. Breathe in through your nostrils and out through pursed lips to calm and center yourself. Before you begin, dab a little massage oil or cream of your choice on your fingertips. If you have never been introduced to castor oil, this is a good time to try it; an occasional facial massage with castor oil is very rejuvenating to the skin. Castor oil is a popular folk remedy for all sorts of skin problems, and it is an ingredient in many cosmetics because of its hydrating and soothing properties. You may also use your own massage oil or plain vegetable oil; see pages 123-125 from Monday: Day 3 for some recommended oils for different skin types.

Now, with your fingertips, gently massage your temples in a circular motion. Move all around the temple area. If you find a sensitive spot, do not avoid it, but bring your attention to that spot and gently massage the tenderness away. Continue your conscious breathing as you feel the relaxation spread through the muscles of your face.

FACIAL MASSAGE

Next, use your fingertips to gently massage between your eyebrows in a circular motion. Then stroke your fingertips across your forehead, moving out from the center toward the temples. Use gentle but firm pressure, as much pressure as feels comfortable to you. Work your way up and down the forehead, stroking across in this manner, so that you cover the entire forehead. Then place the fingertips of each hand along the corresponding eyebrow and with firm but gentle pressure slide the fingertips from the eyebrows into the hairline. Cover the entire forehead with this sliding motion, to relax the forehead and smooth out the wrinkles in your brow.

Massage your cheeks by sliding the fingers upward on each side, from the chin up over the cheeks, out to the temples, and into the hairline. Repeat this movement several times, covering the sides of the face completely. Then massage in a circular motion over the cheekbones, beginning below the outer corners of the eyes, moving across the cheek and down to the base of your nose. Massage in a circular motion back out and down to the hinge of the jaw. Spend some time massaging here, noticing any tender spots. Many people hold a lot of tension in the jaw.

As you massage your face, feel the muscles relax and the blood flow into all the tissues, nourishing them and bringing a glow to your complexion. This facial massage is also helpful for freeing the sinuses of congestion.

Finish your facial massage by placing your thumbs under your chin and pulling them up, first on one side and then the other, along the jawline toward the ears. The longer you continue this alternate chin stroking, the greater will be the toning effect if you have a tendency to a sagging chin line.

Continue your facial massage for a full five minutes. Then, still lying on the slant board, use your fingertips to massage your scalp. Use the pads of the fingers, being careful not to damage the scalp with your nails. If you find tender spots, concentrate on those. Massage in a circular motion over the entire scalp, being sure to go all the way down to the neck and behind the ears. This scalp massage encourages hair growth and improves scalp problems. Keep up the scalp massage for two to three minutes. It is a very relaxing and pleasant way to enhance your natural beauty.

Quick Oriental Massage Remedies

Pressure-point massage techniques are derived from shiatsu and acupressure. During the 21-Day Program, you may experience some minor discomforts as your body is ridding itself of toxins. Try these massage remedies for drugless first aid the next time you have the indicated problem.

CONSTIPATION

HEADACHE

HAND PRESSURE POINTS

Headache

Press your left thumb onto the back of your right hand, in the web of flesh between the base of the thumb and the bone that connects to the forefinger. Hold firmly for five seconds to two minutes, and you should feel your headache pain subside. This acupressure point was known in ancient times as the "Great Eliminator."

Constipation

Move your left thumb just up from the Great Eliminator point, so that you are pressing with the thumb into the inside edge of the metacarpal bone of the right index finger, just beyond the V where this bone meets the bone from the thumb. Hold this point firmly while attempting to move the bowels, to ease tension in the large intestine.

Low Energy

Massaging specific points in the abdomen and the chest is a great substitute for coffee, whenever you are groggy and want to stay awake—while driving, working, or dozing off at a concert. The first points, used to stimulate the adrenal glands, are located two and one-half inches above and one inch to either side of the navel. Hold your hands with the palms across the abdomen, with the fingertips pointing toward each other. Now

BODY PRESSURE POINTS

using a circular motion, massage with the fingertips of each hand deep into the abdomen in this area, just below the rib cage. Do not massage these points too close to bedtime, as you may not be able to go to sleep.

The second set of points that stimulate the brain is located on each side of the chest, running from a point on the collarbone directly below the ears vertically down to the armpit. Use your thumbs or fingers to massage with firm pressure in a circular motion all the way down this line. These points may feel rather sensitive or painful at first, but as the massaging takes effect, the tenderness will decrease, and you will become more alert.

Sleeplessness or Emotional Upset

Place the tips of the four fingers of each hand over the frontal eminence on each side of the forehead. This is the slight bulge on either side of the forehead, between the eyebrows and the hairline. Feel for a faint pulse in this area, and hold with gentle fingertip pressure on these points for two to five minutes. Usually, within a few minutes you will begin to feel relaxed enough to sleep, or your troubling thoughts will begin to melt away. Pressing these points helps to normalize the adrenal glands after an upsetting event.

HEAD PRESSURE POINTS

Another point for sedating the adrenal glands is located on the posterior fontanel on the top rear of the head—the "soft spot" on the back of a baby's head. Feel for the slight pulse, and hold for two to ten minutes, to calm upset or ease yourself into sleep.

Yoga Self-Massage

Yoga and massage are similar in many ways. Both activate areas along the spine, directing nourishing blood and nerve impulses to the body's organs. Both help to "wake up" the joints and connective tissue and improve the circulation of blood and lymph. While massage does this through direct manipulation, yoga postures achieve the same results by targeting specific organs, joints, and areas of the body with specific postures. The gentle stretching movements of yoga help to stimulate areas that are difficult to reach and energize through walking or other forms of exercise. The following series of yoga postures provides an "internal massage" for the spine, joints, and internal organs. Use it as a warm-up before your exercise today. You may want to read the following instructions into your tape recorder and play it back while you perform the movements.

Spinal Stretch

Lie on the floor with your arms relaxed at your sides. Breathing in through the

SPINAL STRETCH

nose, slowly raise your arms over your head so that they are stretched out on the floor behind you. At the same time that you are inhaling and bringing your arms back, point your toes so that you are stretching from the waist down to your toes and from your waist up to your fingertips. Hold in your breath and feel the tension of the stretch in your spine and in the entire length of your body. Release the tension without changing position, and relax around the held breath for a moment. Then exhale, bringing your arms back to your sides. Lie flat, breathing normally, and relax, enjoying the benefits of the stretch. This lying position, known as the Resting Pose, is one of the most important postures in yoga. Take the time to experience the total relaxation that the name implies. Repeat the spinal stretch three times.

Knees to Chest

Lying on your back, bring both knees to the chest, with the arms clasped around your knees, holding one wrist with the other hand. Relax in this folded-up position, breathing in and out normally. Feel the invigorating stretch in your lower back. Now, still holding this position, rock gently from side to side to wake up the spine.

KNEES TO CHEST

Release your knees and straighten the legs, lowering them slowly to the floor, returning to the Resting Pose. Rest for a while and enjoy the feeling of relaxation. Repeat three times.

COBRA

Cobra

Roll over onto your tummy. Lie flat with your toes together, your forehead on the floor, and your palms flat on the floor next to the armpits. Breathe in, slowly raising the head and neck. Open your eyes and look up through the eyebrows. Continuing to breathe in, rise farther, lifting the chest off the floor and curling the spine back as far as possible without lifting the hips or pelvis off the floor. Hold your breath in this reverse stretch, looking up through the eyebrows and jutting the chin out with the teeth together to tense the throat and neck. Hold this position for several seconds, then begin to exhale. Lower the stomach to the floor, then the chest, and finally allow the head to roll forward to the floor. Relax in a lying position on your tummy with your head to one side. Repeat this posture three times.

Canine Stretch

Still lying on your tummy on the floor, place your palms next to your armpits and push yourself up, with your weight on your hands and the balls of your feet. Straighten your legs and raise your buttocks in the air, as if a rope were lifting your lower spine toward the ceiling. Hold this position for a few moments. Really push up your lower back area, feeling the spinal stretch. Then bend your knees, lower your body to the floor position, and

CANINE STRETCH

relax. Breathe in and out normally throughout this exercise; do not hold your breath. For a different stretch and a different sensation, try drawing your heels down to the floor in the raised position, rather than keeping your weight on your toes. Repeat the Canine Stretch three times, ending in the floor position.

Prenatal Posture

From lying on the floor, push yourself up into a kneeling position, so you are sitting relaxed on your feet, with the tops of the feet flat on the floor, the toes touching, and the heels turned out to the sides. Take a deep, slow

PRENATAL POSTURE

inhalation. Extend your arms out in front of you with the fingers lightly touching, exhale slowly, and as you exhale, bend forward until your forehead is resting on the floor with your arms extended. Relax in this position, breathing normally, for at least one minute. Repeat three times. This position, known as the Prenatal Posture, stimulates the circulation of blood to the head, making your mind alert and your eyes rested and bright.

Warm Soak and Stroke

A wonderful way to relax before bedtime is to do a self-massage in your bath. You can use these self-massage techniques anywhere, at any time during the day, to work on easily reached trouble spots that accumulate tension.

Be sure that your bathroom is nice and warm when you begin. Add one pound of Epsom salts and today's leftover Rejuvelac to a warm (not hot) bath. Periodically add a little hot water if necessary to maintain the temperature for twenty to thirty minutes. The Epsom salts promote the eliminative activity of the skin, carrying through on the work of elimination begun by stimulating the circulation of blood and lymph with massage. You do not need to use oil for this massage, since the bath water will provide lubrication.

Sitting up in the tub, begin with the neck. Using the thumb and fingers, grasp the muscle on either side of the spine at the back of the neck. Move gradually up and down each side of the spine, pinching and releasing the muscle, going down as far as you can and up to the base of the skull. Concentrate on the areas that feel tight and sore. Bend your neck back and hang your head forward as you continue to pinch and knead the muscles. Do some neck rolls to the sides to loosen up the neck, then massage the neck muscles some more.

From the neck, move out toward the shoulders. Rest the heels of the hands on the tops of the shoulders against the neck, with the fingers curled over the back of the shoulders. Now, slide your hands forward with a firm, smooth, sliding pressure, so your elbows come down over the chest. Repeat this sliding movement, gradually working out from the neck to the shoulder, pressing as hard as you wish. Feel the heat in your skin as you slide your hands firmly over the muscles.

Now, work on one shoulder at a time with the opposite hand, squeezing all around the shoulder joint. Begin with gentle squeezing, then increase until you are squeezing as hard as is comfortable.

Next, work on the arms, always moving toward the heart. Work on one hand and arm and then switch to the other. Begin by massaging each finger from the tip up to the palm. Take the time to squeeze, stroke, and shake each of the fingers and the thumb, working the blood and lymph back toward the heart. Now, squeeze and massage the hands, stroking firmly along the bones, always moving toward the heart to flush out the wastes and stagnant blood. Work your way up the arm, kneading and squeezing the muscles. Work around the elbow, massaging any tender spots you find, and moving up toward the armpits. Finish with strong upward strokes, using the whole opposite hand, with the fingers wrapped around the arm, to push the blood and lymph back toward the heart. If you feel tender spots, you may be encountering areas of congested lymph. Work on them, and then move everything onward, squeezing and stroking toward the heart. Take the time to do some shoulder rolls to loosen up your shoulders as you work.

Next, massage your legs. Use both hands to work on one foot and calf, then go on to the other. Bend one knee so that you can rest the foot on the opposite thigh. Squeeze and massage the toes from the tip toward the foot, to force the blood back toward the heart. Slide your index finger back and forth between the toes, feeling the wonderful relaxation spreading through your body. Grasp all your toes with one hand, and with the other hand bend the foot back and forth. Massage along the bones on the top of the foot and knead deeply into the sole, gently moving up toward the leg.

Keeping your knee bent with the foot resting on the opposite thigh, massage the calf, kneading and squeezing. Then use strong, firm strokes with both hands to move the circulation up the calf into the thighs. When you have finished one calf, work on the other foot and calf.

Now, straighten the legs in front of you to work on the knees and thighs. Work on one knee at a time, squeezing and kneading with both hands behind and around the sides of the knee. Next, grasp the top of one thigh between thumb and fingers, squeeze, and let the muscle slip out of your hand. Work your way all over the thighs in this manner to stimulate the circulation. Then stroke strongly up the thigh with both hands curved around the leg. Finish by stroking the insides of both thighs, up toward the groin. Remember that massaging toward the heart helps to flush the veins, promoting circulation and cleansing.

After your massage, get out of the bath and dry briskly with a coarse towel. Wrap in a robe or towel and get into bed and relax for fifteen minutes, or prepare for sleep. The skin-cleansing properties of the Epsom salts, activated by the self-massage, will continue to draw wastes out of your skin through the night.

Closing, Week One

Tonight marks the end of the first week of your 21-Day Program. Your body is building new cells, and your systems of elimination are working more efficiently to keep your tissues and body fluids clean and clear. Many of the toxins and wastes stored in your body have been released and eliminated. As you lie in bed relaxing after your Warm Soak and Stroke, take time to be aware of your body. Breathe deeply and notice any changes that have occurred since you began the program.

Do you feel more energetic, less achy, lighter, and more limber? Draw your breath into every part of your body, noticing any areas that seem sore or tense. As you exhale, breathe out the tension and notice the wonderful feeling of cleanliness and relaxation produced by your bath and massage. Let go of all your stress, negativity, and doubts tonight. Tomorrow you will be moving on to new challenges as you enter a new, more intense phase of your cleansing program.

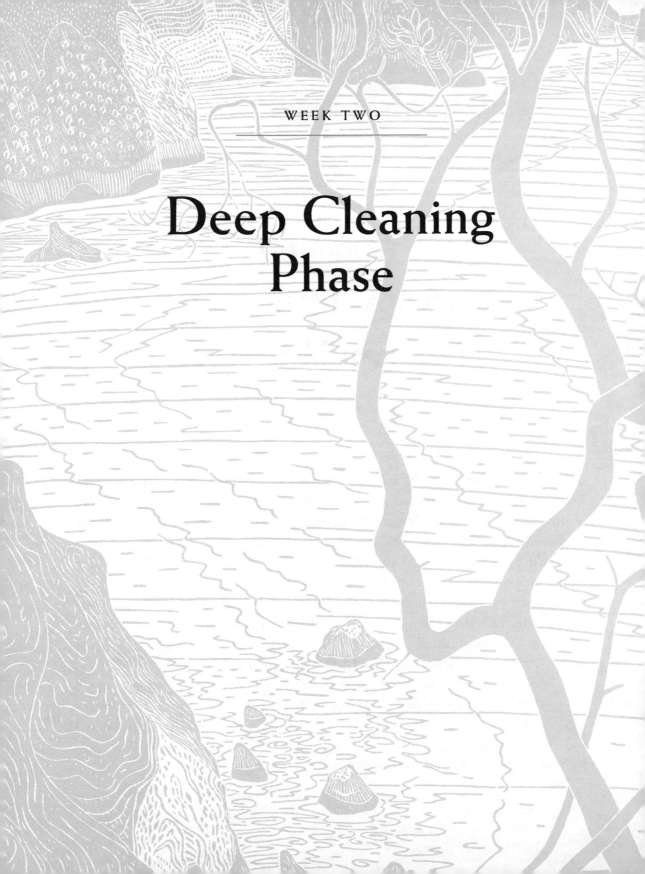

Deep Cleaning Phase

INTRODUCTION:
Inner Cleansing, Outer Beauty

This week you will begin the intensified cleansing phase of your 21-Day Program. Every meal, every beverage, every activity is designed to gently flush and cleanse your organs, tissues, and cells. Even your thoughts and feelings will take on a renewed brightness and clarity.

Last week, you prepared yourself for cleansing by following the Rejuvenation Diet, which eliminated unnecessary contaminants and congesting foods and taught you how to combine foods properly, so they would not leave behind undigested wastes in your system. This week's diet eliminates animal protein and focuses on simple, cleansing foods. Your daily menus will progress from a combination of cooked and raw fruits and vegetables to raw foods only. The final two days, you will be on a fast of juices and thin vegetable broth. This progressively lighter diet—leading to a liquid fast—is designed to give your systems of elimination a deep rest and allow them to release the toxins and wastes they have accumulated. This cleansing process will be assisted by a variety of beverages to flush your body. I will also introduce you to special detoxifying baths and to techniques for colon cleansing.

This week's therapeutic cleansing regimen is not the sort of program you would follow all the time, but it does contain rejuvenation and weight-loss techniques that you will be able to use both for periodic touch-ups and for special health boosts in the future.

During Week 1, you learned many methods for promoting the correct functioning of your systems of elimination. I explained how you can use exercise to stimulate blood and lymph flow and to encourage your skin to excrete waste through sweating. I taught you breathing exercises to help you cleanse your blood and lungs of waste and introduced you to a Cleansing Inhalant to clear your breathing passages. I presented several stretching exercises based on yoga to stimulate the organs of elimination and massage techniques to move the lymph, enhance blood circulation, and release tension. I showed you how to do dry brush massage and how to prepare a variety of stimulating and cleansing baths to promote the eliminative function of the skin and lymph. This week's schedule intensifies these activities as you step up the cleansing of your body and mind.

Each day, I want you to take a brisk walk or to work out on your mini-trampoline. Rebounding on the trampoline really keeps the lymph moving and helps to expel the waste that is being flushed out of your cells and tissues. You will also do a Lymph-Cleansing Warm-up before your daily exercise, using special movements that pump the lymph throughout your body. In addition to the massage techniques you have already learned, I will teach you procedures for cleansing the upper lymph system and emptying the colon through gentle massage. A Hot Castor-Oil Abdominal Wrap will help to move waste out of the lymph system, induce pleasant relaxation, and prepare you for colon cleansing. You will also do the breathing exercises that you learned last week, and you will use your daily baths and showers to stimulate your blood, lymph, and skin function and to reinforce a wonderful feeling of inner and outer cleanliness.

Although this week's program may appear rigorous at first glance, your daily diet and activities will be similar to those you would be following at an exclusive spa. Yet you will still be able to go to work, socialize with friends, eat meals out, take care of your family and your personal needs—all with increased energy and an enhanced sense of well-being. And best of all, you will discover revitalizing life-extension techniques to integrate into your daily life.

The Deep-Cleansing Diet

Now that your body has been prepared and strengthened by a week on the Rejuvenation Diet, you will follow a progressively lighter diet, allowing all of your systems of elimination to rest and be restored. Although you will lose weight on this diet, that is not its main purpose.

Because this one-week Deep-Cleansing Diet eliminates many foods to which people have sensitivities, it also rests the immune system, which may have been producing low-level allergic reactions. Mild allergic reactions to specific foods can cause fatigue, sleeplessness, anxiety, indigestion, and many other symptoms.

Continue your regular supplement program throughout Week 2. In addition, be sure to use one tablespoon of flax seed oil every day this week with your Protein Drink, and take a GLA/EPA supplement with your evening meal. You will be getting GLA oils from the Liver Flushes and salad dressings, but because you will be eating no animal protein, you will not be getting EPA from fish in your diet. An adequate supply of the beneficial GLA and EPA oils helps to shrink fat cells that cause your figure problems. And, because toxic waste is often stored in the fat, using GLA/EPA supplements also helps to reduce your overall toxicity level through their fat-flushing properties.

I want to re-emphasize that this week's diet of raw foods, broths, and juices is a special therapeutic cleansing treatment. I do not recommend it as a regular diet for the rest of your life, although you will find many opportunities to use it in the future. If you have overindulged during the holidays, you can cleanse your system with raw foods and juices. If you are anticipating a trip or special event and want to lose some weight quickly, you can use this diet. It is also a wonderful diet for healing and nourishing your body when you are sick. However, a raw food and juice regimen is a difficult program for most people to follow on an everyday basis. I speak from personal experience. For two years, I tried to eat nothing but raw foods. I thought I was doing the best thing for myself, even though I was troubled by constant cravings for sweets and starches. I didn't realize it at the time, but my energy level was not good, I was easily over-stressed, and I felt out of balance and "spaced" most of the day. It wasn't until an observant acupuncturist saw that I was not doing well that I was finally persuaded, very reluctantly, to change. I began eating more protein foods and came back into better balance. Please pay attention to the messages your body gives you. Some people do very well on raw foods for longer periods of time, but others simply need more cooked foods and protein in their diet.

The most important determining factor in individual metabolism seems to be our ancestry. Although people have moved from their ancestral homeland, genetic and ethnic conditions persist. For example, if your ancestors lived in Scandinavia, you inherited a need for more essential fats, such as those found in fatty fish, than did those whose ancestors came from the Mediterranean, where grains, legumes, and olive oil are widespread. It's really just common sense that the diet of an Indian from Mexico who runs miles every day would not be suitable for an executive of Norwegian descent who sits at a desk all day.

According to other studies, your blood type may hold another key toward creating your most efficient nutritional program and balanced weight. According to Dr. James and Dr. Peter D'Adamo, type O is the oldest known blood type, having evolved when humans were predominantly hunter-gatherers. As a result, those with blood type O have a genetically increased need for animal protein and fat and find it virtually impossible to remain healthy on a vegetarian diet for long. Type A blood evolved later and is the predominant type in Europe and Africa. Those with type A may do very well on a vegetarian regime and, with individual variation, may find that adding fish, chicken, and turkey a few times a week is helpful. Type B evolved less than 10,000 years ago and can handle a wide variety of foods, including dairy. Type Bs need to make an effort to find a balance among several different foods rather than focusing on just one group.

When you have finished the 21-Day Program, you will be much more sensitive to the personal effects of various foods. I will encourage you to pay close attention next week as you begin to add foods back. You are the one who will best recognize the signs that something is either missing from your diet or is too heavy for your system.

Overview of Deep-Cleansing Diet Schedule

At the same time that you are giving your system a rest by eating clean, simple foods, you will be using special beverages and herbal preparations to gently flush all of your systems of elimination and clean away the toxic debris. Drinking large quantities of fluid this week, including generous quantities of your Hydrating Drink, is key.

You will begin your second week by adding a powerful detoxifying herb, chaparral, to your Inner Beauty Herbal Tea Blend. Then on Monday: Day 10, the Inner Beauty Tea will be replaced by an Herbal Purification Tea that flushes the lymph system and removes congestion and toxicity from the digestive system. Also beginning on Monday, you will start each morning with a Liver Flush, based on fruit juices, which helps trigger the liver to release stored toxins. To cleanse the kidneys and urinary system, you will drink a Diuretic Tea of special water-flushing herbs. All these beverages will be used during the cleansing period, along with an Intestinal Cleanser made up of fiber-rich seeds, which will gently sweep and tone the intestinal tract.

Later, I will describe procedures for colon cleansing, to complete the process of flushing and detoxifying all your systems of elimination.

Saturday and Sunday

You will eat only fruits and raw and cooked vegetables, eliminating animal proteins. A diet high in protein places extra stress on the kidneys, which must remove the toxic by-products of protein metabolism. Vegetables and fruits contain their own enzymes, so plant proteins are already in a predigested state and place less burden on the kidneys. Vegetables and fruits are also high in fiber content and help to clean out the intestines. Be sure that all the fruits and vegetables you eat this week are organically grown or are soaked in the hydrogen-peroxide cleanser. Pesticides and other chemicals used in commercial agriculture are very toxic and place extra stress on the liver. It is very important to avoid stress on the system during this week of cleansing.

In addition to fruits and vegetables, your menu includes protein drinks made from nuts and seeds. These high-energy beverages are an excellent source of protein. They are already partially digested, because the seeds are soaked overnight to release their enzymes. Be sure to have at least one protein drink each day, in the mid-morning. Now that you have begun to pay closer attention to your body, you may notice when your energy level drops between meals. If you feel your energy dropping in the mid-afternoon, have a second protein drink for an extra boost at that time. To assist the cleansing process, I will be asking you to add two tablespoons of granulated lecithin to one protein drink each day this week. If you do not choose to have a protein drink in the mid-afternoon, have a glass of Rejuvelac instead, to keep your intestines supplied with beneficial bacteria and promote a youthful, glowing complexion.

Your dinners this weekend are tasty vegetable soups based on Potassium Broth. Repeating the process from last Saturday, you will prepare a large batch of the Potassium Broth—some of it in the thick bisque form for the weekend soups, the thin broth set aside and frozen to use later in the week. If you would rather simply use the Potassium Broth than make any of the recommended vegetable soups, you will still get wonderful results. I am providing the variations for those who prefer them.

Your lunches for Saturday and Sunday will consist of mixed steamed vegetables. Choose as wide a variety as possible of non-starchy vegetables—broccoli, cauliflower, carrots, string beans, beets, zucchini or other summer squash, turnips, greens of all sorts, and eggplant. Include vegetables of different colors to help ensure that you are getting a wide range of nutrients. Top your steamed-vegetable plate with pressed garlic and toppings from the recipe section. If you eat lunch in a restaurant, ask for a mixed steamed vegetable plate, and bring along some topping from home, or ask for olive oil, garlic, and lemon at the restaurant.

Monday through Wednesday

You will now begin to eat only raw foods. By progressing from cooked vegetables to raw, you reduce the stress on your system even further. Heating destroys the valuable enzymes and vitamins in fresh, wholesome foods.

Your fruit breakfast will be replaced by a morning Liver Flush, based on fresh fruit juice. For lunch, have a Super Salad with the dressing of your choice. Sprinkle some granulated lecithin on your salad for additional cleansing benefits. If you usually eat your lunch in a restaurant, try to visit a salad bar that has many of the Super Salad ingredients. If you have time, this would be an excellent week to prepare some salad and dressing and bring it with you to work.

I have found that for some people a diet of raw foods exclusively can be dehydrating and even irritating. Years of improper eating can produce irritation in the ileocecal valve, between the small intestine and the colon. Raw foods can sometimes irritate the ileocecal valve even further, producing soreness and tenderness in the left side of the abdomen, about halfway between the pelvic bone and the navel. To check for an irritated ileocecal valve, press into your abdomen in this area and feel for any soreness. If you find that raw foods are irritating for you, it is perfectly all right to steam your vegetables on the raw food days. Eventually, as your intestinal tract continues to heal itself from the effects of congestion, you will be able to eat raw foods without any discomfort.

Thursday and Friday

Your diet now progresses to consuming only liquids—juices and broth. Continue with your Liver Flush for breakfast, followed by a mid-morning protein drink. For lunch, choose from a variety of tasty and healthful fresh-squeezed vegetable juices. You may also have another glass of vegetable juice or Rejuvelac in the mid-afternoon as a pick-me-up, and for dinner you will have thin Potassium Broth, as much as you wish, to which you may add a little miso for extra flavor and energy.

It is very important that you use organically grown vegetables, so your juices are free of contamination from pesticides and other chemicals. If you do not already have a juicer, I strongly recommend that you buy one. For the purposes of this program, a relatively inexpensive juicer will provide you with delicious fresh juices you can enjoy every day. For the times that you eat out, locate a juice bar in a health food store, or select from the fresh-squeezed juices that are available daily in the refrigerator section of any health food store.

Fresh raw vegetable juices have a well-deserved reputation for their powerful healing properties. Because they are rich in enzymes, they allow the digestive system to take a rest from its constant production of hydrochloric acid and digestive enzymes. Fresh juices also contain high concentrations of vitamins, minerals, trace elements, and other nutrients that help to regenerate and cleanse your entire system.

SHOPPING LIST AND INVENTORY

This weekend's shopping list includes all breakfasts, special beverages, and the base ingredients for protein drinks. Please check your daily schedules and refer to the indicated recipes so that you can buy the fresh ingredients and staples you will need for the meals you will prepare at home. As in Week 1, I want to remind you that there is room for your individual variations to the program.

If you need to make fresh juices with a juicer, check the recipes for Cleansing Juice Blends to determine what additional vegetables you will need. If you are making more Potassium Broth, replenish your supply of ingredients. If you do not wish to make the nut and seed milks and would rather substitute ready-made almond milk or soy milk in your protein drink recipes, please add them to your shopping list and omit almonds, sesame seeds, and sunflower seeds. If you are extremely busy, delicious, ready-made protein drinks available in many health food stores and juice bars would be acceptable as an occasional substitution.

Check the items marked with an asterisk and replenish them if necessary up to the quantity indicated. The Equipment Inventory lists equipment you will need for this week's activities.

cont'd.

Nuts, Grains, and Cereals

*Almonds, 1 pound
*Barley, 2 pounds
*Sesame seeds, ½ pound
*Sunflower seeds, shelled,
   unsalted, 1 ½ pounds

*Fruits and Vegetables
(organic, if possible)*

Cucumber, 1
*Garlic, 3 bulbs
Ginger, fresh, 1 large piece
Lemons, 6
Oranges, 3
Papaya, very ripe, 1
Pineapple, very ripe, 1

Vegetable Oils (cold-pressed only)

Safflower oil, 16 ounces

Beverages and Miscellaneous Foods

Apple juice, organic, 32 ounces
Carob powder, 2 ounces
Eggs (for facials), 6
*Milk (for eye packs), 1 pint
Tahini, 1-pound can
*Water, bottled if you do not have
   a water purifier, 3 gallons

*Herbs, Supplements, and
Health-Care Items*

Baking soda, 16 ounces
Castor oil, 1 small bottle
Cotton balls, sterile, small box
Dried Herbs:
   chaparral, dried, 2 ounces
   fennel seeds, 1 ounce
   fenugreek seeds, 1 ounce
   flax seeds, powdered, 3 ounces
   juniper berries, 1 ounce
   licorice root, 2 ounces
   parsley root, 1 ounce
   peppermint leaves, dried,
   2 ounces
   psyllium seeds, powdered,
   3 ounces
   uva-ursi leaves, 1 ounce
*Epsom salts, 4 pounds
Essential Oil: juniper
Petroleum jelly or lubricating
   (K-Y brand) jelly

Equipment Inventory

Balloons, thick, 1 dozen
Electric heating pad
Enema bag
Flannel, soft wool, piece 16 inch-
   es wide by 12 to 18 inches long
Garbage bag or dry cleaner's bag,
   plastic, large
Juicer (optional)

Saturday: Day 8

On Awakening: One 8-ounce glass of Hot Lemon-Water Flush (page 42). Prepare Inner Beauty Herbal Tea with Chaparral (page 49); drink throughout the day between meals. Use Cleansing Inhalant (pages 168-169).

Morning Cleansing: Dry Brush Massage (page 127). Follow with Alternating Hot and Cold Shower—begin with three to five minutes of hot water; switch to ten to fifteen seconds of cold water. Repeat three times, ending with cold water. Dry briskly with a coarse towel.

Breakfast: Sliced Fresh Pineapple Breakfast (page 54).

Mid-morning Snack: Carrot Shake (page 73) based on seed or nut milk of choice. Add one tablespoon of granulated lecithin.

Lunch: Steamed mixed vegetables with Golden Goddess Topping (page 66).

Mid-afternoon Snack: Optional—Carrot Shake (page 73) or Rejuvelac (page 47), one cup.

Afternoon Activities: Shop for week's food and supplies, see Shopping List And Inventory (pages 208-209) and Schedules for Days 8 through 14. As in Week 1, if you have decided to alter the meal plan in any way, make the necessary adjustments to your shopping list. Use Cleansing Soak for Fruits and Vegetables (page 116) for nonorganic produce. Prepare barley water for Cleopatra's Milk Bath (pages 133-134); make four times the recipe. Use one cup tonight, and freeze the other three in separate containers for later in the program. Prepare Potassium Broth (pages 44-45) for the week; refrigerate two batches of thick bisque for tonight and Sunday and freeze two batches of thin broth for later this week. (If you have any Potassium Broth left from Week 1, adjust the size of this week's recipe accordingly.)

Dinner: Carrot Bisque (page 58), as much as you wish. Make the bisque with thick Potassium Broth. Add one tablespoon of granulated lecithin.

Exercise: Precede exercise with Oxygenation Cocktail (page 47); follow with Lymph-Cleansing Warm-Up (pages 221-223) and thirty minutes of brisk walking or twenty minutes of Rebounding Workout (page160).

Evening Activity: Drink one cup of Rejuvelac (page 47). Add the remainder to tonight's bath. Tummy Massage (pages 240-241). Follow with Cleopatra's Milk Bath (pages 133-134); while in bath apply Milk Eye Packs (page 236). Just before going to bed, do Alternate-Hemisphere Breathing (pages 174-175) and take Intestinal Cleanser (page 52).

Relieving Cleansing Reactions

As you begin to eat a lighter, fiber-rich diet and to cleanse your body of the toxins and waste that have accumulated over years of abuse, clogging up your systems of elimination, you may notice certain symptoms that can be annoying or even uncomfortable—headaches, skin eruptions or other blemishes, coated tongue, low energy, grouchiness or anger, and cold or flu-like symptoms, such as runny nose and body ache. These reactions occur because the toxins are being released from the cells and dumped into your system.

Do not be disturbed if some or all of these minor symptoms appear during the course of your cleansing program. Welcome them as a good sign; they are telling you that your body is really freeing itself of wastes and toxins that may have been stored in the cells and tissues for a long time. Any minor discomfort you experience now means you will have fewer problems in the future. Be sure to drink plenty of liquids and get adequate sleep to help your body deal with the added stress of removing these toxic substances.

To help you get over these cleansing reactions as quickly and comfortably as possible, I am stressing the intense use of cleansing preparations to flush the systems of elimination. This is also why it is important for you to do colon cleansing during this program. If you do not remove the toxins promptly from the system, they will be reabsorbed.

In addition to the cleansing beverages in this week's schedule, be sure to drink plenty of Hydrating Drink. Make it a habit to drink this sweetened purified water on arising, in the mid-morning, mid-afternoon, and just before bedtime.

The granulated lecithin you will add to your protein drinks this week will help to minimize cleansing reactions by emulsifying toxins and flushing them out of your body. If you do have uncomfortable symptoms, take three 1,200-milligram lecithin capsules with a cup of black tea (the small amount of caffeine in the tea serves as a carrier for the lecithin). Lecithin helps to detoxify the liver, so it will help to relieve symptoms without interfering with the cleansing process. Additional daily colon cleansing will also be helpful in keeping symptoms to a minimum. Some people may be bothered by bad breath or offensive body odor as part of their cleansing reaction during this week. Remember that chlorophyll-rich vegetable juices can help. Refer to the list of Cleansing Juice Blends for fresh green vegetables that help to eliminate unpleasant body odors.

This week you will be cleansing all your systems of elimination. Your daily skin brushing will remove dead cells and waste that are being eliminated through the skin. You will also use several special cleansing baths and steams that speed the elimination of toxins from your system. Every morning when you brush your teeth, also be sure to brush your tongue, to remove the buildup of waste that has coated it during the night. Tongue cleaning is an ancient custom in India. Be sure not to swallow the residue you remove from your tongue; rinse your mouth thoroughly with clean purified water.

If you should get blemishes or other skin eruptions as part of your cleansing reaction, please do not resort to chemical-laden cosmetics to mask the problem. It is perfectly all right to use cosmetics made of all-natural products to cover up any blemishes. Do promote the proper functioning of your skin by keeping it absolutely clean and by getting plenty of exercise to promote sweating. The simple complexion-enhancing facials you will use during your evening activities this week will also help to cleanse and tone your skin without the use of synthetic products.

Massage will aid in flushing the toxins out of your system. This week you will perform the Lower-Body Lymph Massage that you learned on Wednesday: Day 5, as well as an Upper-Body Lymph Massage. You can also use the Quick Oriental Massage Remedies from Friday: Day 7 for help with specific problems such as headache or low energy.

Rely on affirmations to reinforce your resolve as you deal with uncomfortable cleansing reactions—"I welcome this sign that my body is cleansing itself of waste and poisons" and "Each day my body is becoming cleaner and younger inside, as my cells are being rejuvenated."

There are, of course, very positive cleansing reactions, which are just as common as some of the seemingly difficult ones. A clarity of mind, an enhanced sense of well-being, and increased creativity and intuition often accompany a cleansing of your systems of elimination, or "body filters." Many of my clients have reported new feelings of clarity and lightness and have resolved to incorporate cleansing into their lives as a result. Truly, a polluted body produces a polluted mind!

Sunday: Day 9

On Awakening: One 8-ounce glass of Hot Lemon-Water Flush (page 42). Prepare Inner Beauty Herbal Tea with Chaparral (page 49); drink throughout the day between meals. Use Cleansing Inhalant (pages 168-169).

Morning Cleansing: Dry Brush Massage (page 127), followed by warm shower.

Breakfast: Papaya Complexion Breakfast (pages 54-55).

Mid-morning Snack: Hot Mock Chocolate (page 72) based on seed or nut milk of choice. Add one tablespoon of granulated lecithin.

Lunch: Steamed mixed vegetables with Tahini-Tofu Topping (pages 67-68).

Mid-afternoon Snack: Optional—Hot Mock Chocolate (page 72) or Rejuvelac (page 47), one cup.

Dinner: Cauliflower Bisque (page 58), as much as you wish. Make the bisque with thick Potassium Broth. Add one tablespoon of granulated lecithin to the bisque.

Exercise: Precede exercise with Oxygenation Cocktail (page 47), Balloon Breathing (page 169), and Lymph-Cleansing Warm-Up (pages 221-223); thirty minutes of brisk walking or twenty minutes of Rebounding Workout (page 160).

Evening Activity: Drink one cup of Rejuvelac (page 47). Apply Egg-Yolk Mask (page 236) to face, leave on while doing Digestion Toning Postures (page 219). Follow with Aromatic Fume Bath with witch hazel (page 135). Take Intestinal Cleanser (page 52).

The Healthy Digestive System

Rejuvenation truly begins within. The key to youthful beauty is a properly functioning digestive system—an "inner spa" that functions around the clock, absorbing the nutrients needed to build fresh new cells and cleansing your body of toxic wastes that age your appearance and drain your energy.

THE STOMACH AND DUODENUM

Digestion begins in the mouth, where the teeth grind the food and saliva is released by the salivary glands. The enzyme ptyalin in saliva begins to break down the starches, converting them to sugars, and some nutrients are absorbed right in the mouth. When the food is swallowed, it travels down the esophagus, moved along by wave-like muscular contractions known as peristalsis. The food enters the stomach, where hydrochloric acid and digestive enzymes break it down into particles to be assimilated. The resultant nutrients are absorbed through the stomach wall.

The food now moves into the duodenum, which is the beginning of more than twenty feet of small intestine. Several small ducts empty into the duodenum. One comes from the gallbladder, a small sac that stores a liver secretion called bile, which helps to digest fats. Another duct deposits juices from the pancreas, which are rich in enzymes that break down partially digested proteins.

After food leaves the duodenum, most of the nutrients are absorbed in the small intestine, through tiny finger-like projections called villi. These nutrients are carried by the bloodstream and the lymph to the liver to be purified, before they are distributed to the cells of the body. Material that is not absorbed while it is in the small intestine is waste, and it passes into the colon. In a healthy colon, this waste is excreted as feces in six to twelve hours.

I am convinced, based on my observations of many clients, that undigested starches and proteins are really the root of much illness and premature aging. If we learn to eat properly, so our food is properly assimilated and eliminated, many symptoms of toxicity will be prevented, and the aging process will be slowed. Bad breath, unpleasant body odor, bags under the eyes, low back pain, obesity, cellulite—all these symptoms are produced by undigested, decomposing food in the intestine.

Dairy products and other foods that produce mucoid deposits line the intestinal walls, preventing the proper absorption of nutrients. Many people overeat simply because the nutrients in their food are not being absorbed through their mucus-coated intestinal walls. They feel hungry and eat more and more because they are starving for vital vitamins and minerals, but only the calories are readily absorbed, and so they gain weight. Eating simple, easily digestible foods in proper combinations helps to prevent the buildup of mucus deposits, so nutrients are properly absorbed and cravings are eliminated.

Place your finger on your abdomen on the pelvic bone just above your right thigh, and trace a vertical line up to just above the level of your navel. Continue across to your left side, and trace another vertical line down to the same abdominal point above your left thigh. Your finger has traced the approximate route of your colon, some five to six feet from beginning to end, including its curves and folds. (This is the area where many people mistakenly say they have a "stomachache.")

When the mixture of food and digestive juices, known as chyme, leaves the small intestine and enters the colon, it is in a semiliquid state. The first part of the colon, in the lower right abdomen, is known as the cecum. The chyme is pushed by peristaltic action from the cecum, past the area of the appendix, and up along the right side of the abdomen. As it moves along, moisture is absorbed through the colon wall into the lymphatic system, to become blood plasma. The colon makes its turn just under the right rib cage, in the area of the liver and gallbladder, and the now-mushy food moves across the abdomen above the navel, turning again just below the left rib cage in the area of the spleen and pancreas. By this time, the stool has become more solid, and as it moves downward toward the floor of the pelvis, it exerts a pressure that finally triggers the muscles to evacuate the contents.

Unfortunately, what I have described is only an ideal digestive scenario. For many people, the waste moves through the colon much too slowly, leading to constipation and irregular elimination. Once the stool gets slowed down, the colon is no longer able to exert its normal peristaltic action, its nerve signals shut down, and hard, dehydrated waste begins to lodge in pockets in the colon and to get plastered on the intestinal wall. This stagnant waste contains many toxic substances, which are gradually reabsorbed by the blood into the system, creating what is known as toxemia or toxicity.

Digestion Toning Postures

Because of mild body toxicity, I observe a wide range of symptoms in my clients who are constipated—fatigue, flatulence, headaches, irritability, nausea, nervousness, depression, protruding abdomen due to bloating, and obesity. They often have coated tongues, bad breath, body odors, dark circles under the eyes, and brittle hair and nails. While some medical authorities in the United States might disagree with this long list of symptoms, a group of England's most eminent physicians, at a meeting of the Royal Society of Medicine, presented an amazingly long list of ailments, affecting virtually every part of the body, that are caused either directly or indirectly by toxemia arising from malfunctions of the bowels.

Many factors can contribute to the slowing of bowel transit time and constipation, including improper diet, inadequate water consumption, failure to respond to the urge to eliminate, emotional stress, lack of exercise, and the use of painkillers and other medications. Regular toning exercises, such as the Digestion Toning Postures you will do this week, help to keep the abdominal organs functioning at their peak, assuring that your inner spa will be cleansing and rejuvenating your whole body.

Performing these Digestion Toning Postures on Sunday night will help to prepare you for the raw food diet you will begin on Monday. These exercises are done in the head-down, antigravity position on the slant board, bringing blood into the abdominal organs to nourish their tissues and carry away nutrients for the rest of the body. The movements are based on yoga postures designed to stimulate and tone the muscles and nerve centers that control digestion. By helping to overcome sluggishness of the stomach, intestines, and liver, these postures encourage proper elimination and speed the purification process.

Abdominal Contraction

Lying on your back on the slant board, exhale all the breath from your lungs and draw in your abdominal muscles, making your waist as small as you can. Keeping your lungs deflated, draw your chest toward your chin, tensing the abdominal muscles at the same time. Pull everything in and up inside. Then relax and breathe normally. Repeat the exercise ten times, then relax in the resting pose.

Leg Raises

Still lying on the slant board, raise both legs together. Keep the legs straight and the toes pointed. Raise your legs slowly until they are vertical with respect to the room, then lower them as slowly as possible, keeping your attention on the slow, smooth movement. Notice the toning pull in your abdominal muscles. Repeat the leg raises ten times.

Bicycling

Lying on the slant board, pedal your legs in the air, holding the legs vertical and allowing your thighs to push forcefully against the abdominal organs with each cycling motion. Pedal briskly, about two cycles per second. Keep pedaling for one to three minutes, depending on your level of fitness, feeling the beneficial toning in the abdominal organs.

Plough Posture

Lying on the slant board, raise your legs up and all the way back behind your head, as far back as you can comfortably go. Keep your knees straight and feel the pull. If you are very limber, you may be able to go all the way back and touch the board behind your head. Keep your arms at your sides, but if you need a little extra support, you may prop up your buttocks with your hands, resting on bent elbows. Once you have your feet all the way back, breathe normally and hold the pose as long as it is comfortable. For an extra stretch in the lower back, try bringing your arms back behind your head. While in the plough position, you may also try to lower your knees down toward the slant board, next to your ears, to provide a different stretch. Do not force your movements; just do what is comfortable for you. With a little practice, this posture will become much easier. Slowly lower your legs back onto the slant board and relax in the resting pose, feeling the effects of this rejuvenating yoga stretch.

Palming

Lying on the slant board, rub your palms together until you feel the heat, cup your hands over your closed eyes, and feel the relaxation spreading to the muscles of your face and all through your body. Continue palming until the heat is gone from your hands.

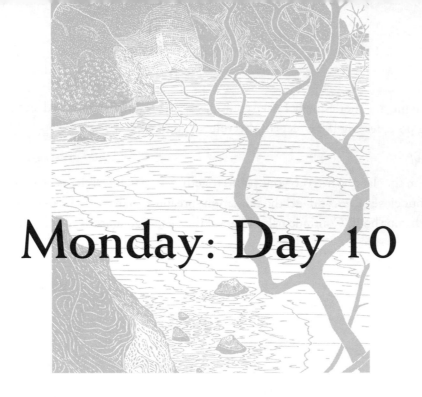

Monday: Day 10

On Awakening: One 8-ounce glass of Hydrating Drink (pages 43-44). Prepare Herbal Purification Tea for the day (page 49). Use Cleansing Inhalant (pages 168-169). Prepare protein drink for mid-day snacks.

Morning Cleansing: Dry Brush Massage (page 127), followed by Morning Cold Splash and Rub (page 185).

Breakfast: Liver Flush #1 (pages 50-51). Follow with one cup of Herbal Purification Tea; drink a second cup of the tea during the morning.

Mid-morning Snack: Tahini Shake (page 73). Add one tablespoon of granulated lecithin.

Lunch: Super Salad (pages 62-63) with Fat-Loss Dressing (pages 63 to 65) of choice. Sprinkle granulated lecithin on salad. If eating in a restaurant, order a raw vegetable salad. Bring your own dressing or use olive oil and lemon juice.

Mid-afternoon Snack: Optional—Tahini Shake (page 73) or Rejuvelac (page 47), one cup. One hour before dinner, prepare and drink one cup of Diuretic Tea (page 52).

Dinner: Raw Vegetable Delight (pages 60-61), as much as you wish.

Exercise: Precede exercise with Oxygenation Cocktail (page 47). Lymph-Cleansing Warm-Up (pages 221-223), followed by thirty minutes of brisk walking or twenty minutes of Rebounding Workout (page 160).

Evening Activity: Drink one cup of Rejuvelac (page 47). Add remainder to tonight's bath. Upper-Body Lymph Massage (pages 222-223); follow with Epsom Salts Soak with Hydrating Bath Salts (page 132). Accompany bath with Easy Steam (pages 135-136), using three drops of juniper essential oil. Drink one cup of Herbal Purification Tea before going to bed. Take Intestinal Cleanser (page 52).

Lymph-Cleansing Warm-Up

You will perform the Lymph-Cleansing Warm-up every day this week to pump the lymph forcefully through your body. Vigorous movement of the arms and legs aids in cleansing the system by encouraging waste-laden lymph to be carried away from the cells for elimination. The warm-up will take about twelve minutes. It is fun to do to music.

Marching in Place

Begin by marching briskly in place. Lift your knees in an exaggerated marching step. As you lift one leg, swing the opposite arm forward, and swing the arm on the same side as far back as it can go. Keep your arms straight but relaxed as you swing them vigorously back and forth from the shoulders. Keep your spine straight and your head high. Continue for about three minutes to really get the lymph moving. Then stop and rest in the standing position for a moment, feeling the effects of this brisk exercise.

Alternate Arm Raises

Lie on your back on the floor with your arms at your sides and your knees up, with the feet slightly separated. Raise one arm up and back so that it rests on the floor behind your head. Now, return this arm to its original position at your side, while you raise the other arm and let it rest on the floor behind your head. Keeping your arms straight, continue this alternating movement fairly rapidly, about one second for each arm raise. Breathe in as you raise one arm, and out as you raise the other. Continue for about three minutes, then relax with both arms at your sides and feel the effects of the pumping movement.

Side Leg Lifts

Lie on your right side with your legs straight and your head cradled on your right arm. Lift your left leg sideways, up toward the ceiling, keeping your toes turned in, pigeon-toed. Go slowly, stretching your leg up sideways as much as possible; take about two seconds to raise the leg and two to lower it. Continue for about two minutes, then repeat while lying on the left side. End by relaxing flat on your back for a few minutes in the resting pose. Breathe normally, feeling the stimulating effects of the leg movements.

Upper-Body Lymph Massage

This gentle upper-body self-massage, which you will perform this evening, helps to flush congested lymph out of the extremities and toward the heart, where it joins the main lymph drainage of the body. Combined with skin brushing and detoxifying baths, lymph massage also assists in rejuvenating the complexion.

Begin your massage at the neck, under the chin, in the areas where you may have sometimes noticed swollen lymph glands. Massage with the fingertips from ear to ear in a gentle circular motion, then gently stroke from the ears under the chin toward the center. Now, with your fingertips, gently stroke downward, from under the chin down the neck. Use these gentle downward stroking movements all around the neck, moving the lymph from beneath the chin and the base of the skull down into the top of your chest.

Next, using your left hand, work on the right arm, beginning at the wrist. Use your fingers to repeatedly smooth and stroke the inside of the arm, from the wrist up to the inner elbow. When you reach the inside of the elbow, gently massage with a circular motion, then continue with a light, feathery, stroking movement up the inside of the arm to the underarm. In the armpit area, gently squeeze with thumb and fingers, releasing the lymph and moving it up and out of the arm. This is another area where many lymph nodes are located, and where you may have noticed swelling when you have been sick. Stroke from the armpit up over the top of the right breast, using light, feathery strokes to bring the lymph out of the armpit and around toward the center of the chest. Guide the lymph from the right shoulder, the right arm area, and the neck, all down toward the middle of the chest.

Now, use the right hand and repeat this process, bringing the lymph up the left arm and into the armpit. Concentrate a little longer on the left side, to work the lymph out of the armpit and along the extensive lymph drainage around the heart. Draw it all in toward the center of the chest, into the area between the breasts. Now, rub in a gentle circular motion between the breasts. It is quite possible that you will feel some tenderness in this area; this simply means that there is some lymph congestion here. Do not be alarmed; just continue to gently massage, and over time the congestion will begin to be relieved. Now, massage beneath the breasts, about an inch or so below each breast, stroking gently around the bottom of the breasts toward the middle, bringing it all down into the abdomen. Stroke gently downward all the way across your chest beneath your breasts, moving the lymph into the abdomen, where the waste will be eliminated by the colon.

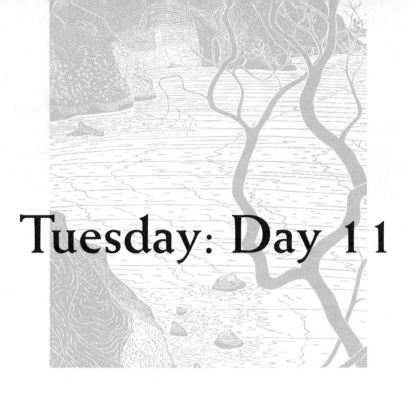

Tuesday: Day 11

On Awakening: One 8-ounce glass of Hydrating Drink (pages 43-44). Prepare Herbal Purification Tea for the day (page 49). Use Cleansing Inhalant (pages 168-169). Prepare protein drink for mid-day snacks.

Morning Cleansing: Hot shower, finishing with a one-minute cold splash. Follow with Dry Brush Massage (page 127).

Breakfast: Liver Flush #2 (page 51). Follow with one cup of Herbal Purification Tea. Drink a second cup of the tea during the morning.

Mid-morning Snack: Carrot Shake (page 73). Add one tablespoon of granulated lecithin.

Lunch: Super Salad (pages 62-63) with Fat-Loss Dressing (pages 63 to 65) of choice. Sprinkle granulated lecithin on salad. If eating in a restaurant, order a raw vegetable salad. Bring your own dressing or use olive oil and lemon juice.

Mid-afternoon Snack: Optional—Carrot Shake (page 73), or Rejuvelac (page 47), one cup. One hour before dinner, prepare and drink one cup of Diuretic Tea (page 52).

Dinner: Raw Vegetable "Cream" Soup (page 61), as much as you wish.

Exercise: Oxygenation Cocktail (page 47). Lymph-Cleansing Warm-Up (pages 221-223), followed by thirty minutes of brisk walking or twenty minutes of Rebounding Workout (page 160).

Evening Activity: Begin preparations for Chaparral Detoxifying Bath (page 227). Drink one cup of Rejuvelac (page 47). Add remainder to tonight's bath. Lower-Body Lymph Massage (pages 162-163); follow with Chaparral Detoxifying Bath. Accompany bath with Easy Steam (pages 135-136), using three drops of rose essential oil. Drink one cup of Herbal Purification Tea before going to bed. Take Intestinal Cleanser (page 52).

Constipation and Aging

Many people think their bowels are moving normally, and yet they may actually be constipated. If you must often strain to move your bowels or if you have a bloated, uncomfortable abdomen, you have symptoms of constipation. Populations who eat healthy diets of clean, whole, natural foods high in fiber do not suffer from such symptoms, and their stools are full, large, and soft.

Ideally, elimination of feces should occur in direct proportion to the amount of food eaten. This means that if you eat three meals each day, you should have three bowel movements each day. It makes sense that your colon would promptly eliminate the waste from what you eat. Of course, this goal cannot be reached overnight by people who have had long-standing problems with constipation. As you follow my suggestions on the 21-Day Program, you should find your own elimination pattern moving toward this ideal.

What happens in your colon can affect every part of your body. Putrefying waste trapped in the colon produces a number of toxic substances, some of which have been implicated as causes of cancer. These substances pass through the colon wall and enter the bloodstream and lymph, where they are carried throughout the body. These poisons can produce symptoms in the nervous system, such as headaches, depression, mental dullness, or a case of the blahs. The liver and the colon are directly connected by their blood supply. It is the liver's job to remove the toxic substances from the body by filtering impurities out of the blood. The liver can become over-taxed and damaged by all the extra toxins from the colon. Toxic and incompletely digested waste can also impair the function of the kidneys, whose job it is to filter waste from the blood before excreting excess water. A high-protein diet also places a heavy burden on the kidneys.

The skin is another organ of elimination that can be over-stressed by a constipated colon. Not only can the complexion develop wrinkles and eruptions or become sallow or blotchy as a direct result of toxic substances accumulating in the skin, but offensive body odor is also a reflection of a congested, unclean colon. Similarly, bad breath is often a sign of a toxic condition in the intestines. When the putrefying waste makes its way through the bloodstream to the lungs, it fouls the breath.

Constipation may also increase the risk for breast disease, including lumpy and cystic breasts and breast cancer. According to a 1981 report in *Lancet*, the British medical journal, a study of fifteen hundred women at a California breast clinic showed that breast diseases were relatively rare among women who had bowel movements at least once a day, while women who had two or fewer bowel movements a week had more than four times greater incidence of breast problems. More recently, the *American Journal of Public Health* reported in January 1989 that a study of seven thousand women showed a slightly increased incidence of breast cancer among women who reported constipation problems, as indicated by infrequent bowel movements or hard stools. The explanation may lie partly in the changes in intestinal flora that occur with constipation. The friendly bacteria in an unconstipated colon help detoxify bile salts and excess estrogen, which have been implicated in the development of breast lumps and cancer.

Poisons from the colon can weaken and stress the heart, cause pain and stiffness in the joints, weaken and fatigue the muscles, rob you of your beauty and your health, and age you prematurely. And it is not just the poisonous substances being reabsorbed into the bloodstream that cause problems, but a constipated colon can also bulge and press on the neighboring organs, further impairing the function of the liver, the heart, the reproductive organs, and the kidneys.

Constipation also affects the bacteria in your colon. Your intestinal tract has two very different types of bacteria. The so-called coliform bacteria are the ones that cause putrefaction, producing toxic substances. These putrefactive bacteria thrive in the oxygen-starved, alkaline environment produced by an improper diet and a constipated colon. The beneficial bacteria are Lactobacillus bacteria, primarily Lactobacillus acidophilus and Lactobacillus bifidus. These "friendly" bacteria, which require an oxygenated, acid environment, manufacture B vitamins and vitamin K in the intestine and produce digestive enzymes.

A healthy colon should contain at least 85 percent beneficial bacillus and no more than 15 percent of the coliform "bad guys." But most people in our society show a reversed ratio of 85 percent coliform and 15 percent Lactobacillus. As you cleanse your colon this week, I want you to realize you are restoring the proper balance of good bacteria. While it is possible to buy Lactobacillus supplements in a health food store, I recommend that you promote the good bacteria in your intestines by drinking Rejuvelac every day, as I have indicated on the schedule. Many health food stores carry ready-made Rejuvelac in the refrigerator section. It is full of Lactobacillus species and other friendly bacteria. It contains natural lactic acid, which helps to destroy the harmful bacteria, and enzymes that help digestion. No wonder Rejuvelac has earned a reputation for promoting a beautiful complexion. Clear, youthful skin is simply a reflection of a clean, healthy colon.

Chaparral Detoxifying Bath

A chaparral soak cleanses and detoxifies the blood, kidneys, liver, lymph, and thymus gland. Because chaparral is a powerful detoxifying agent, it helps to minimize cleansing reactions. Many people report that they feel "like new" after a chaparral bath, thanks to its restorative and deep-cleansing action.

Chaparral promotes immune-system functioning and fights bacteria and viruses. It contains a substance called NDGA, which prevents harmful oxidative processes that can lead to aging of the tissues.

Prepare a strong batch of chaparral bath tea at least one hour ahead of time, as follows:

4 tablespoons dried chaparral herb or 4 droppersful of tincture
1 quart purified water

Boil the water, remove from the heat, add the chaparral, and steep, covered, for one hour. Add the entire batch of chaparral tea (with the herb strained out) to a medium-to-hot bath. Soak in the tub for about twenty minutes, then dry quickly, wrap in a warm robe or towel, and lie down. Because chaparral flushes toxins out of the tissues so efficiently, it is a good idea to rest for ten to twenty minutes after your soak.

Wednesday: Day 12

On Awakening: Drink one 8-ounce glass of Hydrating Drink (pages 43-44). Prepare Herbal Purification Tea for the day (page 49). Use Cleansing Inhalant (pages 168-169). Prepare protein drink for mid-day snacks.

Morning Cleansing: Warm shower followed by Dry Brush Massage (page 127).

Breakfast: Liver Flush #1 (pages 50-51). Follow with one cup of Herbal Purification Tea. Drink a second cup of the tea during the morning.

Mid-morning Snack: Maple Nut Shake (page 72). Add one tablespoon of granulated lecithin.

Lunch: Super Salad (pages 62-63) with Spa Salsa (page 66). Sprinkle granulated lecithin on salad. If eating in a restaurant, order a raw vegetable salad. Bring your own dressing or use olive oil and lemon juice.

Mid-afternoon Snack: Optional—Maple Nut Shake (page 72) or Rejuvelac (page 47), one cup. One hour before dinner, prepare and drink one cup of Diuretic Tea (page 52).

Dinner: Raw Vegetable "Cream" Soup (page 61) with variation of choice, as much as you wish.

Exercise: Oxygenation Cocktail (page 47). Lymph-Cleansing Warm-Up (pages 221-223), followed by thirty minutes of brisk walking or twenty minutes of Rebounding Workout (page 160).

Evening Activity: Drink one cup of Rejuvelac (page 47). Add the remainder to tonight's bath. Professional Colon Cleansing or a Cleansing Enema (pages 241-243) accompanied by Tummy Massage (pages 240-241). Follow with Cleopatra's Milk Bath (pages 133-134). While in bath apply Milk Eye Packs (page 236). Drink one cup of Herbal Purification Tea before going to bed. Take Intestinal Cleanser (page 52).

Colon Cleansing

A great deal of the waste that you want to remove from your body during the cleansing program will end up in the colon—not only the residue from your food, but also toxic waste that has been delivered into the colon by the lymph system. Your body cannot be completely clean as long as your colon is blocked, so it is essential during any cleansing program to remove all the debris from the colon. I also consider colon cleansing an essential part of any truly effective weight-loss program, since it helps to remove toxins from the body that might otherwise end up being stored in the excess fat cells.

Laxatives are not sufficient for cleaning the colon; in fact, laxatives dehydrate the body and often leave old layers of dried feces on the colon wall, allowing only more recent waste to push through and evacuate. Even though the bowels are being evacuated, a condition of constipation exists, causing degeneration of the nerves and muscles of the colon, so that even more laxatives are needed.

A much better way to cleanse the colon is to flush it with clean, purified water. Colon hydrotherapy was first recorded in 1500 B.C. in the Ebers Papyrus. In the fourth and fifth centuries B.C., Hippocrates reported using enemas for treating fevers, and the Essenes used water therapy to rid the colon of uncleanliness and the body of disease. In modern times, colonic irrigation was quite popular among some physicians in the 1920s, 1930s, and 1940s, and then it fell out of favor. Now, with safe, effective, and sterile equipment, colonic irrigation is once again being recognized as a valuable adjunct to health care.

In fact, many Hollywood stars since the early 1900s have used colon cleansing as their "secret" for maintaining their youth and beauty until well into their 70s and 80s. Mae West was well-known for her gorgeous complexion. According to her biographer, George Eells, she often taunted reporters with her beauty secret; she finally revealed that her much speculated-on secret lay in her obsession with a clean colon. She took one colonic weekly for many, many years. Many stars since Mae West, including Gloria Swanson, have been dedicated to regular colon cleansing as the key to their beauty and health. In fact, although I am not at liberty to divulge their names, I know that many of today's Hollywood stars and top New York models have weekly colonics to help maintain their youthful complexion and vitality.

Colonic irrigation is a gentle warm-water washing of the colon that cleanses the entire length from the rectum all the way up to the cecum at the beginning of the colon. To receive a colonic, you lie on your side and the colon hygienist inserts a small disposable tube in the anus. At the foot of the table, a hygienic colonic-irrigation machine regulates the water pressure, temperature, and volume. As you relax on your back, the water is slowly and gently infused into your colon. Before any excessive pressure is felt, the direction of water flow is reversed, and the contents of the colon are evacuated through the tube. The most important thing for you to do during this process is to relax.

Most people are amazed at how much mucus, feces, and excess gas is removed from the colon during their first colonic. And after expressing their initial skepticism, most people find a colonic to be a very pleasant, relaxing experience.

You may wonder whether you will become dependent on colonics, but actually the opposite is true. When colonics are done properly, with a low-pressure technique, they exercise and tone the muscles of the colon, improving its peristaltic activity. Remember, one colonic is not enough to completely empty the colon. At the Inner Beauty Institute, we usually recommend that our clients begin with four to six sessions over about a four-week period. Clients who choose to go on to do a deeper cleansing after that usually require many more sessions, depending on their health history, age, and personal objectives. I remind my clients that it took many years to build up the congestion and it will not disappear in only a few sessions. Your 21-Day Program is a wonderful beginning, and I encourage you to discuss a longer series with your colon therapist.

There are many rumors circulating about colon hydrotherapy. For example, you may have heard that a colonic will wash away the beneficial bacteria in the colon. On the contrary, if your colon has been constipated for some time, it is really helpful to flush away the putrefactive bacteria that have accumulated there. A colon-cleansing program, along with a proper diet, will help to change the environment in the colon to make it more hospitable to the beneficial Lactobacillus bacteria. Colon therapists generally recommend supplementary bacteria for nutritional support while the colon is getting back into proper balance.

Colonic irrigations not only clean the colon, they also produce a feeling of well-being. We tend to have a lot of negative mental programming about our eliminative systems, and in fact, the taboos about elimination often contribute to constipation problems. Colonic irrigations can help to create a new awareness of how it feels to release and let go of the waste that has been trapped in your body. After a series of colonic irrigations, you may also feel an increased energy level, your skin will be radiant and your eyes clear, and your digestion will be better than ever.

People bothered by protruding abdomens and excess weight find immediate relief with a colonic. During a cleansing program, they often eliminate as much as five to fifteen pounds just from cleaning out their intestines, and when the accumulated gas is removed along with the excess feces, their tummies become flat.

One of the most rewarding parts of my work is seeing the truly miraculous changes that occur after clients have had colonic irrigations. One of my clients, named Marlene, is the owner of a travel agency. She does a great deal of traveling in the course of her business, and a combination of restaurant and airline food, jet lag, and stress had caused her to develop a severe constipation problem over the years. Even before she came to me for help, she had known that her body was toxic. Marlene had begun to clean up her diet, and she was making an effort to get more sleep and regular exercise. Even though she had improved her lifestyle, it had not really helped her constipation problem. She still was not eliminating more than a couple of times a week. As a result, her system was very toxic. She had terrible headaches, and she dreaded her menstrual periods because they were so uncomfortable. Her skin was very blotchy, and she felt generally sluggish.

Marlene heard about my clinic in Sausalito from friends in the airline industry who were my clients, and finally, she came to see me in desperation. After consulting our physician, she began her cleansing program with a series of colonics. After about three months, Marlene's skin was really beginning to clear, its texture had improved, and she had developed a healthy glow. Her headaches had also gone away, and her periods were becoming much more comfortable. For someone else with similar symptoms, who had not already made an effort to improve her diet, it might have taken much longer to eliminate the symptoms of toxicity. In Marlene's case, the colonics made all the difference in turning things around and changing her whole outlook on life.

While having your colonic, use the breathing techniques and affirmations you have already learned during this program. Take nice deep breaths into the abdomen, especially if you feel any cramping. Practicing deep-breathing techniques will help you to achieve a deeper release. If you feel a little apprehensive because this is your first colonic or because you are not accustomed to having a stranger touch that part of your body, use your affirmations and breathing to calm and center yourself. Do not be afraid to discuss your feelings with the therapist; it is part of the colon hygienist's job to help you relax and to allay your anxieties.

How to Select a Colon Therapist

On Wednesday: Day 12 this week, and Saturday: Day 15 and Tuesday: Day 18 during Week 3, you are scheduled for a colon cleansing. Ideally, all three of these cleansings should be performed by a professional colon hygienist. Three professional colon cleansings may cost more money than you can afford at this time, or you may not be able to locate a colon hygienist in your area, so I have also provided instructions for giving yourself a cleansing enema at home (see Day 14). If it is at all possible, however, please arrange for at least one colonic irrigation with a professional, since this will be a much more effective cleansing treatment than an enema. Preferably, if you can have only one professional colonic, schedule it ahead of time for Saturday: Day 15. If you find that you are only able to have your professional colonic(s) on a different day than I have recommended, it's absolutely fine. You may even decide to have more than the three sessions I have scheduled. That's great! Remember, you will get excellent results from this program even if you do it differently than I have suggested.

As always, the best source of information about a colon hygienist is through personal referrals. Ask your friends if they can recommend a colon hygienist in your area. If not, contact the International Association of Colon Hydrotherapy at 210-366-2888 for a referral. If no one is listed in your area, look in the yellow pages of your telephone directory under Colonic Irrigation. In some states, you will not find this listing. In that case, look under Naturopaths, Chiropractors, Holistic Health Care, or Health Spas—these practitioners and facilities may be able to refer you to a colon therapist. You can also ask for referrals at your local health food store or look in the classified section of an alternative newspaper such as *Common Ground*. You might also call a local hospital and ask to speak with a nurse on duty; at least one nurse will probably know of colonic-irrigation facilities in the area.

Once you have the name of a colon therapist, you are ready to phone and ask questions to determine whether this person is the right professional for you. Here are some questions to ask and points to cover in the conversation.

1. Ask if the colon hygienist uses modern equipment, as opposed to the older gravity-style equipment, which is harder to sterilize. The newer kind of equipment is characterized by separate inflow and outflow water systems and, when entering the colon, uses low water pressure.

2. Ask whether the hygienist uses disposable tubing and speculum. Disposable equipment has become the standard for the modern practice of colon therapy. If the therapist does not use disposable equipment and is the only person available, ask how the tubing is sterilized. The only acceptable method is autoclaving.

3. Ask if the hygienist uses filtered water for the colonic irrigation. This has become a standard of good practice.

4. Ask the hygienist if he or she provides nutritional counseling in the session. Prevention of future constipation problems is one of the primary objectives of colon hygiene, and proper diet is the key.

5. Ask if the hygienist is familiar with the use of abdominal massage during the colonic. Massage helps to release trapped material from the colon.

6. Ask whether the therapist offers an herbal steam in addition to the colonic irrigation. Many do not, but if you find someone who does offer it, be sure to take advantage of it, because it really enhances the cleansing process.

If a colonic irrigation is a completely new experience for you, it is important that the hygienist put you at ease about the procedure. But no matter how pleasant the therapist sounds on the phone, look elsewhere if he or she is not using modern, disposable, or properly sterilized equipment.

Thursday: Day 13

On Awakening: One 8-ounce glass of Hydrating Drink (pages 43-44). Prepare Herbal Purification Tea (page 49). Use Cleansing Inhalant (pages 168-169). Prepare protein drink for mid-day snacks.

Morning Cleansing: Dry Brush Massage (page 127). Follow with Alternating Hot and Cold Shower—begin with three to five minutes of hot water; switch to ten to fifteen seconds of cold water. Repeat three times, ending with cold water. Dry briskly with a coarse towel.

Breakfast: Liver Flush #2 (page 51). Follow with one cup of Herbal Purification Tea. Drink a second cup of the tea during the morning.

Mid-morning Snack: Sesame Seed Milk (page 71). Add one tablespoon of granulated lecithin.

Lunch: Cleansing Juice Blend (page 53), as much as you want.

Mid-afternoon Snack: Optional—Eight ounces of Cleansing Juice Blend (page 53) or Rejuvelac (page 47), one cup. One hour before dinner, prepare and drink one cup of Diuretic Tea (page 52).

Dinner: Potassium Broth (pages 44-45), as much as you wish. If desired for an extra boost, add miso to taste, up to one teaspoon per cup.

Exercise: Oxygenation Cocktail (page 47). Lymph-Cleansing Warm-Up (pages 221-223), followed by thirty minutes of brisk walking or twenty minutes of Rebounding Workout (page 160).

Evening Activity: Drink one cup of Rejuvelac (page 47). Add remainder to tonight's bath. Apply Oatmeal-Egg White Pack (page 236); leave on while doing Yoga Self-Massage (pages 194-199). Remove facial and take hot Epsom Salts Soak (pages 132). Accompany bath with Easy Steam (pages 135-136), using three drops of chamomile essential oil. Drink one cup of Herbal Purification Tea before going to bed. Take Intestinal Cleanser (page 52).

Using Affirmations: A Cleansing Diet for the Mind

Perhaps this week's diet is a completely new experience for you. You may find it difficult to let go of foods that have always been sources of comfort and security. An excellent tool to help you hold to your resolve is to use affirmations every day. Affirmations are simply positive statements that keep you focused on your purpose and help to remind you that you are doing something wonderful for your body. You first used affirmations on this program when you repeated positive phrases such as "Peace, harmony, and well-being" on your daily walks. Now I will show you some other ways to use these powerful self-programming tools.

Every time you sit down to eat a meal, use an affirmation to dedicate the food to your well-being. In your mind or out loud, say something like "I am giving my body a wonderful gift by following this program" or "I am rejuvenating my body with this wonderful cleansing food." When you wake up in the morning, use affirmations to create a positive, optimistic frame of mind. Tell yourself something like "My body feels alive and wonderful. I feel healthy and rejuvenated." When you are tempted to stray from your diet or to ignore other elements of this program, use an affirmation to keep yourself on track, such as "I release all negative thoughts" or "I will feel wonderful after I do my exercise."

As you cleanse your body this week, negative thoughts and emotions may come up. Use affirmations to reprogram your unconscious mind, to truly express love for yourself and recognize that you are taking care of yourself. When you experience negative thoughts or disturbing emotions, use an affirmation such as "I welcome the opportunity to cleanse myself of old negative feelings."

Fill your journal with affirmations and bring it with you to work, so you can reinforce your resolve during the day. Filling your mind with positive thoughts actually changes the way you feel. Try it—affirmations are a powerful tool and a wonderful habit to develop.

Beauty-Bonus Facials

During a cleansing program, it is important to pay close attention to your skin, since some toxins released from your cells will be excreted through your pores. Facials help to tone and balance your skin, keeping it silky, healthy, and clean.

Egg-Yolk Mask

Separate the yolk from the white of an egg and save the white for use in the oatmeal-egg white pack listed below. Beat the yolk until it is frothy, and dab it onto your face, allowing it to dry and harden. Rinse the dried egg yolk from your face with cold water. The egg-yolk mask helps to moisturize dry skin.

Oatmeal-Egg White Pack

Mix one handful of raw oatmeal with one egg white and a few drops of fresh lemon juice to form a paste. Spread the paste on your face and throat, rubbing it into the areas around the chin and nose. As you allow this facial mask to dry, you will feel it soothing and tightening your skin. Remove it with splashes of cold water. This facial mask helps to smooth rough, bumpy skin and tighten wrinkles and furrows.

Milk Eye Packs

Dip cotton balls in warm or cold milk and place them over your eyes while you soak in your bath. Milk helps to cleanse and nourish the delicate skin around your eyes.

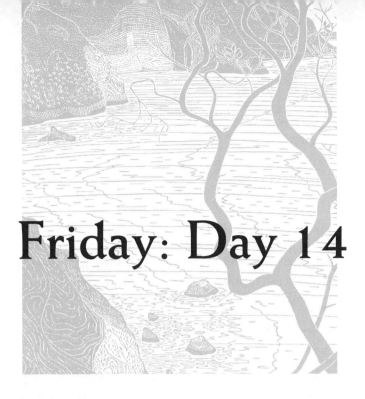

Friday: Day 14

On Awakening: One 8-ounce glass of Hydrating Drink (pages 43-44). Prepare Herbal Purification Tea for the day (page 49). Use Cleansing Inhalant (pages 168-169). Prepare protein drink for mid-day snacks.

Morning Cleansing: Morning Cold Splash and Rub (page 185), followed by Dry Brush Massage (page 127).

Breakfast: Liver Flush #1 (pages 50-51). Follow with one cup of Herbal Purification Tea. Drink a second cup of the tea during the morning.

Mid-morning Snack: Carrot Shake (page 73). Add one tablespoon of granulated lecithin.

Lunch: Cleansing Juice Blend of choice (page 53), as much as you want.

Mid-afternoon Snack: Optional—Eight ounces of Cleansing Juice Blend (page 53) or Rejuvelac (page 47), one cup. One hour before dinner, prepare and drink one cup of Diuretic Tea (page 52).

Dinner: Potassium Broth (pages 44-45), as much as you wish. If desired for an extra boost, add miso to taste, up to one teaspoon per cup.

Exercise: Oxygenation Cocktail (page 47). Lymph-Cleansing Warm-Up (pages 221-223), followed by thirty minutes of brisk walking or twenty minutes of Rebounding Workout (page 160).

Evening Activity: (At-home night)*:* Begin preparations for chaparral detoxifying bath (page 227). Drink one cup of Rejuvelac (page 47). Add remainder to tonight's bath. Hot Castor-Oil Abdominal Wrap (pages 239-240). While wrap is on, do Three-Part Breathing (pages 172-173) and Complete Breath (pages 173-174), and simply relax. Follow with Chaparral Detoxifying Bath. Accompany bath with Easy Steam (pages 135-136), using three drops of rosemary essential oil. Drink one cup of Herbal Purification Tea before going to bed. Take Intestinal Cleanser (page 52).

Dinner: Potassium Broth (pages 44-45), as much as you wish. If desired for an extra boost, add miso to taste, up to one teaspoon per cup.

Exercise: Oxygenation Cocktail (page 47). Lymph-Cleansing Warm-Up (pages 221-223), followed by thirty minutes of brisk walking or twenty minutes of Rebounding Workout (page 160).

Evening Activity: Drink one cup of Rejuvelac (page 47). Add remainder to tonight's bath. Apply Oatmeal-Egg White Pack (page 236); leave on while doing Yoga Self-Massage (pages 194-199). Remove facial and take hot Epsom Salts Soak (page 132). Accompany bath with Easy Steam (pages 135-136), using three drops of chamomile essential oil. Drink one cup of Herbal Purification Tea before going to bed. Take Intestinal Cleanser (page 52).

Self-Cleansing Methods

You are scheduled for three colon cleansings as part of this 21-Day Program—on Wednesday: Day 12, Saturday: Day 15, and Tuesday: Day 18. I recommend that at least one colonic irrigation be with a professional, but I've provided the following instructions for giving yourself an enema at home. The Hot-Castor Oil Abdominal Wrap and Tummy Massage are excellent ways to prepare yourself for this procedure.

Hot Castor-Oil Abdominal Wrap

A perfect way to end your cleansing fast on Friday: Day 14 and to prepare for a colonic irrigation is to use a Hot Castor-Oil Abdominal Wrap. This abdominal wrap has the same benefits as expensive herbal wraps in a salon, but its effects are more lasting. The Hot Castor-Oil Wrap helps to break down the toxins stored in the tissues and to loosen the waste in the colon, so it can be flushed away. The wrap also helps to detoxify the lymph system, since the major lymph drainage goes into the colon. At the Inner Beauty Institute, we have observed that the results of colon cleansing are enhanced when a Hot Castor-Oil Wrap is used the night before.

This castor-oil wrap was popularized by the renowned psychic Edgar Cayce, who recommended it in thousands of his health readings. Many health practitioners, including myself, follow some of Cayce's recommendations. This wrap is useful for a wide variety of problems, including headaches, abdominal tenderness, problems with the digestive system and the sex organs, menstrual cramps, and muscular tension. In addition, the Hot Castor-Oil Wrap has a particularly relaxing effect on the nervous system. It is sometimes available in health food stores.

To make your own Hot Castor-Oil Abdominal Wrap, you will need the following materials:

4 ounces of castor oil	*Electric heating pad*
Bowl or pan	*Large plastic bag (such as a garbage bag or*
Piece of large, soft wool flannel,	*dry cleaner's bag)*
16 inches by 12 to 18 inches	*Large towel to lie on*

Pour some of the castor oil into the bowl or pan and soak the flannel cloth in the oil. Then wring it out thoroughly, so that the cloth is just moist; it should not be dripping wet. Now, fold the cloth in half, so it measures eight inches in one dimension. It will reach from the groin up to just under the breasts. The long side, twelve to eighteen inches, will reach all the way across the abdomen. Place a towel on your bed to avoid soiling. Plug in the heating pad by your bedside.

Lie down and place the folded cloth over your abdomen, then place the plastic bag over the cloth, and tuck it underneath you. Finally, position the heating pad over the entire arrangement and set it to medium heat.

Enjoy the wonderfully soothing benefits of the abdominal wrap for at least one and one-half hours, or up to two to three hours if you wish. Relax, watch TV, read, do some gentle breathing exercises, or just do nothing. Some people simply fall asleep because the Castor-Oil Wrap is so calming.

While this wrap is designed to be used over the front of the abdomen, you can apply it to other parts of your body as well. For example, if you are having low back problems or kidney problems, it is fine to use it on your back.

When you are finished using the Hot Castor-Oil Abdominal Wrap, place the moist flannel cloth in a plastic bag and keep it in your refrigerator. You can use it over and over, as many times as you wish.

Remove the castor oil from your skin by taking a bath with two tablespoons of baking soda dissolved in it, or simply let the castor oil continue to soak in overnight for extra moisturizing benefits.

No one really knows exactly why this Castor-Oil Wrap works. The oil from the castor bean has long been a popular folk remedy. It has been applied externally for all sorts of skin problems, rubbed on the breasts to increase the flow of milk, and rubbed into the chest to relieve chest colds or bronchitis. It is also used as a base in lipstick and other makeup, because it is so stable and soothing to the skin.

Although I am recommending the Hot Castor-Oil Wrap specifically for the purpose of cleansing, it also has a tremendously calming effect on the central nervous system, helping people to fall asleep with ease.

Tummy Massage

Become familiar with this Tummy Massage before attempting to give yourself an enema. A colon therapist will administer a similar massage when you receive your professional colonic irrigation. When used along with colon cleansing, this Tummy Massage helps to loosen deposits in the colon and to gently work the waste down toward the rectum to be eliminated.

Lie on your back on a firm surface with your knees up, to relax the colon and abdominal organs. Warm a little castor oil in your hands and start on the lower right side of your abdomen, massaging with your fingers in a circular motion. Press as deeply as is comfortable. As you massage deeply, you may encounter areas that are tender. Do not be alarmed by this; just make note of the tender places. Breathe into them and massage them away.

Continue to work your way up the right side to just below the rib cage, then move across the upper abdomen above the navel, massaging deeply in firm circular motions, again noting any tender areas. You may feel some hard masses as you move across the abdomen, which may be congestion in your colon. Move across the tummy to your left side. Work slowly, trying to relax into any area that feels tender. These tender areas provide you with feedback on where your colon may be congested.

Now work your way down along the left side of your abdomen. Massage deeply, all the way down to the pelvic bone on the left. You have now massaged all along the course of the colon, following the natural direction in which the waste moves out of your body.

Once you have gone around the colon, go up again under the rib cage on the right. This area is the home of your liver. Massage there and feel if there is any hardness or tenderness. Then massage below the rib cage in the middle of the abdomen. Press in under the rib cage; this is the solar plexus, where the diaphragm is located. We often hold a lot of tension and stress in this area. If anything feels tender or tight, breathe into it to loosen it up and really relax. As you massage, you will feel a release of tension. Massage under the left side of the rib cage, in the area of the spleen, breathing and relaxing into any tender spots.

Allow fifteen or twenty minutes for your Tummy Massage, ending with palming of the abdomen. Generate heat in your hands by rubbing your palms together, and then lay your hands on your abdomen in any area that feels tight or where you feel you want to direct healing, loving energy. Allow the warmth to go into your tummy, into all your abdominal organs, helping them to let go of the waste, congestion, and tension.

How to Give Yourself a Cleansing Enema

In our culture, we do not grow up associating colon cleansing with regular health maintenance. Yet many of the great natural-healing clinics insist that clients on fasting programs take one or two enemas every day to facilitate the detoxification process. I realize that many people still cling to the old destructive taboos and fears about this part of their body. If you do have inhibitions, try to break through and allow yourself to do colon cleansing during this program. The overall benefits will be greatly enhanced.

If for some reason you are not able to obtain colonic irrigations, you can give yourself a gentle cleansing enema at home instead. You can also have both colonics and enemas. Enemas are not able to flush the entire colon as effectively as a colonic, but they can still be very helpful. Do not hesitate to give yourself an enema every day this week if you happen to be troubled by cleansing reactions. The enema will really help to clear up any uncomfortable symptoms.

To give yourself an enema, use any standard enema bag from the drugstore. Also buy some petroleum jelly or lubricating (K-Y) jelly.

I recommend that you give yourself the enema lying on your slant board, since lying in the head-down antigravity position helps the water to travel farther into the colon. You can also lie on the floor or in your bathtub—wherever is more comfortable for you. Prepare the area where you will be doing the enema by arranging a towel to lie on. Find a place where you can hang the bag so that the bottom of the bag is about one or two feet above your rectum. It is very important not to hang the bag too high, because you want the water to trickle in slowly and gently.

Fill the enema bag with warm purified water. Add a couple of drops of fresh lemon juice to help break up fecal impactions. Be careful not to get any seeds in the bag. Unclamp the tube and let a little water run out of the enema nozzle to remove air from the tubing. Then clamp the tube shut, hang the enema bag, and lie on your back with your knees up. Apply a small amount of petroleum jelly or lubricating jelly to the tip of the enema tube and gently insert the tip into your rectum. Release the clamp and let the water trickle in slowly, as much as you can comfortably hold. This first fill will be going into the lower portion of the colon, on the left side of the abdomen. Let the water run in until you just begin to sense discomfort—perhaps pressure at the rectum or a general feeling of fullness. Stop at this point, clamp the tube, and go to the toilet. If you are able, hold the water in for a moment, and massage your abdomen gently on the lower left side to work the water up into the colon and loosen the material before you go to the toilet.

After you have evacuated your bowel, return to the enema setup and lie on your left side. Once again let the water gently trickle in so that you stop just before you sense discomfort or urgency. This time hold the water in if you can. Massage from the lower right abdomen up the right side, across the top of the abdomen, and down the left side, as you did when you practiced your Tummy Massage. You will be loosening the waste and working it out of your colon. Evacuate again, and then fill your colon one more time, this time lying on the right side. Let the water run slowly in, as much as you can hold. You will feel the water gurgling around. You want it to go as far in as it can, down into the right side of the colon. Massage once again up the right side, across the top of the abdomen, and down the left side, to break up pockets of hardened waste.

On the second and subsequent fills with the enema, use as much water as you comfortably can, and then allow your bowels to completely empty themselves. With each successive evacuation, you will be able to hold more water in your colon, since more space will be emptied out. The more water you can get into your colon, the more effective the enema will be.

You may find it somewhat awkward to lie on your side on the slant board. However, as you become more familiar with the entire enema procedure, you will be able to move around a little more easily and do more massaging.

After your enema, you may feel quite sleepy, or you may feel surprisingly invigorated. Allow time after your enema to relax quietly, and do not get too far away from the toilet, because you may still feel the urge to evacuate your bowels.

Closing, Week Two

As you practice effective and safe cleansing of your systems of elimination, you will become more sensitive to the miraculous workings of your body. Just as you have released the waste from your cells, tissues, and organs, you have also released negative emotional and mental patterns. The cleansing process brings body, mind, emotions, and spirit into greater harmony. You should now be feeling lighter, clearer, and wonderfully rejuvenated.

Integration Phase

INTRODUCTION:
Awaken Your Sleeping Beauty

Congratulations! You have arrived at the third and final week of your Rejuvenation Program. If you have followed the program faithfully, I am sure you are now feeling wonderfully light and clear. I remember that when I first experimented with juice fasting many years ago, I was amazed at how dramatically different I felt. I experienced a sustained clarity of mind that was entirely new for me, and a constant flow of energy replaced my usual daily ups and downs. During the first two weeks of the 21-Day Program, you have eliminated the foods that generally cause people problems. This week, as you begin to add foods back, you have an opportunity to discover how these various foods have been affecting you.

The goal of this program is to rid your body of toxins, awakening the sleeping beauty within you. This beauty may have been concealed by layers of internal pollution from years of incorrect eating, stress, and accumulated waste. Each chapter of this book has focused on a method of cleansing and detoxifying your body, to free the lovely, vital you who slumbers within. This week you will begin to integrate these techniques into your everyday life.

To complete the intensive releasing and cleansing process of Week 2, you will begin Week 3 with a professional colonic irrigation on Saturday or an at-home enema if you have not been able to locate a professional colon therapist. On Sunday, you will reward yourself with a relaxing professional massage, which will help to flush the toxins out of your system. Remember, if you find that it is more appropriate for you to schedule your colonic or massage on other days, it's absolutely fine. If you wish to have more colonics and massages than I have recommended, that will only enhance the results. I encourage you to discover your individual rhythm with the program.

This week's diet plan returns gradually to the Rejuvenation Diet (or Elimination Phase), which you followed during Week 1. You will break your two-day liquid fast with two days of raw fruits and vegetables, followed by two days of raw and cooked fruits and vegetables. Be sure to have at least one protein drink on these days, in the mid-morning or mid-afternoon or both—whenever you feel the need for an energy boost. If you tend to be hungry or to have a drop in energy in the mid-morning or mid-afternoon, you may continue one protein drink each day when you return to the Rejuvenation Diet, Days 19 to 21. If you do not choose to have a protein drink at either of these times, have a glass of Rejuvelac to help cultivate friendly intestinal bacteria and keep your complexion smooth and glowing. To aid in digestion when you re-introduce proteins to your body, you will have a glass of Apple-Cider Vinegar Drink before each mid-day meal.

This week, I will show you how to vary the Rejuvenation Diet to meet your body's particular needs and to make it easier to practice proper food combining for the rest of your life. I will ask you to pay attention to any cravings you may experience and to watch how you feel as you re-introduce various foods into your diet. By noticing how your body reacts, you will be able to find the foods that bring out the very best in you.

During Week 2, you flushed your systems of elimination with cleansing beverages, detoxifying baths, an intestinal cleanser, and an enema or colonic. To help you preserve your light, high feeling, I will show you how to keep your eliminative systems clean and clear by making the right choices in diet and health practices, so toxic waste never builds up in your system again. Unfortunately, we are not taught simple tools for cleansing in our culture. If constipation has been a problem for you in the past, I will give you specific guidelines that will end constipation once and for all.

This week, you will also learn how to fight cellulite—that lumpy, puckered fatty tissue that you may have been trying to get rid of for years without success. I will recommend specific diet choices to help control cellulite, and I will provide many tips about how to keep cellulite out of your body forever, including a technique for cellulite self-massage to help break up and dissolve those unsightly bulges. If you are one of the lucky few who do not presently have cellulite problems, I will help you to prevent the formation of cellulite.

Last night, you treated yourself with a Hot Castor-Oil Abdominal Wrap—an excellent way to end your juice-and-broth fast and to prepare for this Saturday's colon cleansing. This wrap is similar to the herbal wraps used for detoxification in expensive spas; it loosens up the toxins in your lymph system and loosens the material that will be rinsed away in your colonic. You will do another Castor-Oil Wrap on Monday: Day 17, before the final colon cleansing of the program.

I hope you were able to arrange for a massage therapist to come to your home this Sunday, so you can benefit from an entire afternoon of relaxation and rejuvenation. To prepare for your massage, you will do Father Kneipp's footbath, to help loosen up the lymph and decongest the lower part of your body, maximizing the cleansing effects of your massage. Sunday evening, after your massage, you will take a fume bath with witch hazel to continue the cleansing and flushing action. You will conclude your Sunday activities with the Yoga Arch Pose Variations, followed by the tensing-and-releasing exercise from the Yoga Stress Releasers. I will teach you special Yoga Rejuvenation Postures and show you other ways to nourish and stimulate your glandular system to guarantee you many added years of vitality.

This week, you will also continue your regular warm-up and exercise activities, and you will practice your breathing exercises, to cleanse and oxygenate all your cells and tissues. Both exercise and correct breathing will help to eliminate constipation and cellulite from your life.

Remember that you do not have to be on a special 21-Day Program to enjoy these self-nurturing activities. You can treat yourself to a massage with a footbath and herbal steam anytime you wish. I recommend that you do so on a regular basis.

As you encourage your body to build healthy, youthful cells to replace the old ones that are constantly dying and being eliminated, you turn back the clock on the aging process. Rejuvenation is the key to a more youthful and more satisfying life.

SHOPPING LIST AND INVENTORY: *WEEK THREE*

This weekend's shopping list includes staple foods that you will need for the final week of the program, including all breakfasts and special beverages, and the base ingredients for protein drinks. Please check your daily schedules and refer to the indicated recipes so that you can buy the fresh ingredients for the lunches and dinners you wish to prepare at home. As in Weeks 1 and 2, I encourage you to allow for your individual variations in planning for your meals and other recipes. If you have decided to purchase ready-made items, make the necessary adjustments to your shopping list. If you are making more Potassium Broth, replenish your supply of ingredients.

Check your stock of all items marked with an asterisk and replenish them if necessary up to the indicated quantity.

Nuts, Grains, and Cereals
*Almonds,½ pound
*Barley, 1 pound
*Sesame seeds, ½ pound
*Sunflower seeds, shelled,
   unsalted, ½ pound

*Fruits and Vegetables
(organic, if possible)*
Apples, 4
*Garlic, 3 bulbs
Grapes, 2 pounds
Lemons, 4
Papaya, very ripe, 1
Pineapple, very ripe, 1
Watermelon, ½

Beverages and Miscellaneous Foods
*Apple juice, organic, 32 ounces
Apple-cider vinegar, 1 bottle
Honey, with royal jelly, 1 small jar
*Milk (for eye packs), 1 pint
*Water, bottled if you do not have
   a water purifier, 3 gallons

*Herbs, Supplements,
and Health-Care Items*
Essential Oil: geranium

Saturday: Day 15

On Awakening: One 8-ounce glass of Hot Lemon-Water Flush (page 42); add one teaspoon honey with Royal Jelly (page 277). Prepare Inner Beauty Herbal Tea (pages 42-43); drink throughout the day between meals. Use Cleansing Inhalant (pages 168-169). Prepare protein drink for mid-day snacks.

Morning Cleansing: Hot shower followed by Friction Air Bath (page 128).

Breakfast: Cleansing Watermelon Breakfast (page 56).

Mid-morning Snack: Tahini Shake (page 73). Add one tablespoon of granulated lecithin.

Lunch: Apple-Cider Vinegar Drink (page 53), followed by Super Salad (pages 62-63) with Spa Salsa (page 66).

Afternoon Activities: Shop for week's food and supplies; see Shopping List And Inventory (page 249) and Schedules for Days 15 through 21. As in Weeks 1 and 2, if you have decided to alter the meal plan in any way, make the necessary adjustments to your shopping list. Use Cleansing Soak for Fruits and Vegetables (page 116) for nonorganic produce. Prepare Potassium Broth (pages 44-45) for the week. Refrigerate one batch of thick bisque for Monday, and freeze two 4-cup batches of thin broth for later this week. (If you have any

Potassium Broth left from last week, adjust the size of this week's recipe accordingly.) Professional Colonic Irrigation or Cleansing Enema (pages 241-243). If you do not have a colonic today, schedule it for Tuesday: Day 18.

Mid-afternoon Snack: Optional—Tahini Shake (page 73) or Rejuvelac (page 47), one cup.

Dinner: Raw Vegetable Delight (pages 60-61), as much as you want.

Exercise: Oxygenation Cocktail (page 47). Wake-Up Shake-Up (page 148), followed by thirty minutes of brisk walking.

Evening Activity: Drink one cup of Rejuvelac (page 47). Add the remainder to tonight's bath. Three-Part Breathing (pages 172-173), Complete Breath (pages 173-174), and Alternate Hemisphere Breathing (pages 174-175). Sea Salt Scrub (page 128), followed by a warm bath with Easy Steam (pages 135-136), using three drops of sandalwood essential oil.

The Power of Positive Attitudes

If you are experiencing the clear, light, clean feeling that comes with a thorough cleansing of your systems of elimination, you now realize that a polluted body can affect the way you think and feel. Truly, a polluted body produces a polluted mind. To preserve your new feeling of clarity and lightness, resolve to follow the "diet for the mind" that I described, using your journal and affirmations regularly to reprogram your thinking.

Think for a moment about how you have been feeling during this program. If you are like me, last week's cleansing has left you feeling better than you have felt for a very long time. If you have had any symptoms from cleansing reactions—troubled skin, mild headache, and so forth—remember that they are just part of getting better. In fact, the stronger your cleansing reactions are, the more toxins you had to eliminate from your body, and the healthier you will be as a result. All the suggestions I have given you in this program about drinking lots of fluids and getting plenty of exercise and rest and relaxation should have helped to minimize any cleansing symptoms. Remember to look at these symptoms from a positive, releasing point of view, and don't sabotage your hard work by becoming discouraged or by using chemical remedies that will introduce toxins into your system, bringing you down from your high, positive feeling.

Just as a congested, toxic body will produce cloudy, negative thoughts, negative thoughts and attitudes can adversely affect your body. Folk wisdom has always taught that negative thinking and stress can lead to illness. Now medical research is beginning to show exactly how this happens. The new field of psychoneuroimmunology studies the interactions between thinking (psycho), the brain and central nervous system (neuro), and the immune system (immunology). We now understand that stress causes the body to produce potent hormones that damage the organs and can lead to disease. Stress can also suppress the proper functioning of the immune system.

In the 1960s, medical researchers Thomas Holmes and Richard Rahe devised a scale for evaluating significant life changes, both pleasant and unpleasant, that produce stress. Different life changes were given different scores, with the highest score being assigned to the death of a spouse. Examples of other stress-causing events include being fired from a job, retirement, a change in residence, travel, and marriage. Generally, the higher a person's Life Change Score for a specific period of time, the greater would be the likelihood that he or she developed a serious illness following these life changes.

We now know that the relationship between stressful events and illness is not quite that simple. It turns out that some people, rather than being made sick by stress, are actually spurred on to higher levels of performance. Why are some people made ill by stress, while others thrive on it? In an attempt to answer this question, psychologist Suzanne Kobasa studied executives at the Illinois Bell Telephone Company during the stressful period of the AT&T divestiture. She found that the stress-resistant executives had certain characteristics in common, which she labeled challenge, commitment, and control. Challenge means that the executives who remained healthy were able to view the potentially threatening situation as a challenge—a stimulus to creativity and high performance. Commitment means that those who successfully survived stress felt deeply committed to their work, their families, their personal well-being, and other important values. Finally, the control factor meant that the healthy executives saw themselves as being in charge of their lives, instead of feeling they were victims of outside circumstances.

The point of this research is that it is not stress itself that can make you ill, but your attitude toward it. This means that by learning to relax and be flexible in the face of change, you can protect yourself to a very large extent from the ill effects of stress.

This is exactly what I have been talking about when I say that your attitude affects the way you feel and look. By programming your mind with positive messages, you will be able to cope with stress, your body will work much better, and you will greatly reduce the danger of developing a serious illness in the future.

Think for a moment about the feelings that have come up while you have been on this program and about how you can use the attitudes described as challenge, commitment, and control to keep you on track. Think also about the things that are causing stress in your life right now and about how affirmations embodying challenge, commitment, and control can help you to cope better. The more you program yourself with a positive diet for the mind, the more you will be able to sail successfully through the potentially distressing events in your daily life.

Take out your journal now and write some affirmations that seem appropriate for you during this last week of the program. Think in terms of the qualities of challenge, commitment, and control. Possible affirmations might be: I am committed to making myself as healthy as I can be, so that I can be better for the people I love; I have the power to control my diet by choosing the foods that are best for me; or I welcome the challenge of walking or bicycling instead of using my car.

Use affirmations embodying challenge, commitment, and control every day. You will be surprised at how much more powerful this diet for the mind will make you feel.

ST. JOHN'S WORT

St. John's Wort is one of the most frequently recommended substances in all of Europe to help people cope with daily life. Most modern research into its properties has been conducted in Germany, where the use of this herb is widespread. Clinical interest in St. John's Wort reached new heights in 1996, when the British Medical Journal published a summary of research findings, concluding that it had a beneficial effect on mental well-being. One double-blind study demonstrated relief from mild to moderate depression in more than half of the sixteen hundred patients studied.

The natural ingredients in St. John's Wort support natural brain function by helping the brain maintain healthy levels of certain amino acids, which act as neurotransmitters within the brain. St. John's Wort also helps support levels of serotonin, a brain chemical that helps maintain a feeling of well-being.

cont'd.

St. John's Wort has been valued for centuries as a mild sedative, an anti-inflammatory, and a wound-healing nervine. It has been especially regarded as an herb to treat irritability and anxiety triggered by menopausal changes. It is increasingly recommended as an alternative to pharmaceutical products such as Prozac and Valium. Although these drugs are effective for some, they are expensive and may have unwanted side effects. For example, Prozac may cause anxiety and digestive disturbances.

Many forms of St. John's Wort are available, including caplets, capsules, tinctures, and teas.

Sunday: Day 16

On Awakening: One 8-ounce glass of Hot Lemon-Water Flush (page 42); add one teaspoon honey with Royal Jelly (page 277). Prepare Inner Beauty Herbal Tea (pages 42-43); drink throughout the day between meals. Use Cleansing Inhalant (pages 168-169).

Morning Cleansing: Dry Brush Massage (page 127). Follow with Alternating Hot and Cold Shower—begin with three to five minutes of hot water; switch to ten to fifteen seconds of cold water. Repeat three times, ending with cold water. Dry briskly with a coarse towel.

Breakfast: Healing Grape Breakfast (pages 56-57).

Mid-morning Snack: Hot Mock Chocolate (page 72). Add one tablespoon of granulated lecithin.

Lunch: Apple-Cider Vinegar Drink (page 53), followed by Super Salad (pages 62-63) with Fat-Loss Dressing (pages 63 to 65) of choice.

Mid-afternoon Snack: Optional—Hot Mock Chocolate (page 72) or Rejuvelac (page 47), one cup.

Afternoon Activity: Father Kneipp's Footbath (page 161) for twenty minutes, followed by professional massage, preferably in your home.

Dinner: Raw vegetable platter with Green Goddess Topping (page 65).

Exercise: Oxygenation Cocktail (page 47). Dancer's Warm-Up (page 149), followed by thirty minutes of brisk walking.

Evening Activity: Drink one cup of Rejuvelac (page 47). Aromatic Fume Bath with witch hazel (page 135). Yoga Arch Pose Variations (page 263), followed by Yoga Stress Releasers (pages 109-111), just before bedtime.

Conquering Constipation Forever

Last week, we examined what happens when waste is not promptly eliminated from the colon and its poisonous contents are allowed to reenter the bloodstream, causing symptoms throughout the body. I truly believe that this internal pollution underlies a great deal of illness. Overweight, lethargy, headache, poor skin condition, unpleasant body odor, low back pain, premature aging—all the symptoms listed in the Toxicity Symptom Checklist that you completed at the beginning of this program—can result from constipation. These symptoms are early warning signs of more serious problems, which can develop if the constipation is not corrected. At the end of this week, you will repeat the Toxicity Symptom Checklist to see what improvements have occurred now that you have begun to incorporate into your life techniques to reduce toxicity and end constipation once and for all.

It was the British physician Denis Burkitt who first called widespread attention to the relationship between diet, constipation, and disease. Burkitt was one of a number of British doctors working with native villagers in Africa. He noticed a striking difference between the elimination habits of the natives and those of the Englishmen. The Africans' meals would pass through their digestive tracts to be eliminated in about twenty-four hours, whereas for the British it generally took three days, and sometimes as long as two weeks. Not only did the Africans eliminate their waste much more rapidly, but their stools were also large and soft, in sharp contrast to the generally small, hard, difficult-to-pass stools of the British doctors. The Africans were eating unprocessed natural foods high in fiber, whereas the Englishmen were eating the typical "civilized" diet high in refined white flour, sugar, and saturated fats. Not only were the Africans free of constipation, but they were also free of many of the diseases that have become plagues of modern civilization, such as heart disease, colon and rectal cancer, appendicitis, hemorrhoids, obesity, and varicose veins. As a result of Burkitt's observations, fiber became a popular supplement in modern Western diets.

I have gone into graphic detail to help you consider the question of whether you have a problem with constipation. Are your stools soft and full, or are they small and hard? A constipated system is one where waste moves through the bowel slowly, and its hard consistency causes strain and eventual damage to your body. Even when your bowel movements seem to be regular and normal, they may be squeezing their way past an accumulation of hardened, dried waste somewhere in the colon.

Moreover, remember that the waste should move through your system to be eliminated promptly after it has been digested. You may think you are doing fine if you have one bowel movement each day, but if you eat three meals a day, that means there are two other meals backed up in your colon, waiting to be eliminated. As you heal and cleanse your digestive system and colon, you will begin to move toward the ideal of one bowel movement per day for each meal eaten each day. It is a natural, common-sense relationship between what goes in and what comes out.

Last week I taught you how to do a Tummy Massage that follows the course of your colon, feeling deep inside your abdomen for areas that seem hard or sore. Now that you know where your colon is located, you may begin to realize that your protruding tummy or your frequent abdominal pains may be caused by a constipated colon. Many people think they have a stomachache, when the problem is not in their stomach at all.

The story of one of my clients, Doreen, illustrates this point very dramatically. Doreen and her husband have their own business, and she also spends a great deal of time caring for a disabled son. From morning to night, Doreen is on the run, taking care of her business and taking care of her family. She is one of those people who had never thought of herself as constipated, even though she would have bowel movements only every second or third day. That was the way it had been for her mother, and she thought it was just normal for her.

Over a couple of years' time, Doreen had had more or less constant pain in her upper abdomen, in the area near the liver. She had been to many different doctors and most recently, had had gallbladder studies. The doctors were very concerned, because they could find no explanation for the pain and had recommended exploratory surgery.

Fortunately for Doreen, her massage therapist noticed congestion in her abdominal area and sent her to the Inner Beauty Institute. We found that she had severely impacted waste in her colon, which had become so hard it was impossible to dislodge with regular bowel movements. After three colonic-irrigation treatments, Doreen's pain went away, and the only time it comes back now is when she becomes constipated. She has learned to know her body well enough to recognize what is causing the pain when it occurs and what foods may have caused the constipation. As an added benefit, Doreen began to experience a much more satisfying sex life with the use of deep breathing, as she learned to release not just the waste from her bowels but also the tension from her pelvic area.

ANTICONSTIPATION DIET

Look over this table of good foods and bad foods for fighting constipation. How many of the Foods to Avoid have been staples in your regular diet?

Foods to Eat

Fresh fruits and vegetables, including raw ones and fresh-squeezed juices

Prunes and prune juice

Whole grains—one serving per day

Sprouts

Fibrous foods in general

Lots of steamed vegetables when you eat protein

Potassium-rich foods, such as vegetables and Potassium Broth

At least eight glasses of water—in the form of Hydrating Drink, purified water, herb teas, broth, and other fluids

Cold-pressed vegetable oils, such as flax seed, olive, sesame, and safflower—
two tablespoons per day

Fermented foods, such as Rejuvelac and sauerkraut

Hot Lemon-Water Flush

Supplements, such as aloe-vera juice, liquid minerals, Lactobacillus supplement, and intestinal cleanser

Foods to Avoid

Bread

Cheese

Salt

Refined sugar

White flour

Candies, cookies, and pastries

Excessive coffee and black tea

Carbonated beverages/alcoholic beverages

Processed foods—canned, salted foods

Salted snack foods

Fried foods

Excessive animal protein

Very hot or very cold foods

Because the focus of the entire 21-Day Program has been on cleansing the systems of elimination, just about everything you have learned so far will help in your battle against constipation. To begin with, be sure to drink at least eight glasses of pure, clean water each day. This fluid intake may be in the form of plain purified water or the sweetened Hydrating Drink, herbal teas, Oxygenation Cocktail, or other beverages recommended in this program. These healthful, toxin-free drinks ensure that your colon is properly hydrated, bathing and cleansing your cells, tissues, and organs of elimination. A correctly combined diet of fresh, natural foods, including plenty of raw fruits and vegetables and fresh juices, provides water content and minerals for proper bowel function, as well as the fiber to move the waste through your intestines quickly and cleanly.

Some foods are very dehydrating and thus, can lead to constipation. A particularly insidious culprit is bread. All the people I have ever worked with on constipation problems have improved when they eliminated bread from their diet. People who are constipated should not eat bread, with the possible exception of dark pumpernickel made without yeast, such as Ruhrtaler pumpernickel, available in many health food and specialty gourmet stores. Also, avoid mucoid-forming foods such as cheese, since they tend to coat the intestinal wall and impair absorption. Hard cheese is as difficult to digest as bread. It absorbs moisture out of the system and produces dehydration. I realize that many people will have a hard time giving up cheese entirely; my advice is to consider it a special treat rather than an everyday staple.

Help your digestive system by adding friendly bacteria in the form of Rejuvelac or a Lactobacillus supplement, and use digestive enzymes if you combine meals improperly or eat a lot of protein. Proper eating habits are essential for eliminating constipation. Always eat slowly and calmly, be sure to chew your food well, and avoid overeating. Adequate exercise, such as walking, swimming, or trampolining, helps to keep your bowel function regular, as do slant-board exercises. Yoga exercises, such as the Yoga Arch Pose Variations and the Digestion Toning Postures, help to promote proper digestion and elimination. Sitz baths, especially the cold "Youth Bath" I described on Friday: Day 7, bring vastly increased circulation to the abdominal organs and can be very helpful in aiding digestion, expelling gas, and encouraging proper bowel function.

Regardless of your busy schedule, always heed nature's call. Repressing the urge to move your bowels when you have to go is one of the most common contributing factors in chronic constipation. Based on extensive research with my clients, I have concluded that constipation problems can often be traced back to early childhood embarrassment about going to the bathroom or to having to "hold it" when it was necessary to wait to use the toilet. This early conditioning can still be undone in adulthood. Establish the habit of trying to have a bowel movement first thing every morning, whether you feel the urge or not. Be prepared to take fifteen minutes if necessary, do not strain, and just be patient. If your bowels are weak, they will take longer to respond. Try breathing deeply and bending forward, and elevate your feet on a low stool if necessary. Also try using the colon-stimulating acupressure massage point that you learned on Friday: Day 7.

CONSTIPATION DO'S AND DON'TS

These tips can help you conquer constipation forever. Incorporate the Do's into your life, and you will begin to notice improved elimination patterns.

Do:

Eat your main meal early in the day—at mid-day, rather than in the evening.

Drink at least eight glasses of fluids each day.

Chew your food twenty to thirty times per mouthful.

Follow food-combining rules.

Use digestive enzymes when you miscombine foods or eat too much protein.

Use a fiber-rich intestinal cleanser.

Promote the friendly bacteria in your intestines by drinking Rejuvelac and using a Lactobacillus supplement.

Exercise regularly—walk, swim, use a trampoline, etc.

Use breathing exercises at least three times a week to relax the abdominal organs.

Practice yoga postures at least three times a week to tone and stimulate the digestive organs.

Practice slant-board exercises at least three times a week to rejuvenate the abdominal organs and strengthen the supporting muscles.

Take hot and cold sitz baths to stimulate the abdominal organs.

Use Hot Castor-Oil Abdominal Wraps to loosen up waste in the colon and relax the abdominal organs.

Use Tummy Massage to help elimination and locate tense areas.

Heed nature's call.

Establish the habit of moving your bowels at a specific time each day.

Use a footstool at the foot of your toilet to elevate your feet when moving your bowels.

Consult a sympathetic physician and a qualified colon hygienist; use colonic irrigations and enemas as needed to cleanse and tone the colon.

Take pride in proper bowel function.

Devote time each day to relaxing quietly and paying attention to managing your stress.

Get enough sleep—six to eight hours a day is the usual requirement for most people.

Think positive thoughts; use affirmations.

Don't:

Eat when you are upset.

Overeat.

Ignore food-combining principles.

Drink liquids with meals.

Use pharmaceutical laxatives.

Give in to worry or stress.

Suppress your feelings.

Put off going to the bathroom.

If you have a problem with chronic constipation, I recommend that you work with a qualified colon hygienist. Colonic irrigations not only clean out the waste, they also exercise and tone the muscles of the colon, encouraging proper function. If you cannot find a colon therapist in your area, be sure to follow the dietary recommendations I have given, use intestinal cleansers, and give yourself at-home enemas when necessary to cleanse your colon.

Use the breathing exercises you have learned to breathe deeply into your abdomen. Notice any areas where you are tight and tense, and use your breath to open up and relax these areas. Yoga postures also help to release tension, as well as stimulating proper function of the abdominal organs.

Above all, learn to manage your stress. It is amazing how many people come into my office seeking help and begin by denying that stress is contributing to their constipation problem. In my experience, constipation is usually caused by nutritional problems or emotional factors or both. Once I have worked with clients on correcting their diet, if there is still a constipation problem, we begin to look at the impact of stress. Most people do not realize how much stress they have and where they are storing it in their bodies. When we are under stress, many of us tend to tighten up in the abdominal area and lose touch with the proper functioning of the abdominal organs. Massage and deep breathing can help to increase your awareness of your body's stress patterns.

Sandy was a young mother who came to my office expressing great frustration with her constipation problem. Sandy was one of those people who denied stress. As we worked together on improving her diet, she came to trust me more and began to open up and talk about how stressful it was to be a mother. Her entire life was devoted to meeting the demands of her kids—taking them one place after another, preparing meals for their differing fussy tastes, and maintaining a semblance of order at meal-times. Somehow Sandy never found the time to take care of her own needs. We did a lot of work on her diet and colon cleansing, and Sandy was showing some improvement, but constipation was still a problem. We were really stumped, because we had tried just about everything. Then Sandy went away for a one-week vacation with her husband, leaving the kids at home in the care of a relative. Enjoying her holiday, Sandy ate everything she wanted, and to her amazement, her bowel movements were regular. When she came back and told me what had happened, I realized that now we knew the real source of her problem. We discussed the possibilities and came up with the idea that she and her husband should eat their evening meal alone, after the kids had been taken care of. No longer having to deal with the children at dinner, Sandy was able to relax while she ate. I was very gratified to see that this simple solution turned Sandy's problem around and ended her constipation. As with so many of my clients, the improvement in Sandy's bowel function was accompanied by an improvement in her sexual satisfaction. She had been so tight and uncomfortable in that part of her body that sex had never been pleasurable for her. Now, as she learned to let go of the stress in her abdominal organs, she also learned to relax and enjoy her sex life.

YOGA ARCH POSE VARIATIONS

The Yoga Arch Pose and its variations are excellent toners of the entire abdominal region. The pose helps to promote digestion and is also very relaxing. Lie on your back on the floor, with your arms resting at your sides. Bring your knees up to a bent position with the feet side by side. Push off your body from the floor with your hips, keeping your knees bent. Bring the pelvis up in the air and arch the back, so your body forms an arch supported by the back of your neck and shoulders and your feet. Hold this position for as long as is comfortable, then

YOGA ARCH POSE

lower your pelvis to the floor and relax. Then go up again, this time arching your back even higher. Come down and rest once again. Now, lift the pelvis again, and this time while you are up, tense your whole body and then relax it, tense it and relax it, finally lowering the pelvis to the floor and resting. Go up again, repeat the tensing and relaxing two or three times, then come down and rest. Finally, raise the pelvis again, and this time as you remain in the arch position, pull the abdominal muscles in and up, giving your abdominal organs an internal massage as you pull in and narrow your waist. Lower your pelvis to the floor and relax, breathing naturally for a few minutes.

Perform each of the variations on the Arch Pose as many times as you wish. You will find it is very stimulating to the abdominal organs and leaves you with a wonderful relaxed feeling.

Monday: Day 17

On Awakening: One 8-ounce glass of Hot Lemon-Water Flush (page 42); add one teaspoon honey with Royal Jelly (page 277). Prepare Inner Beauty Herbal Tea (pages 42-43); drink throughout the day between meals. Use Cleansing Inhalant (pages 168-169).

Morning Cleansing: Dry Brush Massage (page 127), followed by Morning Cold Splash and Rub (page 185).

Breakfast: Papaya Complexion Breakfast (pages 54-55).

Mid-morning Snack: Carrot Shake (page 73). Add one tablespoon of granulated lecithin.

Lunch: Apple-Cider Vinegar Drink (page 53), followed by Super Salad (pages 62-63) with Fat-Loss Dressing (pages 63 to 65) of choice. If you eat at a restaurant today, select one that has a salad bar and assemble a Super Salad from the raw vegetables and greens provided.

Mid-afternoon Snack: Optional—Carrot Shake (page 73), or Rejuvelac (page 47), one cup.

Dinner: Hijiki Stir-Fry (pages 69-70); accompany with thick Potassium Broth (pages 44-45), as much as you want.

Exercise: Oxygenation Cocktail (page 47). Yoga Self-Massage (pages 194-199), followed by thirty minutes of brisk walking.

Evening Activity: (At-home night)*:* Begin preparations for Chaparral Detoxifying Bath (page 227). Drink one cup of Rejuvelac (page 47). Add remainder to tonight's bath. Hot Castor-Oil Abdominal Wrap (pages 239-240). While Castor-Oil Wrap is on, do Three-Part Breathing (pages 172-173), Complete Breath (pages 173-174), and Alternate-Hemisphere Breathing (pages 174-175). Follow with Chaparral Detoxifying Bath (page 227).

Food Sensitivities and Your Optimal Diet

Do you have annoying little symptoms that always seem to be there, that you have accepted as "normal" for you? You may have constantly clogged sinuses or mood swings or a rapid heartbeat or a tired feeling sometimes after eating. You may dismiss these problems by saying, "That's just the way I am; I have to live with it." But the real problem may be food sensitivities. One of the benefits of the light diet and the thorough cleansing program of Week 2 is that they eliminated many of the foods to which people are often sensitive. Essentially, I have helped you to do what allergy doctors do—to give your immune system a rest and cleanse your body before you begin to reintroduce foods to which you may be sensitive.

The most common problem foods are dairy products and wheat; others include corn, eggs, soy products, shellfish, and yeast. As you return to the Rejuvenation Diet, you will continue to avoid dairy products and wheat, the two most common offenders. In fact, part of the reason you feel so wonderful now may be that you are no longer experiencing uncomfortable symptoms that food sensitivities may have caused in the past. Food sensitivities can cause a tremendously wide range of symptoms, including skin rashes, gastrointestinal problems, respiratory symptoms, fluctuations in blood sugar, swollen and painful joints, and food cravings.

I am sure that you have lost weight on this program. Part of this weight loss may have been the result of giving up foods to which you are sensitive. Although no one seems to understand it completely, I believe that much excess weight is caused by the body retaining fluid in its tissues to protect itself against foods to which it is sensitive. When you eliminate these substances from your diet, the fluid is flushed out of the tissues. This is why you can lose weight so rapidly on a highly restricted diet. Of course, if you go back to eating the same foods again, you will put the weight right back on, as your body retains fluid to protect itself.

I know this is true from personal experience. I once lost fifteen pounds in three weeks, and the only change I had made in my diet was to give up eating wheat entirely, including all breads, pastas, and muffins. The weight just fell away as my kidneys eliminated the excess water from my system. Such experiences have shown me that wheat is a problem food for me. I also know that since childhood wheat bread has been the food I have turned to for comfort when I am upset. I am not alone in having this problem with bread and other wheat products. In fact, I consider bread the number-one enemy for anyone who has problems with weight control, constipation, and cellulite!

Besides the physical reactions that food sensitivities can cause, you may be surprised to learn that they can have very profound psychological effects. Wheat products are particularly troublesome in this regard. Research in the 1940s showed that many hospitalized schizophrenic patients' symptoms were relieved when they stopped eating wheat and related grain products. If they ate a little bread, they would experience their mental symptoms once again. Food sensitivities are now recognized as a very important factor in all sorts of mental and behavioral problems. Several years ago, Dr. Ben Feingold created a sensation when he developed the so-called Feingold diet, which eliminates foods to which children are often sensitive. On this diet, many children with hyperkinetic behavior problems settle down and improve markedly. Correctional and probation officers have found that special restricted diets can help to control criminal behavior, and some marriage counselors are now taking a look at nutritional factors in dealing with family discord.

As you return to eating a full range of foods, both this week and after you have finished the 21-Day Program, you can experiment cautiously to try to discover your food sensitivities. If you suspect that you are sensitive to a certain food, eat quite a bit of it during one day—for example, eat some at breakfast and again at lunch—and then take note of your reactions. Pay attention not only to physical symptoms, such as digestive upset or headache, but also to any mental or emotional changes—whether you get sleepy or your energy drops or you become irritable. These reactions can all be signs that you are sensitive to the food in question. Be careful with these experiments. Now that your body has been cleaned out, you no longer have the mucoid coating in your intestines that protected you against these offending substances (as well as inter-fering with the absorption of essential nutrients), so the reactions you experience may be more pronounced than they were in the past.

If you do discover a food to which you are sensitive, that does not necessarily mean that you can never eat it again. You simply do not want to expose your body to too much of it, too often. Medical allergists generally recommend that once you have stayed away from a problem food for some time, you can begin to add it back into your diet as long as you only eat it once every four days. This is the so-called rotation diet, which is based on the principle of allowing your body to rest after exposure to a food to which you may be sensitive. In my practice, I have observed that it works better to eat suspect foods no more than once a week. Also, if there are two foods that you know you are sensitive to—for example, dairy and wheat—try not to eat them together, so you do not place an added burden on your body.

As you return to a regular diet, it is still best to rotate even the foods to which you are not sensitive, especially proteins, which are the hardest to digest. It is better to eat a different protein food every day and not to repeat the same protein more than once every four days. Generally, for foods that you are not sensitive to, repeating them no more than once every four days will avoid any possible problems. This principle of food rotation not only protects your immune system by allowing it to rest from food-sensitivity reactions, but it also ensures that you receive the full spectrum of vitamins, minerals, and amino acids, which are provided in perfect balance when you eat from all the foods in nature.

There will be times in the future when you cannot observe the food-rotation principle or you will miscombine foods or eat too much protein. An excellent aid at such times is a good digestive enzyme. After you have completed your 21-Day Program, you may also experiment with some variations in the food-combining rules that I introduced on page 81. One variation is to combine acid fruits such as pineapple, berries, or oranges with light nut and seed proteins. Once your digestive system has been cleansed and healed by following the 21-Day Program, you can try making a smoothie using a protein drink base with strawberries, pineapple, or orange juice added. You can also make a fruit salad that combines acid fruits with nuts and seeds. Because papaya contains a great many enzymes, many people can combine papaya with proteins of all kinds without experiencing bloating. Pay attention to your physical reactions to determine whether these combinations work for you.

Many allergy-oriented health professionals believe that people crave the very foods to which they are allergic. I do not necessarily agree with this point of view. I think that your body has an innate, built-in wisdom, and that if you crave something, what you crave is not necessarily harmful for you. Rather, I believe the craving is an indication that your body needs some particular kind of nutrient to restore its natural balance.

Cravings for sweets are a good example of this "body intelligence." Most people with whom I work in my practice, particularly women, tend to have sweet cravings, especially before their menstrual period. These cravings are not necessarily a sign of poor self-control; they are often a signal that something is lacking in the diet. I generally find that my clients' sweet cravings are a sign that they need more protein, especially early in the day. When my clients balance out their diets and find what is best for them, then sweet cravings usually go away.

Many people, for excellent philosophical reasons, try to follow a pure vegetarian diet or a raw foods diet and find that it simply does not work for them. Their philosophical commitment may prevent them from noticing the warning signs, such as sweet or starch cravings, that their bodies need certain foods they are not getting.

Some studies show that vegetarians are generally healthier than those eating the standard American diet, yet others oppose this trend. There may, indeed, be certain nutrients in animal foods necessary for optimum health. For example, the vegan diet, which contains no animal foods whatsoever, lacks the omega-3 fatty acids known as EPAs and DHAs. Vegetarians who consume eggs ingest only small amounts of both of these ingredients. The body can manufacture these necessary nutrients to a small degree, but that amount may not be adequate for sustained good health. If you're a strict vegetarian, remember that the human body evolved on an omnivorous diet. If your beliefs prevent you from adding fish to your diet, please investigate supplementation with the essential fatty acids EPA and DHA. Be sure to get enough protein from soy products, other legumes, nuts and seeds.

We are all looking for the diet that is best for our physical and mental well-being. We are also all unique individuals, and what is best for one person may not be best for another. Many health professionals, after extensive experimentation on themselves, become very tuned in to their own bodies. They proceed to write a book about having found the perfect diet and act as though what they have discovered is best for everyone. I do not want to do that with you; that is why I keep asking you to notice how you feel.

After cleansing your body, you will be much more sensitive to the personal effects of various foods. Pay particular attention this week as you add foods back to your diet, and continue to be vigilant after you complete this program. You are the one who can best recognize the signs that something is not right.

By becoming sensitive to your body's own needs, you will learn to make proper adjustments in your diet. You will know when you need an extra protein drink to pick up your energy or balance your nutrient intake. Use digestive enzymes when you miscombine foods or eat too much protein, and use natural aids such as Rejuvelac or the Apple-Cider Vinegar Drink to enhance the work of your digestive system.

If you have a severe problem with food sensitivities or with finding the right balance of foods for you, you may want to seek guidance from a nutritionally-oriented holistic physician who has expertise in identifying food sensitivities and nutritional needs. If you do not have serious problems, you can use the tips I have provided in this chapter to experiment on your own, abstaining from the foods you suspect and then noticing what happens when you reintroduce them.

PROBLEM FOODS AND THEIR SYMPTOMS

While food sensitivities can produce a wide and often unpredictable range of symptoms in different people, some foods seem to show reaction patterns in the symptoms they provoke. The following are some of the common patterns that have been observed:

Milk and Dairy Products, Including Cheese: Respiratory symptoms such as runny nose, sinus problems, asthma; ear infections; gastrointestinal symptoms such as gas, cramps, bloating, diarrhea, constipation.

Wheat: Mental and behavioral problems; water retention.

Nightshade Foods (potato, tomato, eggplant, bell peppers): Arthritis and joint pain; headache.

Citrus Fruits (orange, lemon, grapefruit, tangerine): Hives, wheezing, headache.

Caffeine (coffee, cocoa, chocolate, cola drinks): Headache, heart palpitations.

DIGESTIVE ENZYMES: A "FORGIVENESS FACTOR" IN YOUR DIET

When you make an educated choice to miscombine foods or when you overindulge in your favorite delicacy, help your digestive system by taking a high-quality, multiphase digestive enzyme.

Multiphase enzyme supplements have two stages. They release hydrochloric acid and acidic enzymes in the stomach, and then, when they reach the small intestine, they release other alkaline enzymes needed for this basic environment. Take digestive enzymes before you eat a heavy meal to prevent bloating hours afterward. Most people are especially deficient in enzymes that produce hydrochloric acid.

Influenced by television advertising, people generally believe their digestive upset is caused by too much stomach acid, and so they take antacids to ease their symptoms. These remedies slow down or stop the digestive process without solving the underlying problems. Digestive enzymes can help you to derive maximum benefit from your food. You can find a variety of digestive enzymes in most health food stores.

BOOKS TO HELP DETERMINE YOUR OPTIMUM DIET

These books will help you find the diet that's best for you.

Carbohydrate Addict's Diet by Dr. Rachael and Dr. Richard Heller (Signet)

Eat Right for Your Type by Dr. James and Dr. Peter D'Adamo (Putnam)

The Zone by Barry Sears (Harper Collins)

Your Body Knows Best by Ann Louise Gittleman (Pocket)

Tuesday: Day 18

On Awakening: One 8-ounce glass of Hot Lemon-Water Flush (page 42); add one teaspoon honey with Royal Jelly (page 277). Prepare Inner Beauty Herbal Tea (pages 42-43); drink throughout the day between meals. Use Cleansing Inhalant (pages 168-169).

Morning Cleansing: Dry Brush Massage (page 127). Follow with hot shower, finishing with a one-minute cold splash.

Breakfast: Cleansing Watermelon Breakfast (page 56).

Mid-morning Snack: Tahini Shake (page 73). Add one tablespoon of granulated lecithin.

Lunch: Apple-Cider Vinegar Drink (page 53), followed by Super Salad (pages 62-63) with Fat-Loss Dressing (pages 63 to 65) of choice. If you eat at a restaurant today, select one that has a salad bar and assemble a Super Salad from the raw vegetables and greens provided.

Mid-afternoon Snack: Optional—Tahini Shake (page 73) or Rejuvelac (page 47), one cup.

Dinner: Miso Sea Soup (page 70); steamed vegetables with warm Garlic Tarragon Dressing (page 64).

Exercise: Oxygenation Cocktail (page 47). Lymph-Cleansing Warm-Up (pages 221-223) followed by thirty minutes of brisk walking.

Evening Activity: Drink one cup of Rejuvelac (page 47). Professional Colonic Irrigation or Cleansing Enema (pages 241-243) accompanied by Tummy Massage (pages 240-241). Follow with Cleopatra's Milk Bath (pages 133-134), using a batch of the barley water you made on Saturday: Day 8.

Rejuvenation through Glandular Health

Researchers are learning more about the endocrine glands all the time, and some of these glands are understood better than others. The pituitary gland, located deep in the brain, regulates the functioning of the glandular system of the entire body. The pineal gland, also located in the brain, is still little understood. It has been associated in esoteric literature with the "third eye" and appears to be sensitive to light. The thyroid, located in the neck, is the gland most directly involved in regulating metabolism, which affects your weight. It is responsible for the burning of fat, and it also controls the activity of the sex glands. The parathyroids, attached to the thyroid, regulate calcium metabolism and control the activity of lymph in neutralizing certain toxins. The thymus, located in the chest, is also little understood, but it is known to be responsible for producing crucial disease-fighting white cells in the immune system. The pancreas not only produces digestive enzymes, but specialized parts of the pancreas also function as an endocrine gland, producing the insulin that regulates your body's use of sugar. The adrenal glands, sitting on top of the kidneys, produce two kinds of substances. The inner part of the adrenals produces adrenaline, the hormone that prepares the body for vigorous activity in response to stress. The outer part of the adrenal glands produces the adrenocorticoids, powerful hormones that, when present in excess, are largely responsible for the organ damage that comes from prolonged stress. The sex glands include the prostate in men and the ovaries in women. When levels of sex hormones diminish, many signs of aging tend to set in.

We hear a lot these days about hormones, especially in relationship to changing moods, attitudes, and bodily functions. In fact, many women are attracted to hormone replacement therapy in hopes of achieving younger-looking skin. Traditional hormone replacement therapy refers to replacing the estrogen and progesterone depleted by menopause. You are probably familiar with these female sex hormones and, perhaps, with the male sex hormone, testosterone, needed in small doses by some women.

Less commonly known are the human growth hormone produced in your pituitary; DHEA (dehydroepiandrosterone), made in the adrenals; and melatonin, produced by your pineal gland. A great deal of research is being done today on the antiaging and health-stimulating factors in all of these hormones; some claim that they may actually contain the secrets of the fountain of youth.

But just what are they and how do they really work? Hormones are tiny chemical messengers continuously secreted into the bloodstream by your endocrine glands. As mentioned earlier, these are the pituitary and pineal in your brain, the thyroid in your throat, the thymus in your chest, and the adrenals deep in your abdomen. Hormones regulate the activities of your vital organs. They stimulate a multitude of life-giving processes throughout the body, which in turn maintain health, healing, growth, and repair. Yet, they also decline dramatically with age, producing many of the problems associated with aging itself, including heart disease, memory loss, osteoporosis, reduced energy, and skin tone deterioration.

Some of the most promising research being done today demonstrates how natural progesterone helps build bone back even in older women, thus reversing some osteoporosis. Natural progesterone, made from the popular wild yam herb, can also restore or prevent the occurrence of vaginal dryness, a common complaint among menopausal women. According to extensive research in England, it can also reduce many symptoms associated with PMS, especially mood swings, depression, bloating, and breast tenderness. A cream containing 3 percent natural progesterone is sold over the counter in many pharmacies and health food stores. You may be surprised that a cream applied to the skin can be so effective. Remember, many medicines are administered through the skin, such as estrogen, nicotine, and nitroglycerin patches.

Two other hormones, melatonin and DHEA, have recently become widely publicized for their antiaging benefits. Melatonin is produced naturally by the pineal gland at the onset of darkness. It is the first effective remedy for jet lag and a safe and effective inducer of natural sleep. It also may increase the activity of some components of the immune system. It is often touted as an antiaging nutrient and appears to be completely nontoxic. Although some health professionals are somewhat reluctant to recommend it as a long-term supplement until more is known, it is certainly a safer alternative for sleep than the pharmaceutical options. It is available in synthetic form in most health food stores and pharmacies, and its proponents are touting it as a chemical fountain of youth. For those people forty and under, I recommend it for occasional use with a few precautions. If you are pregnant or nursing, have an auto-immune disorder, suffer from depression, use drugs, or have diabetes, you should not use melatonin. People over forty can consider using melatonin on a regular basis with the same precautions.

DHEA is sometimes called the "mother of hormones," because it is used by the body to manufacture other hormones, such as estrogen, progesterone, testosterone, and corticosterones. It is of enormous interest today because it is being called the "youth hormone." Researchers claim that it lowers serum cholesterol, reverses aging symptoms, promotes energy and libido, and stimulates the immune system. Recently, research has also shown the importance of DHEA in the prevention of cancer, heart disease, and Alzheimer's. Although supplements are widely available in health food stores and by mail order, I encourage you to use DHEA only with the supervision of a medical doctor or health practitioner who is familiar with it and can test you for your blood levels of DHEA. If you take too much, it can suppress your body's ability to make its own and encourage adult acne and excess facial and body hair. Wild yam contains the precursors that help the body produce its own DHEA and may be a safer, more natural way to rejuvenate the system.

Scientists tell us that we are as young as our glands. Your body's endocrine glands secrete hormones directly into the bloodstream and lymph system, exerting wide-ranging effects on other glands and on virtually every organ in the body. Many of the rejuvenating benefits of the 21-Day Program come from providing your endocrine glands with what they need to function properly—not just specific foods and nutrients, but also freedom from stress, adequate exercise, and cleansing of the systems of elimination.

Glandular Nutrients

Some of your glands require specific foods or nutrients to stay healthy. The thyroid gland requires iodine to maintain balanced activity. Sea vegetables are particularly rich in iodine. On Monday of this week, your dinner will include a Hijiki Stir-Fry, which is an excellent food for stimulating proper thyroid function and helping to regulate your metabolism, your weight, and your sex glands.

WILD YAM: A FOUNTAIN OF YOUTH

In 1940, an American scientist found that a species of Mexican Wild Yam contained a steroid precursor known as diosgenin, which could be used in the development of synthetic hormone products such as birth control pills, testosterone, and progesterone.

Today, Wild Yam is valued both in the herbal and scientific communities for its powerful effect on regulating hormone production. Though primarily regarded as a progesterone-producing herb, it acts to regulate the ratio of progesterone to estrogen in the system. According to Dr. John Lee, M.D., an authority on natural hormonal therapies, the progesterone taken from the Wild Yam is nearly identical to what the body produces; the body easily converts it into the identical molecule. It is most helpful in balancing symptoms of PMS, peri-menopause and menopause.

Wild Yam is also known to contain the natural precursors of the adrenal hormones, including natural cortisones. The long-term use of this herb can be highly beneficial for anyone in very stressful conditions. These hormone precursors are natural building blocks, which the body can use while the gland is being restored to its natural function.

Wild Yam has been used by the Chinese as a liver tonic, a digestive aid, and a muscle relaxant. It is known for its ability to strengthen, tone, and stimulate the secretive functions of the liver. This most important organ is intimately involved in all bodily functions and the health of all tissues.

Wild Yam remedies are derived from the long, twisting roots or various perennial species that are also known as Mexican Yam. They are unrelated to the sweet potato. Wild Yam is now finally available in a form that can survive the digestive process and deliver it as needed to the endocrine system.

Many vitamins are important for maintaining glandular health. Vitamin C helps all your glands to work at the peak of their capacity, as well as protecting your body against aging in general. Vitamin C is known to be necessary for adequate sex-hormone production and to help the adrenal glands produce their hormones. The bioflavonoids, including rutin, work to increase the biological effect of vitamin C and help to overcome premature aging. Vitamin A is another all-purpose rejuvenating and protective vitamin. Vitamin-A deficiency has been specifically shown to impair the ability of the thymus gland to produce the crucial disease-fighting T-lymphocytes of the immune system. Vitamin A also aids communication between your cells, protecting against the growth of mutated or malignant cells.

The B-complex vitamins are extremely important for glandular health. Vitamin B1, or thiamine, is known as an age-fighting vitamin, and it helps the pituitary gland to regulate the sex organs. Pantothenic acid protects against stress, and it has been known to help women delay the onset of menopause. PABA and folic acid, two other B vitamins, are reported to help keep the sex glands functioning effectively. Vitamin B6, or pyridoxine, helps protect against impotence in men and against PMS in women, and it specifically helps the liver to convert potentially harmful excess estrogen into harmless substances. In fact, all the B vitamins help to support the detoxifying function of the liver and the body overcome the effects of stress. Obviously, it is a good idea to take a high-potency vitamin-B complex supplement to promote glandular rejuvenation.

Lecithin is a very important rejuvenation food. It is present in all the endocrine glands, especially in the pituitary, the pineal, and the male and female sex glands, and it is an important component of semen. Lecithin is claimed to help improve virility and to prevent impotence. Continue to sprinkle granulated lecithin on your salads or soups and add it to your protein drinks to ensure an adequate supply of this life-extending nutrient. Its bland taste blends with any food you add it to.

Vitamin E protects against the aging effects of damaging free radicals in the body. In animal studies, vitamin E has been found to be essential to proper function of the reproductive glands.

When you see how important all these vitamins are to the health of your glands, you will understand why I recommend that you take a comprehensive multivitamin supplement every day.

Of the minerals, I particularly want to call attention to the importance of zinc. Many male sexual problems, including prostatitis and impotence, can often be traced to zinc deficiency. Seafood, especially shellfish, is an excellent source of zinc, but beware of possible contamination in shellfish. Nuts, legumes, and whole grains are other good zinc sources, and pumpkin seeds are very rich in zinc. A zinc supplement may prove helpful for men who are having sexual problems. Zinc also is healthful for the immune system.

In addition to B-complex vitamins, women should be careful to get plenty of calcium-rich foods and calcium supplements to guard against osteoporosis in later years, which so often occurs as the hormone balance changes after menopause. Stress also depletes calcium. Women should also not overdo their protein consumption, because protein can remove calcium from the bones.

Far too many Americans develop diabetes in middle age, especially if they are overweight. Diet is undoubtedly one of the causative factors. The incidence of diabetes tends to be measurably higher in populations eating a "civilized" modern diet low in fiber and high in refined sugar and starch than among native populations eating high-fiber diets based on whole, unrefined foods. Once diabetes develops, it not only limits what foods you can eat for the rest of your life—restricting you of necessity to a healthy Rejuvenation Diet—but it also dramatically increases the risk of heart disease. To avoid this terribly destructive disease, keep your weight within a normal range.

ROYAL JELLY: THE YOUTH FOOD

Royal jelly is the miraculous substance that is fed to the chosen female bee, transforming her into the queen of the hive and making her extremely fertile. Royal jelly extends the bee's normal life span of a few weeks to more than five years. Rich in B vitamins, amino acids, and minerals, royal jelly is a popular rejuvenation and nutritional aid in China and Japan. You can purchase it either in capsule form or in a honey base and add it to your drinks as a sweetener.

To keep your glands young, it is very important that you maintain a positive mental attitude. The health of your adrenal glands, and hence of your entire body, depends on your ability to control stress. When you are under stress, the adrenals first secrete adrenaline, and then, as the stress reaction continues, they begin to secrete cortisol, a compound that can have a damaging effect on all the organs of the body. Certain kinds of stimulants, such as caffeine, can produce chronic stress on the adrenal glands. This is one of the very good reasons to keep your overall caffeine consumption to a minimum.

If you would like professional guidance in evaluating your glandular health and establishing a program for glandular rejuvenation, I recommend that you contact a holistic doctor. These doctors are skilled at evaluating glandular functioning and prescribing special high-dose vitamin supplement programs to correct any possible imbalances.

Wednesday: Day 19

On Awakening: One 8-ounce glass of Hot Lemon-Water Flush (page 42); add one teaspoon honey with Royal Jelly (page 277). Prepare Inner Beauty Herbal Tea (pages 42-43); drink throughout the day between meals. Use Cleansing Inhalant (pages 168-169). Prepare four cups of Diuretic Tea (page 52); let steep all day for use in tonight's footbath.

Morning Cleansing: Dry Brush Massage (page 127), followed by warm shower.

Breakfast: Fresh Apple Breakfast (pages 53-54).

Mid-morning Snack: Optional—Maple Nut Shake (page 72) or Rejuvelac (page 47), one cup. Pour off today's Rejuvelac and prepare a batch for tomorrow. Have a protein drink in morning or afternoon only if you are hungry or need an energy boost.

Lunch: Fish, chicken, or tofu with steamed or raw vegetables.

Mid-afternoon Snack: Optional—Maple Nut Shake (page 72) or Rejuvelac (page 47), one cup.

Dinner: Vegetable Bisque (pages 57 to 58) of choice.

Exercise: Oxygenation Cocktail (page 47). Dancer's Warm-Up (page 149), followed by thirty minutes of brisk walking.

Evening Activity: Drink one cup of Rejuvelac (page 47). Add the remainder to tonight's footbath. Cellulite Self-Exam (pages 281, 283), followed by Cellulite Massage (pages 284-285) with Cellulite Massage Oil (page 283). Follow with Hot Foot Soak (page 161). Add Rejuvelac and Diuretic Tea you made this morning. Soak feet for twenty minutes.

How to Beat Cellulite

By this time in the 21-Day Program, I am sure that you are feeling very good about the weight you have lost. This is an ideal time to begin to attack your cellulite problem, if you have one, and to learn how to prevent the formation of cellulite in the future.

Cellulite (pronounced "sell-you-leet") is a term coined in the European health spas to describe the unsightly fatty deposits that do not go away, even after extensive dieting and exercise. Cellulite tends to form in specific parts of the body—buttocks, upper thighs, knees, upper arms, and more rarely on the lower legs, abdomen, back of the neck, and ankles. Cellulite is easy to recognize once it has become fairly advanced. It has a characteristic doughy consistency and a lumpy, dimpled appearance, like cottage cheese. If you have it, you know exactly what I am talking about.

Cellulite is a very controversial subject in the United States. Although cellulite is still not recognized by the American medical establishment as a health problem, European doctors and health clinics have been treating it for years as a disease of the connective tissue, or "fat gone wrong." Most of my recommendations are based on the breakthrough research and treatment that has been done in Europe.

Cellulite is a gel-like substance made up of a combination of fat, waste material, and water that is trapped between strands of fibrous tissue just beneath the surface of the skin. Women tend to get cellulite much more frequently than men—about 80 percent of women have this problem to some degree. There are several reasons why cellulite is largely a feminine problem. To begin with, women have more fatty tissue than men. Cellulite forms in the layer of subcutaneous fatty tissue just below the skin; it is this tissue that provides the typical rounded feminine contours.

The female hormone estrogen also seems to contribute to the formation of cellulite. Women's bodies are flooded with estrogen before the menstrual period and sometimes also at ovulation. Just as estrogen is responsible for the psychological discomfort of premenstrual stress, it also encourages cellulite formation by promoting excess water retention in the tissues, leading to congestion of the lymphatic system in the legs and the groin region. Because the lymph system is responsible for removing protein waste from the body, this congestion causes the waste to be deposited in the surrounding connective tissue. The protein waste combines with fat cells, and the protein attracts water, forcing the cells to swell. The swelling causes the surrounding blood and lymph vessels to constrict, cutting down on circulation, and eventually the entire connective tissue network enclosing the fat cells begins to atrophy and harden, forming a gelatin-like network with pockets of fat cells puffed up with water.

Out of desperation, trying to rid their bodies of these unsightly bulges, women go on crash diets. Their bodies produce enzymes to break down body fat for energy, but these enzymes cannot reach the stagnant cellulite deposits of fat, water, and waste, because the circulation to these areas is already impaired. As a result, the fat melts away from other parts of the body, such as the breasts and the facial tissues, creating the haggard, aged appearance that is so characteristic of crash dieters.

The formation of cellulite is very closely connected to constipation and the resultant toxicity. The more toxic waste is allowed to accumulate in the body, the greater the chance that it will find its way into the subcutaneous fatty tissue and get trapped in stagnant cellulite deposits. This is an excellent reason to avoid all foods containing chemicals and pesticides and hard-to-digest refined and processed food and to observe the rules of food combining, so wastes are flushed out of the system as rapidly as possible.

The renowned French herbalist and healer Maurice Messegue did extensive experiments on cellulite control with women from all over Europe. He found that it was only when these women gave up eating foods that contained pesticides and other chemicals that they were able to begin to reduce the cellulite in their bodies. Such chemicals create extra stress on the liver, preventing it from doing its job of breaking up fatty deposits and removing excess estrogen and other hormones from the body. Excess estrogen increases the tendency to water retention, promoting the formation of new cellulite.

GLA and EPA not only keep your skin, hair, and nails strong and healthy, but they also help to prevent the formation of harmful fatty deposits in the blood vessels and to burn the subcutaneous fat that can provide a home for waste material and turn into cellulite.

Our sedentary lifestyle also contributes to the formation of cellulite. Prolonged sitting causes the blockage of blood and lymph circulation in the thighs and buttocks. If you have a sedentary job, it is particularly important to get regular exercise to promote circulation in these cellulite-prone areas. Do slant-board activities to promote drainage of lymph and blood, use full-body massage and lymph massage to aid the flushing of wastes, and practice yoga postures that stimulate circulation and tone the muscles that control elimination. Detoxifying baths, herbal steams, Hot Castor-Oil Abdominal Wraps, sitz baths, and footbaths also help to promote circulation and drain waste from the lymphatic system. Daily skin brushing is an essential routine for cellulite control, removing waste from the skin, so the skin is fresh each day to do its job of eliminating the body's debris.

In addition to the general measures that you have learned in the 21-Day Program, I am now going to give you specific techniques for dealing with any cellulite in your body. Many massage therapists use a specialized form of massage to help break up fatty cellulite deposits and bring circulation into the affected areas to carry away the waste that has been trapped there. You can do the same kind of massage yourself on a regular basis to help rid your body of these unsightly deposits.

Your evening activities tonight will be devoted to learning cellulite-control techniques. Before I show you how to do a cellulite self-massage, you need to know where cellulite is located in your body and what kind of cellulite it is. The Cellulite Self-Exam will enable you to take stock of your cellulite situation. Do not despair if you find deposits of cellulite. This 21-Day Program is designed to help you break up this cellulite and flush the debris out of your body, as well as to discourage the formation of new cellulite.

Cellulite Self-Exam

To locate cellulite deposits on your body, stand undressed before a full-length mirror. If you do not see any obvious areas of ripples, lumps, or cottage-cheese skin, try squeezing the tissues of your upper thigh between the thumb and index finger or between the palms of both hands. If cellulite is present, the skin will dimple and have a characteristic quilted appearance. Try this squeezing test on all the areas of your body where cellulite is most likely to occur—the outer parts of the upper thighs, the buttocks,

CELLULITE-CONTROL DIET

Proper digestion and elimination of toxins are the keys to banishing cellulite from your body. Make a commitment to eat the Foods to Eat and beware of the Foods to Avoid, and you can take control of your figure problems.

Foods to Eat:

Organically grown fresh fruits and vegetables—no chemicals or pesticides

Whole grains

Fresh juices

Fibrous foods in general

Sea vegetables and other iodine-rich foods

At least eight glasses of fluids each day—juices, herb teas, Hydrating Drink, purified water, broth

GLA oil in salad dressing and GLA-EPA supplement

Supplements: aloe-vera juice, liquid minerals, digestive enzymes, vitamin B6 for detoxifying excess estrogen, intestinal cleanser

Liver-Flush drinks, for special periodic cleansing

Foods to Avoid:

Processed foods—synthetics, preservatives, additives

Nonorganic meats or poultry

Fish from shallow or possibly polluted waters

Fatty foods

Tap water

Sugar

Salt

Bread

White flour

Salted snack foods

Fried foods

Candies, cookies, and pastries

Cheese

Excessive animal protein

Excessive alcohol

Excessive caffeine

the inner knees, the upper arms, the abdomen—unless you can actually see the dimpling effect without squeezing. Not every fatty area will dimple, only those areas with toxic cellulite.

There are two kinds of cellulite, solid and soft. Solid or firm cellulite generally appears on women who are in good physical condition. You may notice that even female marathon runners with muscular, sinewy legs may show the telltale signs of puckered skin on their outer thighs. People with solid cellulite generally do not have much fatty tissue and cannot easily lift the cellulite away from the underlying muscle. Squeezing or pinching the skin in solid cellulite areas may produce pain or sensitivity. The skin in these areas is generally dry and sometimes rough, due to poor nourishment, and it may have stretch marks.

Soft cellulite is not as concentrated or compact as solid cellulite. It tends to occupy large areas and to hang loosely, shaking with every body movement. Soft cellulite tends to affect women with poor muscle tone and soft skin; they may have been active in the past but have been inactive for some time. People who go on crash diets often end up with soft cellulite, because the yo-yo weight changes cause the tissues to lose their elasticity.

After looking at yourself in the mirror and trying the squeeze test, you probably have a good idea of whether you have any cellulite and whether it is solid or soft. To tell how advanced a case of cellulite you have, notice whether there is any sensitivity on touching or pinching the skin in the cellulite areas. The more advanced the cellulite, the more tender and painful it is when pinched or squeezed.

Cellulite Massage Oil

If you have cellulite, prepare this aromatic oil to use for the Cellulite Massage below. Massage the oil liberally into any areas affected by cellulite to help break up the fatty deposits and mobilize the waste into the lymph system.

1 ounce olive oil   *12 drops rosemary essential oil*

1 ounce almond oil   *12 drops geranium oil*

1 ounce peanut oil

Combine all ingredients and store in an airtight container.

In addition to the moisturizing and beautifying benefits of the vegetable oils, the essential oils in this recipe have special detoxifying properties. Rosemary oil stimulates the function of the liver as it breaks down fat, regulates hormone balance, and synthesizes new proteins to build healthy skin. Geranium oil helps to maintain proper hormone balance and is used to relieve the excessive fluid retention that produces premenstrual stress. These oils stimulate the lymphatic system and aid the elimination of waste and fluids in general.

Cellulite Massage

Please understand that cellulite massage by itself will not miraculously make your cellulite problem disappear. To get rid of cellulite, you must make a serious commitment to the Rejuvenation Diet and to the entire program I am recommending. Only if you have laid the groundwork by doing everything else right will the cellulite massage be able to help, and you must do the self-massage diligently and regularly to break up the cellulite deposits.

Your cellulite massage will be concentrated on the areas where you have identified cellulite. You can do it any time you want—during your bath or whenever you have a few minutes—to help increase the blood and lymph flow to these circulation-starved areas, break down the cellulite, and move the resultant waste out of your body.

Do not press too hard when doing a cellulite massage. Begin with moderate pressure and increase only as you know you can tolerate it without bruising or discomfort.

Before you do your first cellulite massage, make up a batch of Cellulite Massage Oil. This special, fragrant formulation not only lubricates the skin but also penetrates the tissue, helping to promote the removal of toxins. Warm some of the Cellulite Massage Oil in your hands. Then begin by stroking lightly over the cellulite areas, to prepare the skin for the movements that follow. Continue to apply Cellulite Massage Oil throughout this massage whenever necessary to lubricate and penetrate the skin. Using the flat of your hand with the fingers curved around the body part, use long, light, smooth, sliding strokes, always moving toward the heart. Stroke upward on your legs, over the hips and buttocks, and in the same clockwise direction over the tummy as you used in the Tummy Massage (working from the navel to the right side, then up and over the navel to the left, down and below the navel and up again on the right side). If you have cellulite on your upper arms or upper torso, stroke upward into the armpit and down the chest toward the heart.

The next movements you use depend on what type of cellulite you have. If you have soft cellulite that you can grasp between your fingers or between your palms, grab a hunk of cellulite tissue, lift it away from the underlying muscles, and squeeze it firmly. You can do this with your fingers or with the whole hand, depending on how large an area you are working on. Using your fingers or whole hand, lift the cellulite tissue and squeeze, lift and squeeze, working all over the area where you see the cellulite. In areas like the inner knee or the upper arm, squeezing with the fingers is most effective. Lift and squeeze with the whole hand to work on the larger cellulite areas over the hips and buttocks. Work upward from the upper thighs and over the hips. When you massage the leg below the upper thigh, rest your foot on a stool or the edge of the tub, or sit with your knee bent, to relax the muscles.

If you can lift large areas of cellulite tissue with both hands, wring it between your hands and twist it around. Squeeze it to break up the deposits inside and encourage circulation. If you cannot pick up the flesh, just squeeze and wring the tissues between both hands. This is no time to be gentle! Squeeze that cellulite out of your body.

If you have solid cellulite, you may not be able to lift the tissue away from the underlying structure at all, and you will need to employ crushing movements to break up the cellulite deposits and encourage circulation. For solid cellulite, do the crushing movements directly after the initial light stroking. Bunch your hands into fists and, with the knuckles, crush the cellulite areas with a circular motion. Go ahead, take out all your aggressions on those bulges! These crushing movements are very effective for the hips, upper thighs, and tummy.

End your massage with deep, firm stroking. Use full pressure, going in the direction of the heart. Use the flat of your hand, with the fingers and thumb curved around the part of the body you are massaging, and slide your hands in long, deep strokes, exerting pressure. Stroke toward the heart, up the legs and hips and clockwise over the tummy. Firm stroking promotes the circulation of blood and lymph and helps drain away the waste matter that has been released by the massage movements.

You may have noticed that my recommendations for a Cellulite-Control Diet, as well as the Cellulite Do's and Don'ts, are very similar to those for controlling constipation, except that the cellulite-control recommendations focus specifically on eliminating toxic substances and balancing hormone function. This similarity is not coincidence. Proper elimination helps prevent the buildup of fatty deposits and removes the toxic wastes that ultimately get trapped in fatty tissue to create cellulite.

By making a strong commitment to observe these recommendations, you will begin to win your battle against cellulite. It can be a long process. Use affirmations to maintain a positive attitude and help control stress, since anxiety and worry and feeling bad about yourself can cause your muscles to tighten and impair circulation in the very areas where you want to flush the waste away. Each time you do a Cellulite Self-Massage, remind yourself that your efforts are going to pay off with smooth new contours and healthy, glowing, youthful skin.

CELLULITE DO'S AND DON'TS

Winning the battle against cellulite requires determination and effort. The suggested Do's in this table will make you feel better all over; the Don'ts just bring you down from your light, clean, and clear feeling and should be avoided.

Do:

Perform daily skin brushing to promote elimination of waste through the pores.

Receive professional massage to promote circulation and relaxation.

Perform Cellulite Self-Massage, using Cellulite Massage Oil.

Take anti-cellulite baths, such as a seaweed bath or Sea Mineral Bath.

Take detoxifying baths, steams, sitz baths (especially cold), and footbaths.

Exercise daily—walk, swim, bike, use a trampoline.

Practice yoga postures at least three times a week for relaxation, circulation, and toning.

Perform deep-breathing exercises at least three times a week to burn up toxic wastes.

Observe food-combining rules.

Take Lactobacillus bacteria supplements.

Maintain colon health, using intestinal cleanser and colonics or at-home enemas as needed.

Make daily efforts to manage and release stress.

Don't:

Allow yourself to get constipated.

Sit for long periods of time.

Breathe polluted air.

Use excessive alcohol.

Smoke tobacco.

Crash diet.

Overeat.

Eat rapidly.

Drink liquids with meals.

Eat when you are upset.

Worry and rush.

Allow yourself to get fatigued.

Thursday: Day 20

On Awakening: One 8-ounce glass of Hot Lemon-Water Flush (page 42); add one teaspoon honey with Royal Jelly (page 277). Prepare Inner Beauty Herbal Tea (pages 42-43); drink throughout the day between meals. Use Cleansing Inhalant (pages 168-169).

Morning Cleansing: Dry Brush Massage (page 127). Follow with Alternating Hot and Cold Shower—begin with three to five minutes of hot water; switch to ten to fifteen seconds of cold water. Repeat three times, ending with cold water. Dry briskly with a coarse towel.

Breakfast: Healing Grape Breakfast (pages 56-57).

Mid-morning Snack: Optional—Carrot Shake (page 73) or Rejuvelac (page 47), one cup. Pour off today's Rejuvelac and prepare a batch for tomorrow. Have a protein drink in morning or afternoon only if you are hungry or need an energy boost.

Lunch: Fish, chicken or tofu with steamed or raw vegetables.

Mid-afternoon Snack: Optional—Carrot Shake (page 73) or Rejuvelac (page 47), one cup.

Dinner: Squash Bisque (pages 57-58) and baked potato With Golden Goddess Topping (page 66).

Exercise: Oxygenation Cocktail (page 47). Wake-Up Shake-Up (page 148), followed by thirty minutes of brisk walking.

Evening Activity: Drink one cup of Rejuvelac (page 47). Add the remainder to tonight's bath. Yoga Rejuvenation Postures (pages 289-292), followed by Balloon Breathing (page 169). Follow with Evening "Youth Bath" (page 186), or if you really cannot stand cold water tonight, a warm Sea-Mineral Bath (page 176).

Yoga for Rejuvenation

The ancient system of hatha yoga had a profound understanding of the importance of glandular health, and many yoga postures are designed to stimulate and balance the function of the various endocrine glands. On Thursday: Day 20, your evening activity will include these rejuvenation postures, which have been used for centuries to preserve youth and extend life expectancy. Practice these postures regularly to keep your glands young and healthy. If you wish, read the instructions into your tape recorder, so you can perform these postures in smooth, flowing movements without interruptions.

Knees to Chest

Lie on the floor in the resting pose, with your arms at your sides. Relax and breathe for a few minutes. Now bring both knees to the chest with your arms clasped around your knees. Relax in this position, breathing in and out normally and feeling the stretch in the lower back. Hold this position and rock gently from side to side for a minute or so. Stop rocking, and with your knees still to your chest, relax

KNEES TO CHEST

again for another minute or two, then release and straighten your knees, lower your legs slowly to the floor, and rest for a few minutes in the resting pose. This knee-to-chest posture is excellent for relaxing the lower back and easing back strain.

Rocking Plough

ROCKING PLOUGH

Raise your legs with the knees straight and grab your ankles, or as far down your legs as you can comfortably reach. Now, slowly pull your legs down toward your trunk, tuck your head forward, and gently rock forward and back on your spine. Rock as far back as you can comfortably go; if you are very flexible, you may be able to touch the floor behind your head with your toes. Do not strain. Now let go of your ankles, and if you can, bring your legs all the way back behind your head with the knees straight, supporting your lower back with your hands resting on your elbows, and relax in this inverted position. While your legs are back there, bend your knees and bring them down toward the ears and relax in this position. Then straighten your knees again, return to the Rocking Plough position, begin to rock gently, and rock forward and sit up.

Seated Toe Pull

SEATED TOE PULL

Sit quietly for a moment, then as you breathe out, bend forward and grab your big toes and pull on them. According to many yoga teachers, this toe-pull stimulates the pituitary gland. Release your toes and sit up. Now, as you inhale, raise your arms above your head. As you breathe out, bend forward, with your arms reaching as far down your leg as they will go and your head as close to your knees as possible. Keep your knees straight and breathe normally. Relax in this position for as long as you can, then breathe in and sit up. Breathe out and bend forward with your head toward your knees again, and relax as long as you can in the down position, breathing normally.

High Shoulder Stand

Lie down again and relax in the resting pose. Now bring your legs up with your knees straight and push off with your arms, supporting your lower back with your hands resting on bent elbows. Push your body up until you are in a completely vertical inverted position, with your weight on the top of the spine and the back of the neck. This is one of the most invigorating and rejuvenating yoga postures, because it reverses the effects of gravity. Support your lower back with your hands and breathe normally into your abdomen. Bend your chin into your neck to stimulate the thyroid gland. With your legs straight up in the air, rotate your ankles, first in one direction, then the other. If you are still comfortable in this position, spread your legs far out to the sides and rotate your ankles. Bring your legs back together, still breathing normally, and do a forward and back split with your legs, with first one leg forward, then the other. Come out of this inverted posture

HIGH SHOULDER STAND

the same way you got into it, letting your legs drop back behind your head, bracing your hands on the floor, and gradually rolling back down on the spine. Pay close attention as you roll back, trying to release one vertebra at a time. Relax in the resting pose, feeling the effects of the posture.

Fish Pose

The Fish Pose is a perfect complement to the shoulder stand. Lie on your back and breathe normally. Begin by doing the "easy fish." Put your weight on your elbows and arch your back, letting your head drop back so that your weight is resting partially on your elbows and partially on the very top of your head. Your back should form an arch

FISH POSE

from the buttocks to the top of your head. Let your hands rest on your hip joints. This is a wonderful position for stimulating the thyroid, the thymus, and the glands in the head. This is also a wonderful opportunity to stretch the muscles in your face. No one is watching you! Repeatedly jut out your chin, open your mouth as wide as you can, blink your eyes, and stick out your tongue. Now slide back down into the resting position and relax, enjoying the benefits.

Full Fish Pose

Cross your legs at the ankles with the knees bent and pull on both big toes. Pull your toes down behind the opposite knees. Now, keeping your hands on your toes, try to drop your knees down to the floor. Feel the stretch and pull on the hip joints and thigh muscles. In this position, go into the Fish Pose once more. Push up with your weight on your elbows and the top of your head. Do your facial exercises again, breathing all the way down into the abdomen. Stretch your neck out; stick out your tongue! This is a great chance to exercise all your facial muscles again. Then slide your head and arms back down, slide your legs forward and relax, feeling the invigorating effects of this posture.

FULL FISH POSE

Friday: Day 21

On Awakening: One 8-ounce glass of Hot Lemon-Water Flush (page 42); add one teaspoon honey with Royal Jelly (page 277). Prepare Inner Beauty Herbal Tea (pages 42-43); drink throughout the day between meals. Use Cleansing Inhalant (pages 168-169).

Morning Cleansing: Morning Cold Splash and Rub (page 185).

Breakfast: Sliced Fresh Pineapple Breakfast (page 54).

Mid-morning Snack: Optional—Tahini Shake (page 73) or Rejuvelac (page 47), one cup. Pour off today's Rejuvelac and prepare a batch for tomorrow. Have a protein drink in morning or afternoon only if you are hungry or need an energy boost.

Lunch: Fish, chicken, or tofu with steamed or raw vegetables.

Mid-afternoon Snack: Optional—Tahini Shake (page 73) or Rejuvelac (page 47), one cup.

Dinner: Beet Borscht (pages 59-60) and steamed vegetables with Carrot-Leek Purée (pages 66-67).

Exercise: Oxygenation Cocktail (page 47). Lymph-Cleansing Warm-Up (pages 221-223), followed by thirty minutes of brisk walking.

Evening Activity: Drink one cup of Rejuvelac (page 47). Add the remainder to tonight's bath. Complete Toxicity Symptom Checklist (pages 117-118). Review 21-Day Goals Contract (page 32). Apply Hot Olive-Oil Rejuvenating Facial (page 295). Leave olive oil on while taking Optimism Bath (page 134). In bath, do Warm Soak and Stroke (pages 197-199).

Closing, 21-Day Program

As you end this week, take time to look back over the entire 21-Day Program to see how far you have come and how much you have gotten out of the program. Go back and review the goals you set on page 32. Which of your goals did you meet or even surpass? Which will you need to continue moving toward in the weeks and months to come? As you review these goals at the end of the program, you will probably have a better idea of what kinds of goals will be realistic for you to set in the future. Make a note of these in your journal. It is always helpful to have positive, realistic objectives in mind to guide your efforts in becoming the very best that you can be.

Truly, by learning to respect, love, and take responsibility for your body, you are also assisting the entire planet. As we attempt to solve the huge problems of our ailing, polluted earth, we must begin by taking loving action on our own individual selves. By clearing up the pollution in your body, you become more aware of the commitment needed to purify and heal our fragile, shared environment.

Finish the 21-Day Program on Friday night by luxuriating in your Inspiration Bath with your Hot Olive-Oil Rejuvenating Facial, and repeat the affirmations that have guided you through this program. Remind yourself that you have rejuvenated your cells, tissues, organs, and thoughts and that you have become cleaner, clearer, and more effective in every aspect of your life. This may be the end of the 21-Day Program, but it is just the beginning of a whole new, more joyful way of living.

HOT OLIVE-OIL REJUVENATING FACIAL

Hot olive oil applied to the face, throat, and neck helps to moisturize and rejuvenate the skin and guard against wrinkles.

Warm a quarter-cup of olive oil. Smooth it over your face and neck, all the way down to the chest.

For added benefit, wrap a hot towel around your neck, so the oil can really seep into this area, which often becomes prematurely wrinkled. Lie back in a relaxing, fragrant bath and enjoy the soothing richness of the olive oil as it penetrates your skin and refreshes your complexion. At the end of your bath, remove the olive oil with cleansing bath gel or other gentle bath soap.

Rejuvenation Tune-Ups

Now that you have finished the 21-Day Program, I am sure you want to know how you can incorporate what you have learned into the rest of your life. Try to develop the habit of lightening your diet and cleansing your body and mind on a regular basis. Many of my clients go on a seasonal cleansing regimen as a means of rejuvenation. Find the cycle that works best for you. Make a commitment to repeat the 21-Day Program twice a year—spring and fall are the traditional times for cleansing.

Keep in mind that you should undertake the Rejuvenation Tune-Up Programs only if you have been following the principles of the Rejuvenation Diet on a regular basis. If you have been eating all sorts of foods, improperly combined, you must prepare your body before you jump into anything too strenuous. I must emphasize that the Rejuvenation Tune-Up Programs are not crash diets. You must do the entire cleansing program, not just change the way you eat, in order to derive meaningful physical and mental benefits.

Experiment with the rejuvenating possibilities offered by these periodic cleansing programs to discover which ones are right for your needs.

One-Day Liquid Cleansing Diet

I recommend that you rest and cleanse your system one day each week with the One-Day Liquid Cleansing Diet. This lifelong rejuvenation strategy is an effective tool for managing your weight and for cellulite control. The day you set aside for this diet is also an excellent time to receive a professional massage, since you are resting your digestive system and releasing toxins and tension. I like to do this diet regularly on Mondays. If I have wavered from the Rejuvenation Diet over the weekend, a Monday cleansing is a great way to begin the week with new energy and inspiration.

- *Breakfast:* Liver Flush #1 or #2 (pages 50 to 51).

- *Mid-morning Snack* (Optional)*:* Fruit juice of choice, freshly squeezed (if you need the extra energy boost).

- *Lunch:* Protein Drink of choice (pages 70 to 73).

- *Mid-afternoon Snack:* Cleansing Juice Blend of choice (page 53). Drink one cup of Diuretic Tea (page 52) one hour before dinner.

- *Dinner:* Potassium Broth or Vegetable Bisque of choice (pages 57 to 58).

- *Throughout the Day:* Drink Herbal Purification Tea (page 49) between meals.

Three-Day Rejuvenation Intensive

The Three-Day Rejuvenation Intensive is a wonderful way to prepare for a special event or to lighten up your body and your mind. If you feel yourself coming down with a cold or the flu, this Three-Day Intensive is also a good way to give your digestive system a rest, so your body can direct its energies toward healing.

Day 1

- *On Awakening:* One 8-ounce glass of Hot Lemon-Water Flush (page 42). Prepare Herbal Purification Tea (page 49) for the day; drink it throughout the day between meals. Use Cleansing Inhalant (pages 168-169).

- *Morning Cleansing:* Dry Brush Massage (page 127). Follow with a hot shower, finishing with a one-minute cold splash.

- *Breakfast:* Papaya Complexion Breakfast (pages 54-55).

- *Lunch:* Carrot Shake (page 73), as much as you want.

- *Mid-afternoon Snack:* Vegetable juice of choice.

- *Dinner:* Super Salad with sunflower seeds (pages 62-63) and Fat-Loss Dressing of choice (pages 63 to 65); Potassium Broth (pages 44-45), one cup.

- *Exercise:* Oxygenation Cocktail (page 47). Follow with Yoga Stress Releasers (pages 109-111). If you are feeling well, enjoy thirty minutes of brisk walking.

- *Evening Activity:* "Hot Foot" Soak (page 161), followed by professional massage.

Day 2

- *On Awakening:* Drink one glass of Hydrating Drink (pages 43-44).

- Prepare Herbal Purification Tea (page 49) for the day; drink it throughout the day between meals. Use Cleansing Inhalant (pages 168-169).

- *Morning Cleansing:* Dry Brush Massage (page 127), followed by Alternating Hot and Cold Shower, ending with cold.

- *Breakfast:* Liver Flush #1 (pages 50-51).

- *Lunch:* Tahini Shake (page 73), as much as you want.

- *Mid-afternoon Snack:* Vegetable juice of choice.

- *Dinner:* Hijiki Stir-Fry (pages 69-70), with one cup of Potassium Broth (pages 44-45).

- *Exercise:* Oxygenation Cocktail (page 47) followed by Antigravity Tone-Up (pages 152-153) and Antigravity Facial Massage (pages 191-192). If you are feeling well, enjoy brisk walking for thirty minutes.

- *Evening Activity:* Tummy Massage (pages 240-241), followed by Hot Castor-Oil Abdominal Wrap (pages 239-240). While Castor-Oil Wrap is on, do Three-Part Breathing (pages 172-173) and Complete Breath (pages 173-174). Epsom Salts Soak (page 132), with one tablespoon of baking soda added.

Day 3

- *On Awakening:* Drink one glass of Hydrating Drink (pages 43-44).

- Prepare Herbal Purification Tea (page 49) for the day; drink it throughout the day between meals. Use Cleansing Inhalant (pages 168-169).

- *Morning Cleansing:* Morning Cold Splash and Rub (page 185), followed by Dry Brush Massage (page 127).

- *Breakfast:* Liver Flush #2 (page 52).

- *Lunch:* Maple Nut Shake (page 72), as much as you want.

- *Mid-afternoon Snack:* Vegetable juice of choice.

- *Dinner:* Vegetable Bisque of choice (pages 57 to 58), as much as you want; small Super Salad (pages 62-63).

- *Exercise:* Oxygenation Cocktail (page 47). Follow with Yoga Rejuvenation Postures (pages 289-292). If you are feeling well, enjoy brisk walking for thirty minutes.

- *Evening Activity:* Professional colonic, followed by Tranquility Bath (page 137).

Eight-Day Shape-Up

To prepare for a special event, when you want to look and feel your best and radiate vitality, follow this eight-day program. If you do not have the time to do the entire 21-Day Program, this intensive shape-up is excellent for seasonal cleansing, for after the holidays or an overindulgent vacation, for recovering from major stress, or for any time you want to devote a special eight days to taking care of yourself. To avoid cleansing reactions, please do not begin this program unless you have been on the Rejuvenation Diet for at least one week. Return to the Rejuvenation Diet afterward, and you will continue to enjoy the physical and mental benefits. Be sure to include all the activities, since they are an essential part of the cleansing process.

Your meals and beverages during the Eight-Day Shape-up are based on the intensive cleansing portion of the 21-Day Program. You begin with the raw foods portion of this cleansing regimen, and return gently to fruits and raw and cooked vegetables after a two-day liquid fast. The evening activities are an intensified and accelerated version of the cleansing and stress-releasing activities used during the 21-Day Program.

To do the Eight-Day Shape-up, follow all the day-by-day instructions for Monday: Day 10 through Monday: Day 17, and add the special activities indicated below.

1. Hot Castor-Oil Abdominal Wrap (pages 239-240), every night if possible. Be sure to include the Castor-Oil Wrap the nights before colon cleansing.

2. Two yoga sessions: Digestion Toning Postures (page 29) and Yoga Rejuvenation Postures (pages 289-292).

3. Upper- and Lower-Body Lymph Massage (pages 222-223 and 162-163), preceded by "Hot Foot" Soak (page 161).

4. Three breathing-exercises sessions: Each time, include Three-Part Breathing (pages 172-173), Complete Breath (pages 173-174), Alternate-Hemisphere Breathing (pages 174-175), and Balloon Breathing (page 169).

The Apple Diet

This Detox Diet was developed and recommended by the renowned psychic Edgar Cayce back in the early 1900s. He suggests that you eat only apples, but as many as you like, for three consecutive days. The Apple Diet is easier for many people to do, especially if you work, than the other diets, because of the suggestion to eat as many apples as you wish. You're able to continue chewing and may feel less deprived.

The Apple Diet will cleanse your digestive system of excess gas, mucus, and waste material and will help purify your blood and lymphatic systems. Apple pectin helps to sweep out and detoxify the alimentary canal.

Apples will keep your blood sugar on an even keel and aid in controlling appetite by producing a satisfying feeling of fullness. They are also good for cleansing the teeth and stimulating the gums. Research has found that apples help decrease blood cholesterol levels.

Buy organic apples that are free of pesticides and other chemicals. Apples grown with chemicals have toxins even in the core. Many supermarkets are now beginning to carry apples and other produce that have not been sprayed. Choose your favorite sweet apples (I prefer Fuji), and eat them raw. Be sure to eat the skin, which is very high in pectin fiber. Some people even like to eat the seeds, because of their rich supply of nutrients.

Days 1, 2 and 3:

- *On Awakening:* Drink one glass of Hot Lemon-Water Flush (page 42).

- Prepare Herbal Purification Tea (page 49) for the day; drink it throughout the day between meals. Use Cleansing Inhalant (pages 168-169).

- *Morning Cleansing:* Morning Cold Splash and Rub (page 185), followed by Dry Brush Massage (page 127).

- *Breakfast:* Apples, as many as you wish.

- *Lunch:* Apples, as many as you wish.

- *Mid-afternoon Snack:* Apples, as many as you wish.

- *Dinner:* Apples, as many as you wish.

- *Exercise:* Oxygenation Cocktail (page 47). Follow with Yoga Rejuvenation Postures (pages 289-292). If you are feeling well, enjoy brisk walking for thirty minutes.

- *Evening Activity:* Professional colonic, enema, or massage followed by a Bath of your choice.

Monthly Retreat for Women

In native cultures, even today, the menstrual period is considered a powerful rite of passage and a cleansing process. In fact, the cyclical cleansing through the loss of menstrual blood may be one reason women live longer than men. I particularly like the Native American traditions of honoring the "moon time." Among many Native American tribes, women retire each month to "moon lodges." This does not mean that they are stuck away somewhere, as people often believe. Rather, the women are given the gift of quiet, peaceful days when they are not expected to carry out their usual chores. In the moon lodge, the women relax and meditate, often coming away with visions that help to guide the future activities of the tribe.

Native Americans understand that the menstrual cycle is linked with the phases of the moon. The full moon is the time of ovulation, when energy is more externally directed, and the new moon is the time of menstruation, a time when energy draws within. Many women, even in modern society, find that personal and spiritual issues that do not come to the surface during the rest of the month seem to become more pronounced around the menstrual time. As you become more aware of how your cycles affect your mind and body, you can use this special time of the month to gain insights about important personal issues.

Several years ago, my sister and a friend developed an idea for a retreat center especially for women during their moon time, where they would be able to get away for a few days and be taken care of. When I told my sister recently about the Indian moon lodges, she was delighted to realize that her idea had really arisen from a need that all women feel for a different pace during the menstrual period. It is important for women to recognize that demanding, high-pressure schedules should not be maintained throughout the entire month. While you may not be able to afford the luxury of getting away on a monthly basis, you can create a protective haven for yourself during your own cycles. During my menstrual period, I schedule fewer clients, knowing that my lighter workload will give me more quiet time to myself.

The first step in turning your menstrual period into a beneficial, cleansing time is to come to know your cycles. It amazes me how many women I work with are not aware of their "moon cycles" and of the changes that take place in their bodies, their dietary needs, and their moods. When they begin to keep track, most women find that they have their period around either the full or the new moon, although the cycle may change over time. By learning to recognize your cycle, you have another opportunity to gain insight about your body. If you are not already doing so, begin to log your menstrual cycle on your personal calendar. Also note in your calendar any symptoms that are associated with the premenstrual period or with the onset of menstruation. Do you become bloated or constipated before your period? Do you notice premenstrual tension and stress? Do you sleep less or more than usual? As you become more aware of the rhythms of your body, you will know when to use natural interventions to make this a more pleasant time for yourself, and you will be able to deal more appropriately with your feelings, your work schedule, and your relationships.

It is also important to know when you ovulate. Regardless of the length of your entire menstrual cycle, ovulation normally occurs about fourteen days before your next menstrual period begins. We have other ways of identifying when ovulation occurs. The basal body temperature, or the lowest daily temperature that the body reaches during waking hours, drops just before ovulation, and then at ovulation rises steadily for the next three days or so, remaining elevated until menstruation begins. Women practicing natural birth control use this basal temperature method to help predict the fertile days of their monthly cycle. Another method used in natural birth control is to observe the changes in the cervical mucus and vaginal discharges throughout the month. The normal vaginal discharge between menstruation and ovulation is white, cloudy, or yellowish, and thick and sticky. A few days before ovulation, the discharge increases in volume and becomes clear and slippery like raw egg white. Classes in natural birth control and fertility awareness, available through women's clinics and Planned Parenthood, can help you to become more aware of your ovulation and menstrual cycle, so your monthly mood and body changes will no longer take you by surprise.

In our society, premenstrual syndrome, or PMS, has come to be viewed as a disorder that encompasses a wide range of symptoms such as mood swings, headache, bloating, breast tenderness, irritability, and depression. It is not so well known that some researchers have found that women also exhibit positive changes during this premenstrual time, such as greater ability to concentrate and increased creativity and assertiveness. Such changes are due to the interplay of hormones. Before the menstrual period, excess estrogen overbalances progesterone, producing the typical PMS symptoms. The body is then flooded with progesterone when menstruation begins, and the symptoms are alleviated.

I find that if I follow the Rejuvenation Diet and practice food rotation as explained in Week 3, page 267, my premenstrual symptoms are diminished almost entirely. Most of my female clients find the same. The liver is responsible for removing excess estrogen from the system. By reducing the burden on your liver produced by improper diet, you enable it to regulate your delicate hormonal balance and detoxify the excess estrogen. A special program of supplements can also help you to prepare for your menstrual period and reduce the symptoms of PMS.

Smooth-Cycle Checklist

In addition to practicing proper food combining and taking your usual supplements, begin to make these special alterations in your diet and supplement program about three to seven days before your menstrual period is due, and continue until the end of menstruation. If you still experience uncomfortable premenstrual or menstrual symptoms, try beginning earlier the next month, until you find the right time to provide your body with this extra nutritional support.

Supplements

- Take 50 to 150 milligrams of vitamin B6, along with a complete B complex, to help control premenstrual mood swings and other emotional problems and support the liver in detoxifying excess estrogen.

- Take a special PMS formula, available in health food stores. Such a formula may contain enough vitamin B6 or other nutrients that you do not need to take these as separate supplements.

- Take a multiphase digestive enzyme to help prevent constipation and reduce the toxic burden on your liver. (Digestive Enzymes are described on pages 215-217.)

- Add two tablespoons of flax seed oil to your daily diet or take 500 milligrams of Evening Primrose Oil twice daily. (These "good fats" are discussed in detail on pages 93-94.)

If your PMS symptoms are not alleviated by supplements alone, consider applying progesterone cream to your skin. (I described the powerful effects of this cream on Monday: Day 3, page 122).

Diet

- Cut down on red meat, because its high fat content increases stress on the liver.

- Eliminate caffeine, because it depletes B vitamins needed to help the liver break down estrogen.

- Eliminate sugar and alcohol, because they aggravate blood sugar reactions and depression.

- Be sure to drink at least eight glasses of water daily, to keep the system hydrated and flush away toxins that may produce symptoms.

- To prevent bloating and constipation before your period, drink one cup of Diuretic Tea daily. Continue until your period begins.

- Reduce your salt intake to discourage water retention.

- Eat watermelon to help flush water out of your tissues.

- Eat extra cucumbers for their diuretic effect.

- Eat extra garlic to support liver function and protect against vaginal infections.

- Eat sea vegetables to help regulate your hormone balance.

- To control sweet cravings before your period, try eating additional protein. You may need to increase your protein intake as early as ovulation time.

- To relieve breast tenderness, try eliminating hard-to-digest foods such as bread and cheese.

Moon-Time Tonic Tea

Herbs are a wonderful aid in preventing uncomfortable premenstrual and menstrual symptoms such as emotional ups and downs, cramps, sore breasts and muscles. Prepare a batch of Moon-Time Tonic Tea blend as follows.

½ cup red raspberry leaf	¼ cup squaw vine
¼ cup licorice root, shredded or broken into pieces	½ cup chamomile
	¼ cup chaparral

Combine all the herbs thoroughly and store in an airtight container. For each cup of tea, add one teaspoon of the herbal blend to one cup of boiling water. Cover and steep for thirty minutes. Strain the tea into a thermos or other container and drink it one cup at a time according to the schedule that follows.

Begin to drink this Moon-Time Tonic Tea about three to seven days before your next period—before you usually experience the onset of symptoms. Drink two cups of the tea each day, between meals, until your period begins. During your menstrual period, continue to drink it, then discontinue until before your next period. If you use this Moon-Time Tonic Tea as directed over a few months' time, you should begin to notice an easing of premenstrual symptoms. If the above schedule does not control your symptoms, begin drinking the tea earlier in the month.

The combination of herbs in this tonic are specifically targeted at the discomforts that may arise during the menstrual cycle. Chamomile is very soothing to the nervous system, and chaparral assists in the cleansing and detoxifying process. Squaw vine and red raspberry leaf are traditional "female remedies" that help to balance the female system, promote uterine activity, and reduce menstrual cramps. Licorice root assists hormonal balancing and imparts a lively, sweet flavor to the tea, helping to overcome a craving for sweets. There are many prepared combination formulas available in your local health food store.

Moon-time Movements and Massage

During your premenstrual and menstrual time, nurture yourself with yoga, breathing exercises, and massage. A yoga exercise that is particularly beneficial for the pelvic organs is the Yoga Arch Pose Variations (page 263). Practice this exercise daily during your menstrual period to alleviate cramping and tone your female organs.

Self-massage is also helpful during this time. Beginning about three days before your period, do the Tummy Massage (pages 240-241) to help prevent constipation. To relieve premenstrual bloating, menstrual cramps, or achy legs, massage around your ankles and lower legs to increase circulation, relieve congestion, and soothe the female organs. The Lower-Body Lymph Massage (pages 162-163), accompanied by a hot foot soak, is great for relieving lymphatic congestion and relieving cramping.

The Soothing "Hot Seat" Bath (pages 186-187) with essential oils is a great remedy for menstrual cramps. Take one as often as you wish during your menstrual period to help energize the pelvic organs and relieve pain. Add six drops of lavender, chamomile, or marjoram essential oil.

The Hot Castor-Oil Abdominal Wrap (pages 239-240) is a great remedy for many menstrual discomforts. It helps to alleviate constipation and promote cleansing, and it is a wonderful way to achieve deep relaxation when you feel irritability creeping up before or during your moon time.

Inner Beauty Douche

The risk of vaginal infections changes in relation to the menstrual cycle. The vagina becomes more alkaline at ovulation and menstruation, and that is when vaginitis and symptoms of yeast infections tend to appear. The vagina is a self-cleansing organ, so I do not recommend douching as a matter of routine. If, however, you have a tendency to develop these problems, use the Inner Beauty Douche at the end of the menstrual period to re-acidify the vagina.

1 quart Rejuvelac (page 47)   *2 tablespoons apple-cider vinegar*
1 quart Moon-Time Tonic Tea   *2 tablespoons liquid acidophilus*
     (page 305)

Combine the above ingredients and warm them if necessary to a comfortable temperature for douching.

Sterilize your douche apparatus by filling it with warm water and adding about one teaspoon of alcohol. Run this mixture through the apparatus to kill any lingering germs. Then fill it with the douche mixture and douche very slowly and gently, so that you do not force bacteria up into the uterus.

You can use this Inner Beauty Douche at ovulation also, if you tend to get vaginal infections at that time. At ovulation time, omit the Moon-Time Tonic from the recipe and use two quarts of Rejuvelac with the apple-cider vinegar and liquid acidophilus.

Moon-Time Cleansing Program

If you are troubled by discomfort during the premenstrual or menstrual period, the Moon-Time Cleansing Program will help you to cleanse and detoxify your body and reduce your symptoms. You may also choose to use this program to ritualize your moon time and honor the monthly cleansing and revitalizing of your body.

- *At Ovulation*—Use Inner Beauty Douche (page 307) if necessary for symptoms of vaginal infection.

- *About 3 to 7 Days Before Next Menstrual Period*—Begin Diuretic Tea (page 52), one cup per day, to prevent or relieve bloating. Continue until period ends. Begin Moon-Time Tonic (page 305), two cups per day between meals, to prevent other symptoms of PMS. If symptoms are not controlled with this schedule, experiment with beginning Moon-Time Tonic, one cup per day, a few days earlier in the cycle.

- *To Relieve Constipation*—The last few days before your menstrual period are an excellent time for a professional colonic, preceded by a Hot Castor-Oil Abdominal Wrap (pages 239-240) the night before. Or use Hot Castor-Oil Wrap alone the night before your period begins.

- *First Day of The Menstrual Period*—Lower-Body Lymph Massage (pages 162-163) with mustard "Hot Foot" Soak (page 161). If necessary, increase Moon-Time Tonic (page 305) to three cups per day throughout menstrual period.

- *For Cramps*—Soothing "Hot Seat" Bath (pages 186-187), with marjoram, lavender, and/or chamomile essential oils. Yoga Arch Pose Variations (page 263). Hot Castor-Oil Abdominal Wrap (pages 239-240).

- *For Heavy Flow*—Soothing "Hot Seat" Bath (pages 186-187), with geranium, cypress, and/or rose essential oils.

- *For Breast Tenderness or Mood Swings*—Apply progesterone cream to skin (follow directions of your health professional).

- *At End of Menstrual Period*—Inner Beauty Douche (page 307) to restore acid balance to vagina.

Preparing for a Healthy Menopause

Just as menstruation is often treated as taboo in our culture, menopause is generally considered a time of loss. Other cultures do not necessarily view menopause in this light; many embrace it as a time when women achieve the peak of their power. Native American lore recognizes the power of older women. In many Native American tribes, when women stop menstruating, they are allowed entry into the revered Grandmother Lodge. These elder women are respected for their wisdom, and are believed to have great power because they are holding on to their "wise blood."

A comfortable menopause is simply an outgrowth of a healthy lifestyle. Menopause does not happen all of a sudden, but takes place gradually over time. Most women undergo menopause between the ages of forty and fifty, but the timing is partly determined by how they prepared their bodies in their thirties and even earlier. While there is nothing to dread in the cessation of menses, it can be delayed for many years by following a proper diet, using supplements, promoting proper elimination, and maintaining a positive attitude. The older you are when menopause occurs, the easier it will be.

The popular perception of menopausal women as depressed, irritable, and sometimes crazy must be debunked! Menopause is a natural, universal event, not a time of acute crisis. All that happens is, over a period of time, you stop menstruating and can no longer reproduce. In a study of twenty-five hundred middle-aged women by the Women's Research Institute in Massachusetts, more than 70 percent of those experiencing menopause reported neutral or relieved feelings at seeing the last of their periods.

Admittedly, some women do have a difficult time of it. But depression and mood swings may have more to do with our cultural attitudes than with hormonal changes. In Africa and Japan, where aging enhances a woman's status, menopause is viewed as an achievement. Not surprisingly, women in those countries report fewer hot flashes and lower levels of discontent.

Experts are beginning to realize that many of the problems of menopause, the ups and downs and the irritability that accompanies them, may understandably result from a lack of sleep due to hot flashes. Up to 15 percent of women experience flashes so severe that they are awakened several times during the night. The effects of sleep deprivation are well documented.

Some 70 percent of menopausal women occasionally experience hot flashes—feelings of extreme heat caused by fluctuating levels of estrogen. These hot flashes come on unexpectedly and last from one to five minutes. During the "flash," heart rates increase and skin temperatures rise. Afterward, body temperatures fall slightly and one may sweat and feel chilled.

Many menopausal women experience decreased sexual enjoyment. The decline in libido is likely to be related to discomfort resulting from vaginal soreness or dryness, which can be treated with topical lubricants and other natural methods.

There are many books written about menopause and women's health in general. Please see page 311 for my favorites. Make it your responsibility to become fully informed. Talking with others who are going through menopause can help make it easier. Finding a doctor who is truly your partner is also very important. You need to be able to have a series of conversations with your doctor, not just a two-minute exchange. Many doctors are now introducing the subject to patients and are spending time explaining treatment alternatives.

Alternative Therapies and Activities for Menopause

In addition to following the "Smooth Cycle Checklist" on pages 304-305, try some of these natural remedies.

Regular sexual activity (including masturbation) helps forestall vaginal dryness and soreness.

If you experience sexual discomfort, rub your favorite vegetable oil or castor oil on your vaginal area.

Kegel exercises, done by contracting the muscles you use to stop your flow of urine midstream, can help prevent urinary incontinence. Do ten repetitions for three seconds each several times throughout the day.

If you do experience a hot flash, please don't fight it. Try to relax until the discomfort eases. Open the windows, lower the thermostat, layer your clothing, and try one of the deep breathing activities I describe on pages 169 through 175. Do the Yoga Stress Releasers on pages 109-111. Remember, it is a natural function and will pass soon.

Stay away from spicy foods and cut back on caffeine and alcohol. These substances will absolutely enhance the hot flashes. I speak from personal experience! Smokers often have more difficulty with menopause.

Increase your physical activity. Studies show that physically active women experience half as many hot flashes as women who do not work out.

Follow the supplement regime I describe on page 304. Vitamin E may reduce hot flashes enormously and relieve vaginal dryness. It may also reduce the risk of heart disease and cancer. In addition to B-complex vitamins, women should be careful to get plenty of calcium-rich foods and calcium-magnesium supplements to guard against osteoporosis in later years, which so often occurs as the hormone balance changes after menopause. Stress also depletes calcium. Women should also not overdo their protein consumption, because protein can remove calcium from the bones.

In addition, take 500 milligrams of Evening Primrose Oil capsules four times daily. Take Royal Jelly daily (page 277).

Plant estrogens, found in soybean products such as tofu and soy milk, are thought to mimic the effects of estrogen and so may help alleviate vaginal dryness and hot flashes. The recipes containing tofu on pages 67 through 68 will be beneficial to incorporate into your diet on a regular basis. I have personally found that eating soy daily is the best protection against hot flashes. If I haven't eaten soy for a few days, I begin feeling quite warm again.

If you are menstruating regularly, be sure to use Progesterone Cream on days twelve through twenty-six of your cycle. If you are irregular, you may use it daily.

Many herbal products are specifically designed to assist in balancing your hormones. Herbs specifically beneficial for menopause include dong quai, red raspberry, licorice root, black cohosh, and wild yam. Check in your local health food store for specific products appropriate for your symptoms.

Many women and men reach the true fullness of their beauty as they age gracefully. The secret lies in maintaining vibrant, radiant health. There is no time in life when following my program will pay off more dramatically than when you are older. As never before, our fellow humans and our overburdened planet need the guidance of healthy, emotionally centered, and spiritually mature elders. Choose now to take your rightful place among those who will show a better way for future generations. Keep your mind and body clean and clear, and bring the world along with you.

BOOKS FOR WOMEN'S HEALTH

There have been many fantastic books written by women for women. The following are some of my favorites.

Women's Bodies, Women's Wisdom by Christine Northrup, M.D. (Bantam)

The New Our Bodies, Our Selves by Boston's Women's Health Collective (Simon and Schuster)

Super Nutrition for Women by Ann Louise Gittleman, M.S. (Pocket)

Healthy Healing by Linda Rector Page (Healthy Healing)

The Pause by Loni Barbach (Penguin)

Super Nutrition for Menopause by Ann Louise Gittleman, M.S. (Pocket)

Referral Guide to Holistic Health Practitioner

If you have decided to seek professional help and cannot find a practitioner near you, contact one of the following organizations. They can refer you to a qualified practitioner in your area.

American Holistic Medical Association
6728 Old McLean Village Dr.
McLean, VA 22101
703-556-9728

American College of Advancement in Medicine
23121 Verdugo Drive, #204
Laguna Hills, CA 92653
800-532-3688

American Association of Naturopathic Physicians
601 Valley Street, #105
Seattle, WA 98109
206-298-0125

American Association of Acupuncture and Oriental Medicine
433 Front Street
Catasauqua, PA 18032
610-433-2448

American Massage Therapy Association
820 Davis Street, #100
Evanston, IL 60201-4444
847-864-0123

International Association of Colon Therapy
PO Box 461285
San Antonio, TX 78246-1285
210-366-2888

Rejuvenation Program Source Guide

I have designed a complete kit of products recommended throughout this book for those of you who do not live near a health food store or would rather shop by mail. If you would like additional information on getting my Rejuvenation Kit as well as other products, please leave me a message at (415) 332-6566. You can also fax at (415) 331-2623, or write to me at POB 3116, Sausalito, CA 94966. I will put you on my mailing list for my newsletter, books, and upcoming retreats. However, what follows are two product kits that can get you started and are truly all you need to minimally follow the 21 Day Program.

Below are two additional products that are all you need to minimally follow the 21-Day Program.

Body Smart Detox Kit

The Body Smart Detox Kit is designed especially for those of you who would rather not make up the internal cleansing recipes recommended in this book. The kit is easy to use and extremely effective when done in conjunction with the other cleansing and rejuvenation practices I teach throughout this book.

The Body Smart Kit combines herbs in a synergistic fashion to provide a complete purification program for the entire body without having to buy many different products. Lab data from an independent study reported in the January 1993 issue of *Natural Health* shows that herbal cleansing programs such as these successfully reduce levels of body toxins by as much as 50 percent and reinvigorate the body's natural cleansing agents, such as microflora in the colon.

I have worked with hundreds of people who experienced fantastic results from using the products in the Body Smart Kit. These results include weight loss, regular bowel movements, greatly improved skin texture and tone, increased energy, mobility, and flexibility, reduction of joint pain, brighter eyes, less bloating, clarity of mind, and improvement of chronic fatigue. When these products are combined with the Rejuvenation Program, the results will be greatly enhanced.

The Body Smart Kit includes Colon Cleanse, Detox Tea, Total Body Purification Caps, and Lemon Salt Scrub. If you would like to order this kit, please contact Crystal Star Herbal Nutrition at 1-800-736-6015. Please tell them that I have personally recommended the kit to you in *Rejuvenate: A 21-Day Natural Detox Plan for Optimal Health.*

Synergy Pak

The Synergy Pak, developed by the Life Plus Company, contains a thirty-day supply of four basic products to get you started and help keep you going on the rejuvenation program.

TVM-29 is a broad spectrum supplement to insure the RDA's of most vitamins and minerals. When I am in a hurry, on the road, or just too lazy to take my individual supplements, I use these and actually feel the difference.

Sustenase is by far the best full spectrum digestive enzyme I have ever used. It supports the production of digestive juices in the stomach and intestinal tract, which improves the breakdown of foods we eat into nutrients that can be absorbed and used by the body more efficiently. It is the only enzyme I have found that also contains pro-biotics such as acidophilus, lactobacillus, and bifidus.

Colodyne contains fiber and special ingredients such as micro-flora, herbs, and enzymes that support healthy bowel hygiene and ecology. It will replace the requirement to make the fiber product which I recommend on page p.52.

Protx Plus provides antioxidants, immune system support, and antiaging nutrients which are important protection from environmental and other contaminants.

You can order the Synergy Pak at the wholesale cost by calling Life Plus at 1-800-572-8446. Please identify your sponsor as Body Smart, code 117100. You will become a member of Life Plus at no charge and will then be qualified to order any of their products, including Forever Young (see page 124).

Index

OTHER BOOKS BY THE CROSSING PRESS

Aromatherapy: A Complete Guide to the Healing Art

By Kathi Keville and Mindy Green

This complete guide presents everything you need to know to enhance your health, beauty, and emotional well-being through the practice of aromatherapy. Kathi Keville and Mindy Green offer a fresh perspective on the most fragrant of the healing arts.

$16.95 • Paper • ISBN 0-89594-692-0

Balance Hormones Naturally

By Kate Neil and Patrick Holford

Nutrition experts Kate Neil and Patrick Holford show you how to treat: premenstrual tension and depression, irregular and heavy periods, infertility, weight gain and bloating, menopause problems, breast lumps and cancer, ovarian cysts and fibroids, and other women's problems by using one simple medicine—food. In this breakthrough book, you will get the information you need to overcome the health issues that all women face today.

$12.95 • Paper • ISBN 1-58091-041-6

Essential Energy Balancing

By Diane Stein

Diane Stein guides readers through proactive meditations designed to cleanse and heal the inner self. Readers will contact the Lords of Karma for release from problematic relationships, troublesome character traits, or persistent financial difficulties, and feel rejuvenated once the spiritual obstacles are removed.

$16.95 • Paper • ISBN 1-58091-028-9

Good Food: The Comprehensive Food & Nutrition Resource

By Margaret M. Wittenberg

An exceptionally well-organized, up-to-date, and easily accessible treatise on food and nutrition. Wittenberg delineates a direct connection between food and quality of life.—Susan Jane Cheney, Food Writer/Columnist

$18.95 • Paper • ISBN 0-89594-746-3

Healing Spirits: True Stories from 14 Spiritual Healers

By Judith Joslow-Rodewald and Patricia West-Barker

Photographs by Susan Mills

In an attempt to turn a fantasy into reality, three women, Judith Joslow-Rodewald, Patricia West-Barker, and Susan Mills, traveled across the United States to meet, learn from, and record the stories of practicing healers. These healers' stories and paths are both ordinary and extraordinary, but what they all share is an unshakable belief in the idea that everyone is a potential healer with an innate ability to move toward wholeness.

$20.95 • Paper • ISBN 1-58091-064-5

The Herbal Medicine-Maker's Handbook: A Home Manual

by James Green

This guide to the kitchen pharmacy discusses the entire process of preparing herbal medicines at home, from methods of growing, gathering, and drying herbs to different ways of extracting their vital essences and making healing balms, lotions, and more. By the author of the best-selling *The Male Herbal* (50,000 copies sold).

Inner Radiance, Outer Beauty

By Ambika Wauters

Ambika Wauters encourages women to seek and nurture themselves by dismissing unrealistic images of their bodies. She helps them find their archetype of beauty from within and express their inner awareness by transforming their physical appearance. Includes a 21–day program for regaining health and beauty.

$14.95 • Paper • ISBN 1-58091-080-7

The Natural Pregnancy Book: Herbs, Nutrition, and Other Holistic Choices

By Aviva Jill Romm

This is an important work for all pregnant women who want to better know their healing selves.—Rick Clofine, D.O.

Written for the woman who wants to take a creative proactive role in her prenatal care, *The Natural Pregnancy Book* describes effective natural techniques, herbal remedies, and nutritional aids to support a healthy pregnancy.

$19.95 • Paper • ISBN 0-89594-819-2

The Natural Remedy Book for Women

By Diane Stein

This bestselling, self-help guide to holistic health care includes information on ten different natural healing methods. Remedies from all ten methods are given for fifty common health problems.

$16.95 • Paper • ISBN 0-89594-525-8

Pocket Guide to Hatha Yoga

By Michele Picozzi

Hatha yoga is a holistic form of exercise tailor-made for modern Westerners. This guide offers a roadmap for the beginner and a comprehensive resource for the continuing yoga student.

$6.95 • Paper • ISBN 0-89594-911-3

Your Body Speaks Your Mind: How Your Thoughts and Emotions Affect Your Health

By Debbie Shapiro

Debbie Shapiro examines the intimate connection between the mind and body revealing insights into how our unresolved thoughts and feelings affect our health and manifest as illness in specific parts of the body.

$14.95 • Paper • ISBN 0-89594-893-1

To receive a current catalog from The Crossing Press
please call toll–free, 800-777-1048.
Visit our Web site on the Internet: www. crossingpress.com